Italian Life

Also by Tim Parks

Fiction
Tongues of Flame
Loving Roger
Home Thoughts
Family Planning
Goodness
Cara Massimina
Mimi's Ghost
Shear
Europa
Destiny
Judge Savage
Rapids
Cleaver
Dreams of Rivers and Seas
Sex is Forbidden (first published as The Server)
Painting Death
Thomas and Mary
In Extremis

Non-fiction
Italian Neighbours
An Italian Education
Adultery & Other Diversions
Translating Style
Hell and Back
A Season With Verona
The Fighter
Teach Us to Sit Still
Italian Ways
Where I'm Reading From
Out of My Head

Tim Parks

Italian Life

A modern fable of loyalty and betrayal

Harvill *Secker*
LONDON

1 3 5 7 9 10 8 6 4 2

Harvill Secker, an imprint of Vintage,
20 Vauxhall Bridge Road,
London SW1V 2SA

Harvill Secker is part of the Penguin Random House group of companies
whose addresses can be found at global.penguinrandomhouse.com

Tim Parks ha ... be identified as the ... his Work in
accord ... 988

A CIP cata ... h Library

ISBN 9781787302136 (hardback)
ISBN 9781787302143 (trade paperback)

Excerpts from *The Tale of Tales* by Giambattista Basile on pages 131 and 354
are translated by Nancy Canepa. All other excerpts in translation, including all
quotations from Natalia Ginzburg, are in Tim Parks' own translation.

Typeset in 11.5/16 pt Bembo
by Integra Software Services Pvt. Ltd, Pondicherry

Printed and bound in Great Britain by Clays Ltd, Elcograf S.p.A.

Penguin Random House is committed to a sustainable future for
our business, our readers and our planet. This book is made from
Forest Stewardship Council® certified paper.

MIX
Paper from
responsible sources
FSC
www.fsc.org   FSC® C018179

For Edoardo, close companion ...

ACKNOWLEDGEMENTS

I'd like to thank all those who read parts of this book as I wrote it and offered me their advice: my brother John, Eleonora Gallitelli, Edoardo Zuccato, James Bradburne, Chris Greenhaugh, Mark Ryan, Jean McGarry, Jay Parini, Anna Webber. They kept me company and helped me make it to the end.

It takes years to penetrate intimately into Italian society.

– Stendhal

CONTENTS

AUTHOR'S NOTE

What's in this book? The fruit of forty years in Italy. But not written up as memoir. I've been that way before. *Italian Neighbours*. *Italian Ways*. I know the charm of the candid personal account, the bemused observer discovering Italy first hand. It's fun. It has its authenticity. But after so long in this country, one wants to go deeper: get to the core of it, the pattern that underlies both the good and the bad, the wonderful human warmth of the place, its systematic cruelty.

We are told again and again that human experience is essentially the same the world over. Happiness. Suffering. It is not true. Or only in part. You don't need to be long in Italy, looking for a job, sorting out your documents, dealing with your in-laws, colleagues, bank tellers, waiters, ticket inspectors, to understand that people behave differently here, expect different things of each other. But it takes many years to understand that they also rejoice differently, are sad in different ways, over different dramas.

You realise this when you notice your own emotions shifting. It would be strange and rather depressing if I had not become to some degree Italian in my many years here. At this point you want to bring in other stories not strictly connected to your own. You want to make sense of it. And you feel you have the right. You have begun to understand the emotion of the young southerner in the north, the pride of the *padrino* who finds jobs for all his friends, the shame of feeling your loved ones are unworthy, the resentment of the child who is excluded. You know what it's like to be asked to pay a bribe, and the consequences of refusing, or agreeing. You hear others tell their stories and at last you see what's at stake.

In short, this book has a richer dramatis personae than my other writing on Italy, so that the Italian comedy, divine or demonic, can be acted out. It does not restrict itself to what has been directly experienced. It's true, there is an Englishman among the many Italians. He has a central role. Readers may feel that's Parks, there he is. But I have taken the liberty of giving this man many experiences that are not mine. Sometimes the only way to pack a book with life is to superimpose one thing on another, fuse characters together, put imaginary situations and people side by side, so they can call to each other, and the reader can hear them calling. None of the characters described here are to be taken as portraits of this or that real life person.

Those odd stories we call myths and fables invite us to move into a new world of feeling, where everything is strange, but also strangely convincing. I am inviting you now to plunge into an Italian fable, to discover a new emotional landscape and become yourself, if only momentarily perhaps, in the final climactic pages, Italian.

PART ONE

Sud e nord

CARITATIVA

In a small town in Basilicata in the far south of Italy a woman in her early fifties meets a child at the baker's whom she recognises as a friend of her younger daughter.

'*Ciao*, Marta,' she says. 'How are you?'

The girl is nine. She is sweet and shy. '*Sto bene*,' she says. I'm well.

'How's your mother?' the woman asks, recalling that the two had sat together at the end-of-year school gala some months ago.

'*Sta bene*,' the girl says. She brushes hair from her face, eager to get home with her bag of rolls.

'And your father?' the woman asks, for politeness' sake, though she has never met the man.

Marta hesitates. She bites a lip, then bravely says, 'I don't know, we've split up.'

The woman is taken aback. So many marriages are falling apart, not least her own. But she's also vaguely pleased. Back home she repeats to her daughters, 'She said "we". *We've* split up.' For some reason the woman is fascinated with this formula. 'We, not they, the parents. We.' And for years to come she will repeat this little anecdote: she had met her daughter's friend, Marta, in the baker's and, talking about her parents' separation, the little girl had said, '*We've* split up.'

★

Here is a Neapolitan fable gathered in the early 1600s by Giambattista Basile. A king is so depressed over his failure to have a child with his now ageing queen that he isolates himself in his castle, ashamed of his sterility. Hearing of this, a bearded sage comes to seek out the king and offer a solution. He need only capture a sea dragon, cut out its heart, have it cooked by a virgin, then give it to the queen to eat. All is done as prescribed. Both the virgin, a humble serving girl, and the queen immediately swell up and in a matter of days give birth to identical boys. This uncanny similarity and the close friendship between two children of such unequal social status soon becomes a problem for the queen. She needs her boy to be unique, and so attempts to murder the other woman's son, with disastrous consequences. In the 2015 film of this tale, directed by Matteo Garrone, the king, who does seem suspiciously responsible for both births, dies, unmourned, as soon as the two women fall pregnant, presumably injured in the struggle with the sea dragon. More elegantly, in Basile's seventeenth-century version, the king simply drops out of the story. Once the offspring arrive, 'we' means mother and child.

'We've split up.'

Perhaps a decade after the encounter with Marta, this mother, Carmela, takes her younger daughter, Valeria, now eighteen, to see Don Gabriele, a priest who has become quite prominent in their southern town. He is a member of Comunione e Liberazione, a militant Catholic organisation, at once proselytising and political, very active in universities throughout Italy. The fact is, Valeria is to go to university, in Milan. She is the first member of her family ever to go to university, though many in the past have gone north to work. Carmela herself spent a year in Milan in her twenties, teaching in a primary school, and often wishes she had stayed.

It's a morning in late May, which means the piazza outside the church – actually a large car park – is being prepared for the festival of Santa Rita, patron saint of lost causes and abused women. The church itself is a low modern red-brick building surrounded by high-rise apartment blocks. As they enter, mother and daughter run into the priest's *perpetua*, a hunched elderly woman with thick lenses and a quavering voice. She takes them to a door at the back of the nave and knocks. In his office, Don Gabriele, wearing a pale blue polo neck, lifts his eyes, recognises them and jumps to his feet, hand extended.

'It's good of you to see us, Father,' the mother begins, meaning, given that we rarely come to church these days. The truth is that Don Gabriele used to be Valeria's Religious Instruction teacher at school. So he knows the family; in fact for many years the girl was a member of Comunione e Liberazione. She sang in the church choir and helped at events for little children, because every member of the organisation must make an offering of their time and talent, a duty for which the word *caritativa* has been coined. But it's been a couple of years now since Valeria came to church.

Her mother goes on: 'We were just wondering, Father, if you had any advice about accommodation. We don't know anyone in Milan. She's enrolling to study Public Relations.'

Don Gabriele eyes the girl appreciatively. She is slim and dark with long curly hair and black eyes, a splendid if fairly standard specimen. Don Gabriele has a reputation with the women, something that in no way impedes his influence in Comunione e Liberazione.

Valeria herself is a little embarrassed by the visit, worrying that given their recent absence from the congregation, she and her mother will likely come across as cheeky and opportunist. However, far from being put out, Don Gabriele greets them with warm smiles. He insists they sit down. He asks the *perpetua* to make coffee. He congratulates Valeria on her ambitious decision to go north. Of course, many members of the Community, he says, becoming more businesslike, have children studying in Milan. He names some prominent folk. A doctor. An entrepreneur. The owner of the city's leading law firm. One young man is at the Bocconi, the Italian Harvard. A dentist's daughter is at the prestigious Università Cattolica. Others at medical school, others studying law.

Carmela nods appreciatively. She is impressed. The idea that her daughter will join these promising young men and women is encouraging. Valeria listens carefully. This will be the first time she has lived away from home. It is also the first time she has gone with her mother to do some, as it were, serious family business. So she is excited and anxious. She finds Don Gabriele rather handsome, glamorous even, but also a bit off-putting. She remembers how he used to chuck her cheek when she was a ten-year-old, and hand out boiled sweets to the kids at catechism.

So yes, the priest is saying. He has pulled out a file and is leafing through what appear to be a number of handwritten forms. Yes, it would no doubt be possible to arrange for Valeria to share a flat in Milan with other students from the Community who have gone north. 'That way they will all have something in common and keep each other company. They won't forget their homes and families.'

Carmela is enthusiastic. She is already thanking Don Gabriele warmly.

But now he frowns. 'I'll be frank, though.' He turns to Valeria. 'We can only do this for committed Community members, you understand. You can't accept a precious place in a flat in Milan, which is not an easy city for accommodation, and then just abandon us the way you have this last year or so. It's been a while since we've seen you, hasn't it?'

There is a silence around the table. Outside in the piazza people are calling to each other as they set up their stalls for Santa Rita. There will be a procession with the saint's statue and lots of food.

'Of course,' Carmela says, turning to her daughter with an expectant smile. 'That's only natural. Isn't it, Valé?'

Valeria feels slightly dazed. She is not quite sure why she stopped coming to Mass and to the organisation's many meetings for young people. She used to enjoy them, particularly the pre-school Masses in

May, the Madonna's month. She liked the early-morning quiet and the incense and the reassuring atmosphere of devotion in the big church. Perhaps it was boyfriends that took her away, or just not having enough time for all the other things she had taken on. Volleyball. Piano lessons.

The conversation is on pause. Valeria is expected to signal her obedience, her return to the fold; no doubt a word or two will be enough, but so far she hasn't responded. The priest is a smooth operator and turns his affable attention to the mother. He talks about the Community's sense of mission. They are presently building their own university right here in town. But of course she must be aware of that. Did she hear that Fabio, a companion of Valeria's, was accepted at the medical school in Rome? 'He has made a big contribution to the Community's activities.' And Marianna, the councillor's daughter, who helps out at the Sunday crèche. 'She will be studying psychology in Padua, where the entrance exam is very competitive.'

Listening to this, Valeria is aware of a growing uneasiness. Many of her friends can scarcely believe that Fabio got into medical school. He isn't bright enough. The councillor is on trial for taking bribes.

Valeria's mother, who runs a small catering business, is saying what an important moment this is for a young person and how all of us are called upon in life to do our duty to the best of our ability every waking moment. 'Aren't we, Valeria?'

It's the kind of thing her mother routinely says. Still Valeria doesn't respond. The opportunity is slipping away. On the table she notices a leaflet listing the events for the Festa di Santa Rita, notably a talk with the title '*Dal sentirsi accolti all'accogliere*' – From feeling welcomed to welcoming others.

Don Gabriele looks at his watch and gets to his feet. 'You'll let me know,' he says coolly.

'Thank you, Don Gabriele,' Valeria says, taking his hand, and it's clear to all three that the girl means, Thank you, but *no*.

Later, after long discussion with her mother, who is confused and upset – *Sarai sola come un cane*, she says, You'll be lonely as a dog – Valeria thinks that if only Don Gabriele had talked about belief, if he had mentioned prayer and charity, some *caritativa* she might do, if he had invited her to think of what was being offered as something more and deeper than a convenient exchange, she might have been able to say yes.

GENTAGLIA

Exactly as Valeria is preparing to leave her southern home, far to the north a foreigner is trying to penetrate Italian society without the help of Don Gabriele, or indeed a bearded sage, or the heart of a sea dragon. This British man lives in a village where, as far as the folk who share his small condominium are concerned, he might as well be an alien from outer space. It hardly matters that his wife is Italian. She comes from an altogether different part of the Bel Paese. 'I grew up in Bologna,' a neighbour tells the young man one day. 'I've never been accepted here.'

The fact is, local people speak to each other in dialect, which is such a peculiar fusion of accent, cadence, wayward syntax and bizarre vocabulary that there is simply no chance of speaking it as a native does. Even the British man's Italian, after years of effort, will never be anything other than a British man's Italian. Dialect is community, and community means exclusion, for those who are not part of it. In this village, every time you open your mouth you are, or in his case you are emphatically not, a member of the community. Perhaps that's why he has recently been thinking of himself as just 'the Brit', the way a father starts thinking of himself as simply Dad. After all, even when the villagers do pronounce his name they offer a dozen different versions, all slightly wrong. Sometimes endearingly so. Sometimes irritatingly. But always wrong. It never quite feels as if they are talking to the person he felt he was years ago in England.

But this is by the by; our Brit, James, isn't really too worried about being part of village life. It might be nice not to be greeted with suspicion by some, with pity by others, but it is hardly a question of life and death. And being an outsider can have its charms. An outsider is not responsible. He doesn't vote. He doesn't have to feel shame over the shortcomings of the society he lives in. *Mi vergogno di essere italiano* is an expression James has grown used to hearing every time there is another corruption scandal. I'm ashamed of being Italian. *Mi vergogno della mia città*, the local people say when their football fans indulge in racist chants. I'm ashamed of my town.

But again, all this is by the by. The Italy James really needs to penetrate, if he is to enjoy some kind of economic ease in his adopted country, is the Italy of the university, of academe. For some years now he has been teaching English to university students. He is a language teacher. *Only* a language teacher is the formula everyone uses. But his background, his degrees at Oxford and Yale, would seem to have prepared him for the nobler and more lucrative destiny of Professor. He talks to the powers that be at the provincial university where he teaches about how he might achieve that goal, but they are sceptical. They point out that despite a system of obligatory and open public '*concorsi*', or competitions, for research grants and professorial positions, the candidates who come out on top are almost always those who have worked closely with the local professor who sits on the interviewing board. To spell it out, whenever, as is legally required, the availability of a position is announced *nationally* in a certain government newspaper, there will tend to be both so-called *external* candidates, applying from outside the university that is offering the post, and just one so-called *internal* candidate, who will be the pupil of some powerful figure inside the university. In ninety-nine out of a hundred cases that internal candidate will 'win the *concorso*' as they say. He or she will get the job, which in the end was always meant for them.

'Regardless of competence?'

'Regardless of incompetence!' a grinning Head of Department tells the young Englishman. But she goes on to add that of course most internal candidates are actually rather good; they know the work environment and very likely have already been assisting their professor, or protector, as you might want to call this figure, for some time. So it's fair enough that they should win the *concorso*, isn't it? Otherwise, when or where would they ever get a job?

'Well, they might make applications to other universities,' James suggests.

'This can happen,' he is told, 'but it's rare, since they won't have allies there.'

'So academic careers tend to unfold in the same university?'

'Of course.'

James is puzzled. 'Why would these external candidates apply, then?' he naively asks, 'if they know they are not going to win?'

'To indicate their submission to the system,' his colleagues tell him. 'They play the game, as if it was fair. They show themselves around. Perhaps they will impress someone on the commission who might then, in the future, invent a *concorso* for them without an internal candidate.'

Show yourself around! James compiles a CV and sends it to thirty universities. He includes a list of publications, a variety of work experiences, a high level of linguistic competence, etc., etc.

He receives one reply. From a university in Milan. Here the Head of the Language and Literature Faculty, a charming anglophile in her fifties, originally from Turin, offers him, not a research position or professorship, but the chance to teach a literature course on a contract basis, paid by the hour, with the vague prospect that if things go well a *concorso* might 'one day' be set up at which he could, perhaps, be the internal candidate, the designated winner. So James begins to experiment with what years later a colleague will describe as a '*un precariato intimidatorio*', which simply means that the condition of not having a permanent job – *precariato* – is used as an instrument for bullying you – *intimidatorio* – for guaranteeing your obedience, your loyalty. You are given just enough encouragement to keep you hanging on.

Fortunately, given this university's rapid expansion and the Head of Faculty's generosity, James's period of *precariato*, commuting twice a week to the distant town for low pay, will last only seven years. A joke. A researcher's position, the first step towards professor, is to be created; a *concorso* will be held, involving a written exam and an interview, and he, James, will be the famous and invincible internal candidate.

All seems well, until a couple of months before the exam his protectress informs him that a bureaucratic glitch has emerged. His degrees, from English and American universities, albeit prestigious, albeit in the subject area in which he is to be employed, are not recognised in Italy, so that he now needs a document which declares the *equipollenza*, the equivalent value, or potency, of these degrees with an Italian degree in English literature. This document has to come from a specific university, as if that university had given him a degree on the basis of the exams taken long ago in the foreign university. In order to get his *equipollenza*, James will have to make an application, then the appropriate faculty in the university will meet and debate whether a BA from Oxford together with an MA from Yale do in fact have equivalent value with a degree from that university.

But which university will do this for him? And do it in the very short time available, since the *concorso* for the position of researcher has already been scheduled and cannot be postponed?

His protectress suggests the local university where he previously taught, in the town where he still lives. They know him, and she knows the Head of Faculty there. She can put in a word.

A frantic scramble to make the application for *equipollenza* begins, and years later, thinking back on this, James will appreciate how often Italian life is characterised by this need to establish legitimate membership of the community by means of bureaucratic process. Needless to say, there are snags. The local university demands a precise list of all the public exams he took at school and all the courses he did at university, with their contents and his results. The list cannot simply be made up from memory, official documents are required: certificates of his grammar school exams and officially stamped communications from his old universities of Oxford and Yale which must be 'authenticated' by the British and American consulates.

Since neither of these august universities routinely provides such documents, this hurdle initially appears to be insurmountable. But much to James's surprise, in response to his appeal, both institutions come up with the goods, inventing the documents free of charge and dispatching with unexpected haste complete lists of the courses he did years ago, their exact content and his exam results. Extraordinary. He himself had forgotten the half of it. Did he really study all these subjects? He takes these documents, personally, to the British and American consulates and is again pleasantly surprised to be able to persuade the employees to write out 'authentications' in a matter of hours. It's rather like one of those fables in which someone is commanded to perform an impossible task in order to win the desired reward, then much to the chagrin of the person doing the commanding, carries out the task without any trouble at all.

But now the whole wad of papers has to be translated into Italian, this despite the fact that all the professors judging him at the university know English, and many of them teach it. Then that translation needs to be 'sworn' as 'authentic and faithful' before an official in the local courthouse by a translator who is a registered and paid-up member of a privileged group of recognised professional translators of legal documents. So James, who himself translates rather well, has translated a couple of books in fact, now has to pay a translator who is a member of the appropriate translators' community to satisfy the community that he wants to join – that of English academics – whose members all, by the very nature of that community, read English anyway.

No matter. He gets his application together and takes it to the administrative offices of the university, where he is informed, by none other than the Head of Administrative Affairs, that his application has come *three weeks too late* to be taken into consideration for degrees handed out at this forthcoming graduation session. He will have to wait until the next, in six months' time.

James points out that the faculty meeting at which the professors were to decide on his fate is still some days away. How can he be too late?

Because, says the Head of Administrative Affairs, there is a deadline for applications of this kind and that deadline passed some days ago.

But have the other applications actually been transmitted to the faculty?

They have not, he is told. They are all there in a file in the administrator's filing cabinet. But that is irrelevant.

At this point James surprises himself. He names the local Head of Faculty, the friend of his protectress. He tells the bureaucrat that this powerful figure, Professor Lonardi, has specifically and *personally* invited him to make this application for *this graduation session*. None of this is true but, removing his letter of application from its envelope, James simply strikes a pen through the date and predates it to a full month before.

And his application is accepted! James experiences a moment of exhilaration, followed by the anxiety that he might be caught out, and then a vaguer concern that he is behaving in ways he never used to.

So all now appears to be well, until, two days before the famous faculty meeting, the protectress phones James and observes with some consternation that he has not yet been in touch with Professor Lonardi, who has been expecting his call for a month and more.

James doesn't understand. Why would he have contacted Lonardi, to what end?

The protectress, who as well as being a professor is a smart society lady, laughs, but with a hint of exasperation behind her Torinese accent, 'Because he is doing you a *gentilezza*, a kindness!'

'But they are obliged to look at applications, aren't they? It's their job. And the papers are all in order.'

Her patience runs out. 'If you want the *equipollenza*, call Lonardi.'

Reflecting on this, James realises she is also telling him, If you want people to help you in general, you have to show that you are an amenable fellow. Of course, if this were a question of asking some small personal favour from a friend – a lift to the airport, a loan to tide him over to the end of the month – James would be the first to agree that it is only right to show gratitude and amenability; when it comes to work and bureaucracy, however – to something that should not be considered a favour – this approach is new to him. What it boils down to is, he is being asked to make a spectacle of his subservience, to genuflect, to kowtow.

Still, he makes the call. He needs the *equipollenza* to give sense and direction to his professional life. After all that effort to get a box full of documents, is he really going to baulk at a small hurdle like this? No. Since mobile phones are still in their early days, the number he is given corresponds to a fixed-line family phone and it is the professor's wife who picks up. When he gives his name, she says, 'Ah, yes.'

The professor comes on the line and is affable. The two have shaken hands on three or four occasions, but never really talked. James is anxious because he doesn't know what Italians say to each other when making calls like these. He wants to say enough to get what he wants, what he feels is due to him, but he doesn't want to say anything he will later be ashamed of. Feeling shame for James is not feeling shame for how others in his community behave, or for having himself behaved in such a way as to let others in the community down. He only feels shame when he feels he's let himself down. Vaguely, he wishes he had read Professor Lonardi's recent book, so he could offer some credible compliment to the man; on the other hand, he doesn't want to become the kind of creep who reads other people's books just to suck up to them.

Gently, the professor shows him the way by asking how things are going in Milan. James says they are going well, he enjoys his teaching there and now of course he is taking part in this *concorso* for a research post and is hoping to win. There is just the problem of the *equipollenza*.

The professor is silent.

James bites the bullet. 'Of course, I'm terribly grateful to you, Professor, for agreeing to look at my curriculum. It will be a great honour to have a degree from your university.'

'Oh, let's not exaggerate,' the professor chuckles complacently. 'If anything it will be an honour for us to welcome you as a graduate.'

So that's done. It wasn't that difficult in the end, was it?

But just as James doesn't really believe it is an honour to be granted a degree in this way from this provincial university, so there are people in the university who are far from convinced that it is an honour to welcome him there. When the faculty's degree commission eventually meets, their decision is not unanimous. Through a friend, James will learn that there had been a fierce debate with one ex-colleague speaking of 'a dangerous precedent', lowering the university's standards to accommodate 'riff-raff from abroad'.

Gentaglia was the word actually used. Bad people. Scum. Years later, in the Internet era, James will remember that comment when he sees the word on a football-fan chat-line where opposing supporters are insulting each other before a big game. *Gentaglia! Zingari!* Riff-raff. Gypsies. And then: *Nomadi alle porte della città!* Nomads at the city gates!

In fourteenth- and fifteenth-century Florence it was understood that when dealing with a foreigner, a foreigner who was not mere riff-raff, the moment would come when the community must decide whether or not he was to be admitted into *le cose segrete della nostra città* – the secret things of our town. So when a new ambassador came from abroad, or simply from Bologna or Rome, but that was abroad enough, or when a foreign trader came to live in the town, or when a new mercenary warlord was hired, the question would eventually arise,

Are we going to share with this man – and in those days it was always a man – the secret things of our town?

What were those secret things in Renaissance Florence? Essentially, the gap between the way things were supposed to be done – the republic, the elections, the people's councils – and the way power was actually administered, by two or three dominant factions who fought to control the city. One day, shortly after winning his *concorso* (against stiff external competition) and becoming a *ricercatore*, James is sitting in his first faculty meeting when a young professor of Art History launches into a long complaint about the way university courses are assigned. She hasn't been given the course she wanted. It's a scandal. At which point, the anglophile lady professor who has more or less single-handedly brought James into the university, leans towards him and whispers, 'You know, I have never been able to work out who protects Lorena.'

Even those initiated in the secret things must be constantly alert to the possibility of further secret things that are hidden from them.

LE TRE ZIE

The story of young Valeria's arrival in Milan is not as simple as I previously made it seem. Prior to her choosing Milan, she had been planning to go to Rome. Why? Because La Sapienza, in Rome, is an excellent university, and because her father has an uncle in Rome and the uncle, who is the powerful chief administrator of a large charitable association, has a spare apartment there, where, it was hoped, Valeria could live. In this way, while leaving home, Valeria would nevertheless be staying, to a degree, in her family.

Valeria and her father had driven to Rome together to enrol her at the university. There was no selection process for this particular degree course at the time, the only requirement being that one pass one's *maturità* at the *liceo*, that is, the final high-school exams, with a reasonable grade. The question of imposing a *numero chiuso*, a 'closed number' on the places available for particular courses, has always been a vexed one. It is clear that not everyone can or should study Law or Medicine. On the other hand, every form of exclusion is understood as a kind of cruelty, and whenever a new limit is introduced, students will occupy their classrooms and 'go on strike' to protect the right of everyone to study.

Arriving in Rome, Valeria finds herself entering a pharaonic palazzo built in Fascist times and ennobled with bas-relief sculptures of horses and warriors representing the national spirit. What was

Fascism after all if not the ambition to include every Italian in one great *fascio*, or bundle? Inside the building, however, the reality is dimly lit administrative offices where harassed employees defended by a wall of glass go back and forth for tattered files, making photocopies and adjusting the dates on rubber stamps, or cursing computers that will not compute.

The queues are long. Valeria has taken ticket number 173 and when after a couple of hours she finally gets to her window it is to find herself confronted by a blonde girl only a year or two older than herself, who immediately tells her, with an air of conspiratorial solidarity, that it would be a very bad idea to enrol in the course she has chosen. She herself, the girl explains, is a student here. She is working part-time in the office to pay her fees. Well, the truth is that there are already too many students for the courses at the Sapienza. 'If you don't want to be sitting on the floor for lectures, or listening in from the corridors, I think you'd better go elsewhere.'

Valeria is thrown. She hasn't been refused a place, nobody can stop her enrolling if she wants to; but she certainly hasn't been invited in either. Confused, she delays her decision, feeling she should talk to her father about it, though her father, who never went to university, doesn't know what to think. He sees the advantages of having a degree these days, but can't see why his daughter doesn't go somewhere closer to home: Lecce, Bari or Cosenza. The idea that she might want to be far away from her family doesn't occur to him.

What settles it is that when they talk to the uncle, who had previously told them the flat in Rome was available, he now says perhaps it is not available after all. They don't actually see the uncle, because he is an important man, but they do speak on the phone. And he doesn't explicitly say the flat is not available, but he says there are problems. He says the property needs renovating. As all the family knows, this uncle, who never married, relies on a cousin, a woman some ten years older than himself, whom he invited to Rome from their southern town, to cook and clean for him. She is not exactly an employee – he doesn't pay her and has no contractual obligations to her – but she does everything for him and he gives her pocket money as she needs it. However, since he doesn't actually want to live with this rather ignorant old maid, doesn't want to share with her, that is, the very large, you might say palatial, apartment provided for him by his employers, he has been allowing her to live in the apartment he himself owns, which is central, but tiny. During the phone call, which Valeria's father is making from a shabby hotel room, he, her father, gets the impression that while the uncle had initially taken some self-important pleasure from the idea of helping a member of one of the family's poorer branches, playing benefactor to his pretty great-niece, now that it comes down to it, giving her the flat is not convenient. It's needed for the cousin, his maid, and not really big enough for two. Or perhaps there are other reasons. Valeria's branch of the family really is irretrievably ordinary, after all. How could they ever repay a major favour like this?

Putting the phone down, Valeria's father curses his uncle with solemn emphasis. The man has abandoned his own, he says. He has reduced his cousin, Zia Giuditta, to a slave. He would sell his mother. He thinks he is too good for them. He is a miserable opportunist hiding behind a blather of charity and utopian political ideology. He is a *stronzo*. And the father vows and swears, there and then, as he hangs up on the call, that he will never speak to his uncle again. *Never.* Nor speak *of* him. 'As far as I'm concerned,' Valeria's father says emphatically, 'Zio Franco is dead. I am ashamed of him. He doesn't *exist*.'

It was given this state of affairs that Valeria, leafing through stacks of promotional pamphlets on the homeward drive through the dry hills of Campania and Basilicata, settled on Milan. 'I'm going to Milan,' she announced. She had found a course that suited her.

Her father shook his head. 'We don't know anyone in Milan.'

'This is a private university, Papà. They have a limit on the number of students.'

Later, when he realised she had made up her mind, he burst into tears.

'I will lose you then. You'll be so far away.'

He had always dreamed, her father told her, of having his children around him in middle age. They would be there as friends, as company, as helpers, having Sunday lunch together, keeping the family show on the road. Why would he have had children otherwise? Why would anyone have children, if not to surround themselves with affection and assistance? He appeals to her to change her mind.

But Valeria is an independent spirit. The truth is her parents have been separated for many years and though her father continues to orbit around the family, his relationship with her mother is, to say the least, troubled; indeed, her parents' interminable arguments are one of the reasons why she is determined to find a university far away.

'I'll always be in touch,' she says, 'I'll come back regularly.'

The following day her father buys her a mobile phone. Milan, as Valeria will soon discover, is teeming with southern students who call their parents every day. Or are called every day. Two or three times. And not just by their parents, but by aunts and uncles and grandparents as well. For years hence Valeria will be expected to exchange goodnight messages with her mother and then her father, declaring that she is safely home and well. Even when she isn't.

Community is not just people. It is place. One belongs to a family which lives in a house, or houses. In Italy, where the apartment dominates, many families like to have more than one flat in the same building, so that sons can bring their wives in on the second floor while parents, uncles and cousins inhabit the first and grandparents or even great-grandparents decay on the ground, or slightly under, in the semi-basement. By the intercom buzzer at the main door, all the names are the same. Logaldo, A., Logaldo, R., Logaldo, G. & M. Altogether it's a honeycomb of warm solicitude and vicious vituperation. For since it is understood that no member can ever really leave the family, not permanently, there is no need to keep each other sweet. Family members, unlike acquaintances and strangers, can be told what you think of them. 'Insulting me is one of the pleasures of his life,' the novelist Natalia Ginzburg remarked of her son. 'Certainly listening to his insults is one of mine.' In her family biography, *Lessico famigliare*, Ginzburg describes her father constantly addressing his children as *voialtri* – you lot – and always in critical terms. 'You lot have no table manners, you lot don't know anything.' Inside the family, he counted himself out. He was ashamed. In the same town, Primo Levi would live his whole married life in his mother's apartment where his wife was constantly quarrelling with his mother and sister. At the time of Levi's suicide his son had taken an apartment on the floor above. The two did not get on.

But what do family members criticise each other *about*?

The friends they make outside the family.

To date Carmela, Valeria's mother, has argued with all her children's girlfriends and boyfriends. It's rare that she approves a child's choice of partner. 'You can't know how it will turn out if you let strangers set foot in your house,' says a king in one Neapolitan fable, and hence he resolves to marry his sister, for safety. So much can go wrong, he says, when blood is crossed. Certainly Carmela feels pretty much everything went wrong in her own two marriages.

But what makes a good partner?

Wealth, education, culture?

Carmela has a sister ten years older than herself, one of eight daughters born to a humble family on the borders of Puglia and Basilicata. In her late teens Raffaella fell in love with the local doctor, an older and infinitely better-educated man. He too was in love with her and proposed marriage. Far from jumping for joy, her parents opposed the match. It must not be. Not that there was anything *wrong* with the man himself – on the contrary; but he was not one of their folk. The daughter would be lost to a posh world with which there could be no mixing.

The families wouldn't be able to speak to each other. It wasn't in the scheme of things.

The doctor's parents likewise were hardly enthusiastic. They were city dwellers and this was a country girl. Sweet and pretty, but so what? Heartbroken, Raffaella turned to the Church and became a nun, but before doing so, she went to the family photograph albums and scratched out her face wherever it occurred. She would no longer be part of them or their celebrations, or even their memories. She was gone. She didn't exist.

That was many years ago now. These days the ageing Zia Lella is one of the people Valeria must call from her mobile, if not quite on a daily basis, then almost. From her convent in Rome, armed with her shiny *telefonino*, the ageing nun keeps watch over her many sisters and their children. She prides herself on being informed and up to date on all their joys and vicissitudes. 'You're not alone this evening, I hope,' Zia Lella says to Valeria when she calls. 'Are you seeing anybody? Is it still that boy whose father is an engineer?'

In Garrone's film of Basile's *Tale of Tales*, a series of long shots shows the castles and villages where the three fables he intertwines take place. They are all hilltop communities, entirely isolated from the landscape around them, protected by walls and moats and drawbridges. What drama occurs is not conflict *between* these distant, spectacularly segregated communities, or even *within* them; it is the drama of the passage from inside to out, or outside to in, dramas of marriage or exile, or both. And the attendant emotions are those of being welcomed or rejected, of leaving to marry a stranger, or inviting one into your bed. Being proud of your choice, or ashamed. Cursing and being cursed.

From the battlements of his castle keep, the handsome king hears a beautiful female voice from the houses of the poor outside his walls. Whoever it is sings so sweetly the king knows at once he simply must have this woman. He hurries to find the house that the song came from; the door is bolted against him. Inside are two ancient and unspeakably ugly sisters. But of course the king can't know that. What would he know about the people outside his castle?

Fired up by the seductive voice, he declares his love. After eight days, one of the women pokes a finger through a keyhole for him to caress, a finger she has spent interminable hours sucking and smoothing. The king is ecstatic. In her tiniest voice, one of the two old hags says she will come to the king's bed if he will agree to have her in complete darkness, since she would be ashamed to be seen naked. He agrees. But when, in the middle of the night, he discovers the grisly truth – and this woman is supremely ugly – he calls his men and has her thrown out of his high bedroom window down into the wild woods beneath the castle.

The story is far from over. In the woods there are fairies. Amused to find an old hag hanging from a tree by her hair, they cast a spell on her, transforming her into the most beautiful woman there ever was. The king, out hunting, falls in love with this splendid damsel. 'Don't bar the door of pity against me,' he begs her in Basile's version. 'Don't raise the drawbridge of mercy against me.' Now it is him praying to be admitted to the stronghold of her graces. Amazed, she lets him in and he takes her home to his castle. The two are wonderfully happy. They marry.

Still the story is not done. You can leave your loved ones and marry into a different world, but you cannot altogether forget them. Hadn't our enchanted beauty spent her whole life with her poor sister? Didn't they work together and cook together and gripe together their whole life long? It's the only company our new queen has ever known, the company she needs now to complete her sense of self. Only her sister's acknowledgement of her present good fortune will make it real.

So the beautiful queen invites the ugly hag to her wedding. Once the poor woman recognises her sister and appreciates the metamorphosis that has taken place, she is overwhelmed with envy. Much to the queen's consternation, she refuses to go back to the hovel where the two once lived together. She is *family*, she says. She is lonely without her sister. She deserves a place in the castle. But this is impossible. The king would never put up with such a loathsome creature. 'How did you do it?' the ancient sister demands. 'I had myself skinned,' the queen lies to be rid of her. 'I was beautiful *underneath*.'

In desperation the old hag goes to a barber and asks him to skin her. These are not easy scenes to watch. True, Garrone shows very little – the barber sharpening his knives, the first incision – but it is the *idea* that is so upsetting. The old woman cannot accept that her sister is now worthy of the king's bed, while she has been abandoned. It is not enough that the queen promises to help her secretly, behind her husband's back. She demands respect. She demands recognition. What she gets is unspeakable pain.

Basile's version ends with the skinning. But Garrone twists the barber's knife once more. Invited to attend the coronation of another queen in a nearby community, during the ceremony our enchanted beauty suddenly and rapidly begins to age. It's as if contact with this authentic queen had forced her to recognise her own falseness. She doesn't belong. We are left to imagine the king's reaction.

Valeria will learn over the years that leaving home is not as simple as moving to Milan. Whenever there is a boyfriend there will always be the question of how he will be seen at her home, how she will be seen at his. Will one or the other be rejected? Or will the parents be so friendly among themselves that the couple will be pushed towards a marriage they don't want, or aren't ready for?

Meantime the train to Milan takes her through a landscape where villages and castles can be seen perched on distant hills. She knows from history lessons that in the fertile valleys there was malaria. That was another reason why they built high up. She has read Ignazio Silone's *Fontamara* about the peasants in the hilltop village who lose their livelihood when a rich politician redirects their only source of water to his own property. Politically, she tends to the left, believing that the rich and powerful inevitably support the interests of their own families and the hangers-on they gather around them. Dreaming of meritocracy, Valeria hopes the north will not be like the south.

When the train pulls into Napoli Centrale, already three hundred kilometres from home, her Zia Nunzia is on the platform with fruit and a bag of *taralli*, tiny twists of biscuity bread. The two embrace while other passengers get off for a quick smoke. Along with the bread, and a huge sandwich, and a bag of persimmons, there are also two small plastic cups in which the espresso is still warm. They are both for Valeria. Zia Nunzia has already taken her coffee.

'But why two?'

'I thought one was rather mean.'

At Roma Termini it is the turn of Zia Raffaella, the nun. She too is on the platform. She has a huge piece of Caciocavallo, a southern cheese. Valeria doesn't tell her that she already has an equally large piece in her suitcase from home. And a loaf of *cuddura*, a soft bread twisted into a kind of crown. And a litre of labelless red wine bottled by an uncle on her father's side. Her aunt speaks excitedly, admiring her thick hair, warning against the poor food and the notorious lack of hospitality in the north. 'Don't forget your family,' she shouts her goodbye, she who left hers to be a bride of Christ.

Later Valeria will describe this journey as the journey of *le tre zie*, the three aunts. Because on the platform at Firenze Santa Maria Novella, Zia Rosa, another of her mother's seven sisters, will be there to greet her. She has a bag of *pettole* she made herself, small doughnuts fried in boiling oil. She asks after Valeria's mother and talks about her cancer until the whistle blows for the Intercity to depart. Valeria goes back to her seat and a textbook on advertising in a global market. Three hours later, it is something of a relief, but almost uncanny, to find, as the train pulls into the huge grimy glass shed of Milano

Centrale, that *no one is waiting for her.* She is beyond her family's reach. Laden with gifts from loved ones, gifts that would have her forever eating southern specialities, as if eating food from home one inevitably remained the same loyal, reliable daughter of old, she trundles her bag down the long platform into blissful anonymity.

LABORATORIO LINGUISTICO DI CONVERSAZIONE INGLESE

Not all universities are the same. James began his teaching career many years ago at a provincial state-run university. He had heard, from a friend at a language school, that a position of *lettore* was available. A language teacher. In the English Department. It was not advertised. He wrote a letter and was called for interview, something that suggested there was no chosen candidate.

Encouraged, James went to the appointment and found seven or eight fellow Brits, Americans, Australians and South Africans chatting in a gloomy corridor. Some seemed to be there quite by chance and had no background in teaching or languages. There was an Australian girl who had studied Art History in Sydney then married and quickly divorced a Sicilian. There was an Indian who had grown up in Hounslow and an Irishman in his forties who had published an experimental novel fifteen years ago. A middle-aged woman from Newcastle explained that she had left the UK because of Thatcher and would never return while the Conservatives were in power. One rather attractive cockney boy seemed possibly to be casing the joint so as to make off with the ornate handles on the doors, or maybe even the doors themselves. Meantime, a birdlike Canadian woman in her late sixties was showing everyone photos of her Italian grandchildren.

It would be hard, then, to imagine a more heterogeneous group, united by the single fact that they spoke the same language, more or less. And James muttered an Italian word to himself to describe them, a word his wife often uses: *spaesati*, literally countryless, or townless, ones. People in the wrong place. Disoriented, without protection.

When his turn to be interviewed came, sitting across a table from three professors in a cavernous room, James set out to show that he was not one of these *spaesati*. He had been in Italy for some years. He was married to an Italian. He had an Italian child. He was in for the long haul. There was no danger, was his implication, that they would need to be replacing him after a month or so. On the professional side, he spoke of his three or four modest academic publications, of the two books he had translated for reputable publishing houses, his eagerness to work in a university environment.

The professors were affable. Waving aside James's willingness to conduct the interview in Italian, they spoke English in the clipped accents that well-to-do Italians would have picked up in London's more expensive language schools in the 1960s and 70s, and after ten minutes showed him out. The job went to the cockney. James was called in again and told that the professors had appreciated his application but felt he was overqualified. 'You would, er, how can I say, chafe at the bit.'

The elderly professor heading the commission repeated the expression with a complacent awareness that it was hardly the kind of idiom a foreigner could be expected to know. 'This post is not for someone of your, er, laudable ambitions,' he advised. 'You would chafe at the bit.'

'Too bad we can't pay the bills with your, er, laudable ambitions,' James's wife observed.

Only a week later, however, James receives a phone call from a professor of English working in the Sociology Faculty. He needs an

English teacher, a *lettore*, urgently. 'My colleagues in the English Department told me you were available.' The job will involve teaching English to absolute beginners. Economics students. There will be no pretensions of literariness and no career track, but a good salary on a contract renewable annually for up to five years, and a first step into the world he is interested in.

James says yes.

'Curious,' he would later remark to this professor, 'that your colleagues thought I was overqualified to help students to read literary texts, but proposed me for the most basic language teaching of all.'

'They are anxious,' he chuckled, 'about anyone who might feel qualified to judge them.'

In his late forties, a tall, handsome, sensual man, Massimo Volpato is eager from the start to present himself as quite different from his colleagues. 'These people have such a high opinion of themselves!' They look down, he says, on anyone like himself who knows how to live, who goes skiing and plays golf and tennis and squash, who enjoys a bit of clubbing at the weekend. So Professor Volpato has renounced, he tells his new assistant, academic advancement, in favour of this rather marginal position running the English-language teaching for students of Sociology. It's a backwater of course, but it pays well and requires very little effort. Above all it allows him to get on with *i cazzi miei* – my own fucking stuff.

James was initially attracted to Volpato, who seemed a colourful figure; he accepted invitations to dinner parties in a beautiful apartment in the *centro storico* where archaeological treasures were on display, Roman busts, terracotta objects from Etruscan tombs. A terraced balcony over porticos looked down into a pretty piazza. In the mothy summer evenings, over Prosecco and canapés, there was much talk of what a rebel our professor had been in the sixties, occupying university classrooms with the extremist fringes of the Communist Party, acting in a subversive theatre company. Every Italian of a certain age must declare what position he took in the so-called 'Years of Lead', the time of terrorism and social conflict. Volpato had been on the side of the young and the people, he explained. Unlike the snobs of the Brit Lit Fairyland. Of course, he hadn't taken part in violence himself, but he understood those who had. Monopolising the conversation, his observations swung effortlessly between generous sentimentality and brutal cynicism. His children, his family, meant everything to him. *Col cazzo* he would do a stroke more than his contract required. The fuck. Nothing was more beautiful than the Italian countryside. *Col cazzo* he would waste the warm summer weeks doing research in rainy England. Who did they think he was? *Lo scemo di turno?* The fool of the day.

Fairly soon attraction gave way to disquiet and eventually repulsion. It was clear that Volpato had not willingly left the English Department; he had been expelled. He was a man alienated from the circle of colleagues he had originally belonged to. Why this had happened, James would never be told. In any event, Volpato was the first manifestation of something he would gradually come to recognise as a common phenomenon in Italian institutions: the person who has withdrawn into a lonely corner, or been forcibly placed in permanent quarantine. Not that he has been eliminated altogether. No one wishes to be guilty of excluding someone from the community *absolutely*; but he plays no part in its larger workings and has no possibility of further advancement.

But it would take a little while for James to grasp all this. For the moment, he bought the textbook he was supposed to be teaching from – 'My name is John,' a glossy opening page declared. 'Is my name Fred? No, it isn't' – and brushed up on the so-called 'direct method' approach he was supposed to be using. *Laboratorio linguistico di conversazione inglese* was the official name of his course. His specific duty was to teach the students to speak; it would be left to the expert, Volpato, to explain the grammar, syntax and finer points of the language. When he found the classroom, or rather auditorium, in one of the

31

university's modern buildings, there were two hundred and fifty students ranged around its rising banks of seats.

So this was a baptism of fire. James took the microphone, turned the volume on the PA to max and asked two hundred and fifty Italians to repeat, 'My name is John. Is my name Fred? No, it isn't.' The students laughed and chattered. They were happy enough to converse, but not perhaps in English. The only hope seemed to be to drill them like a troupe of performing monkeys. Parrots rather. He pointed at specific students. 'Is her name Marta?' The PA was deafening. 'No, it isn't. Is his name Giovanni? Yes, it is.'

To their credit the young Italians were not ill disposed. They knew they needed English. They tried to follow the questions their teacher was hurling at them with great speed and intensity. But a minority chattered away. Others drifted in and out of the classroom as if to check, between cigarettes and phone calls, what this odd foreigner might be up to. Since the lesson was immediately after lunch, many still had food with them. Sandwiches. Crackers. Bottles of water. Cans of Coke. Italian girls in particular seem never to be without a pack of crackers, carefully cleaning crumbs from their lips, or the desktop in front of them. Finally, three or four, far away at the back of the class, began to play the fool. They laughed, they threw chewing gum.

James, floundering, asked two of these troublemakers to leave the room. At that time he had no sense of the significance of such a request. Expulsion. It was a purely practical question. If he lost control of the lesson, he was done. The two refused to leave. They had a right to study, they said. They had paid their university fees. One passed a remark in a dialect that James couldn't understand and titters spread round the auditorium.

James insisted that he would not continue the lesson until the two left. For the first time there was something like silence in the big classroom. It was a showdown. 'My name ees John,' one of the two giggled. 'No, eet eesn't!' the other cried. General laughter. James waited. He mustn't relent. He wouldn't continue. The last voices subsided in a hush of whispers. Eventually, the two jumped to their feet, as if the decision were entirely theirs, and left in a rush, slamming the door behind them.

'Never do that again,' his wife told him afterwards. She was horrified as to the possible repercussions.

James had three of these lessons, each two hours long, every week. He was not the only one. His two hundred and fifty students covered the alphabet from A to M. A South African colleague, Jerry Marlow, had N to Z. How this diffident, laconic, somehow beaten man handled his rumbustious students, James never knew. Vast amounts of energy seemed to be required to get through those two hours with the feeling that some kind of ground had been covered. Never had money seemed so hard earned.

James remarked on this to Volpato. Volpato laughed. Of course at the beginning everyone made a big effort, he said. But this was largely a question of misplaced self-regard. Why should you worry if you lost control of the lesson? It was clear that you couldn't teach conversation to two hundred and fifty students. A teacher wasn't obliged to entertain, he said. *Col cazzo.* Just to teach. It was up to the students to get what they could from the lesson.

Curious, James asked one or two students what Volpato's lessons were like. They didn't go to Volpato's lessons, they said. He asked a number of students, but none of them went. He asked Jerry to ask his students, which he did, but like James he couldn't find anyone who went to Volpato's lessons. These were timetabled for Friday afternoon, when everyone was already heading off for the weekend. Eventually, however, a girl was found who did attend Volpato's lessons, with a handful of others, she said. The professor read from the grammar book that he himself had published, if not perhaps, as James would later discover, altogether written.

Then there was the exam. Exams rather. Because very shortly James was also asked to teach a third-year class. In this case fifty or so students came to study articles on social behaviour in the British and American newspapers. It was altogether a more gratifying proposition, though it has to be said that over the years James would derive a great deal of pleasure from leading eager young Italians to speak their first sentences in English. A new language on the lips, a new tongue in the mouth, is a wonderful discovery. And for some it would be the first step on a line of escape from the narrow provincial community they moved in.

The exams then. An enormous amount can be understood about a society from the way it assesses its children's educational achievements. When James thinks back on the exams of his youth he recalls grim-faced teachers striding up and down lines of single desks set up for the occasion in the assembly hall. Every pupil had to be isolated from every other. Kept under constant observation. He remembers being hauled from his place and marched to the headmaster's office because his mediocre translation from Livy had turned out to be suspiciously similar to another boy's mediocre translation. Had the two copied? No. They didn't have that kind of courage. Their translations were just mediocre in the same English schoolboy way.

Otherwise he remembers O-level oral exams with external examiners, in French and German, who invariably failed him when he was unable to pronounce a single word with a decent accent. And at Oxford he recalls more of the same. Exams morning and afternoon, one after the other, Monday to Friday. The whole year's work, the whole three years' work, crammed into a few anxious days and nights, his head so full of dates and quotations and theories he was unable to sleep.

Still, at least back then you had known the marking would be impartial. It was your candidate number you wrote on the exam paper, never your name. The papers were sent off to examiners in distant places, people who didn't even know if you were man or woman, white or black. Conversely, you couldn't know what they wanted, what they thought the best answers were. So you were free to study your subject and simply answer what seemed best to you.

BOCCIATO

Having survived his specifically Anglo-Saxon ordeal, James initially feels that Italian students are having it rather easy. The first-year English exam in the Sociology Faculty will be entirely oral and will be carried out by the very teachers who have taught the lessons – he and Jerry, that is – and who will then teach further lessons in the following years. So the assiduous student will likely have worked hard to establish some relationship with the teacher. He or she will have asked a question or two in class, come to see the teacher in his office hours, greeted him in the corridor, made him- or herself recognisable.

The oral exam is the norm in Italy. Where there is a written exam it will often be preliminary to an oral. And this oral exam is almost always with one's own teachers. And always public, which is to say, in the presence of fellow students. This can be quite a trial, but also presents certain opportunities. One risks being humiliated before one's peers, but one can also calculate that a teacher with whom you have established some rapport will be uneasy about humiliating you. Performance will be as important as content; you may not know very much, but you can show off that little with confidence. On the other hand, if you're naturally nervous and timid, the orals will be a nightmare.

Not surprisingly, the art of rhetoric is a respected subject in Italian schools. Students appreciate that it is a valuable acquisition. And one studies one's teacher as much as one's subject, the way a public speaker must study his audience as much as his brief. 'I know *exactly* what's expected,' James's son objects, when his father tries to correct him as he repeats a lesson out loud in preparation for an *interrogazione*. 'But you've got your facts wrong, kid!' 'Dad, I mean I know exactly *what my teacher wants me to say.*'

Some students also think they know exactly what their teacher wants them to wear. When James turns up to conduct his first oral exam he finds many of the girls dressed quite differently from the way he is used to seeing them at lessons. In class they wear trainers and jeans, T-shirts and sweaters. Today there are heels, skirts, décolleté, hairdos, glossy lipstick, even sunglasses. An exam is an occasion, a show. It is not unknown for a weary professor who has spent all day asking the same dumb questions to reward a girl whose charming presence and subtle perfume have cheered him up for a minute or two. Not that all young women play this card. Many turn up in the same old jeans and T-shirts. A puritan professor, James has heard some of them reasoning, might feel irritated by a young woman who makes too evident an appeal to his senses. There is so much to think about, so much to calculate in this kind of encounter. So much that has nothing to do with English grammar.

James takes his place behind a table on the dais in the huge auditorium where he teaches. Do they see him as a puritan? He reads out names in the order in which the students signed up for the exam. Or as a ladies' man? Those who signed first will be examined first. Those not in the first ten, he suggests, can happily scoot off for a coffee. Those not in the first fifty can come back this afternoon. His colleague Jerry is with him at the other side of the dais sitting at another table, so that often, between one student and another, James hears the questions Jerry is asking his students. And the answers they are giving him. But not when the chatter from the auditorium is so loud as to drown them out. The fact that the students are present does not mean that they are paying attention. Some will be planning to take the exam at a later date and have come along just to check it out. Others are friends and family whom today's candidates have brought along for moral support, or simply because it's nice to do things together. From time to time James is obliged to quieten them down. 'I can't hear myself speak!' He invites anyone too bored to listen to go and take a walk. His admonitions achieve the required result. For a minute or two.

How can you pay careful attention to ten people an hour, to forty people in a morning, eighty in a day, assessing, for each one, their range of vocabulary, their syntactical correctness, their fluency, their accent? 'Good morning.' 'Hi, Prof, how ya doin'?' someone answers in perfect Texan. Her parents sent her to study in Dallas for a year. 'How do you do, Professor,' responds another, unaware of the difference between the formal initial greeting and a simple good morning. There is no content to this exam; the students are not, for the first year, expected to discuss aspects of sociology. It's merely a question of whether they can speak.

Merely.

So what to ask them beyond where they live, what they plan to do for the summer, how many brothers and sisters they have? It's considered unwise to ask about a parent's job. The student might be embarrassed because his father is unemployed, or sweeps the streets. This fact might then influence an examiner's perception of the student's competence. Teachers are warned not to discuss politics, the logic being that if one does the students will try to produce the ideas the teacher holds. They need to please to get the result. 'I love London,' is a classic opening line from those who know James is a Londoner. In general, it's such a relief when a student wants to lead the conversation that he lets them go ahead and describe their enthusiasm for Camden Market and free museums, their horror at the price of an espresso in Oxford Street. Do some candidates tell Jerry they love Cape Town, he wonders? Does Jerry try to check if they have really been there? 'I have been going to England every year ...' one student opens, successfully fielding the present perfect progressive ... 'since I am twelve.'

'Since I was ...' James smiles.

Painfully aware that there are those in the first row watching him, he makes desperate attempts to vary his questions, always bearing in mind that they must be kept innocuous. Tell me how you travel to the university every day. Talk to me about a pet you have. No pets? OK, that a relative has. A friend? You don't know anyone with a pet? Describe your kitchen. Describe your bedroom. The young man across the table opens his mouth and closes it again.

'Your room, you know? Where you sleep. Tell me about it.'

Silence.

'Photographs? Posters? Is the bed under the window? Do you have a desk?'

'I have the room,' the boy finally gets out, 'but I am not sleeping in there.'

'So where do you sleep?' James smiles.

'In the room of my mother,' the student says. 'My father is dead many years ago.'

One girl comes forward with a surname that sounds familiar. Where has he heard it? He can't remember. He rolls the ball down the middle. Where do you live? Have you always lived in that house? What kind of car do your parents have? How many brothers or sisters?

'I have one brother,' she says with surprising emphasis.

Just as it is dawning on him where he has heard the name, she says, 'And no, he is not the murderer. My brother is a very kind, very correct person. It is only the police need a guilty one.'

Knifed to death, a black prostitute had been thrown into the canal behind the football stadium with a concrete post tied around her waist.

'I guess,' Jerry observes over a coffee mid-morning, 'when you shoot the bull with so many people, stuff is bound to come out. I ask them all what they think about the food in the university canteen.'

'All of them?'

'Every single one. They love talking about food.'

'I hadn't thought of that.'

'It's amazing how varied their answers are. Someone should do a thesis.'

After five or six minutes' conversation each student has to be given a grade. The mark is out of thirty. The pass level is eighteen. But to be given eighteen, students say, is to be *cacciato con un calcio in culo*, sent off with a kick in the arse. Eighteen is shameful, thus rarely used. And nineteen even less so, since nineteen is just a no man's land between eighteen and a barely respectable twenty. Essentially, then, it's a question of assigning the students a mark between twenty and thirty. At which point, you would say, it might as well be zero to ten. And in fact, this was how it all began. Until the 1960s there were always, officially, three professors examining, each giving a result out of ten, where six was the lowest possible pass. Hence eighteen when the three marks were summed. Now there is one professor, but the thirty remains, even though you never actually record a mark lower than eighteen. When a student fails, they are just sent away to try again.

Bocciare is the word most commonly used for fail, in the context of exams. Oddly, the idea seems to have come from the game of bowls, *bocce*, where *bocciare* means to use your ball to push an opponent's ball away from the objective. It's a sneaky, aggressive move that prevents another person from winning. *Sono stato bocciato.* I've been pushed away. I've been, if not actually excluded, then distanced. *Mandato via*, sent away, is another expression for failing an exam. Or *respinto*, rejected. I've been rejected. In all these expressions there is the suggestion of an agent – a professor, a teacher, a commission – who has done this unkind thing to you. One never says, as in English, the simple, intransitive, I failed.

'I'm afraid I'll have to ask you to repeat the exam.'

James has learned not to use unpleasant terms.

'Please, Prof, give me another chance,' the young man says, in Italian. And he adds, 'This has been a difficult period for me.' Meaning, things are not well in his private life.

James reflects. He still has another thirty students to talk to. 'OK,' he sighs. 'Explain why.'

The student – handsome, muscular – looks blank.

'Explain why this has been a tough period for you.'

'*Veda, la mia nonna ...*'

'In English! *This* is your extra question.'

Again the boy looks blank.

James spells it out. 'Explain, in English, why you feel you deserve an extra question.'

'My, er, my grandmother ...' The boy stops. 'My grandmother ... eel ... *cancro* ... has dead.'

'Died,' James corrects.

LIBRETTO

After each exam James must ask the student to give him his or her *libretto*. This is a small passport-sized document in which the teacher writes down the title of the exam, the date, the result – or *voto* – and his signature. Theoretically, before he gives his mark, a professor might flick through the *libretto*, read the scrawls of his fellow professors, the twenties, the twenty-fives, the thirties, and make comments on the student's achievements. Some professors do this. Some will base the result of their exam on the trend they find in the *libretto*. For to see that a student invariably gets thirty is to feel more confident about giving her another thirty. And vice versa, of course. A student who only has twenty-twos and twenty-fours very clearly does not deserve thirty. Needless to say it is against the rules to check a student's previous results before deciding your own, but common practice all the same.

James takes the *libretto* and carefully avoids looking at the other results. The student waits, anxiously, studying his examiner's face. Likewise those who are paying attention in the front rows of the auditorium. They want to know what mark this student will get for the performance he gave. Because before writing down the mark, the teacher has to announce it out loud to the student. He can't just write it down and have done. These are moments that define a culture. James tends to lower his voice when he gives the mark, though, legally, the exam is public. At least those in the first rows must be able to hear.

These are delicate matters. James knows that some parents will insist on seeing their children's *libretti*. He knows that some students will resist showing it to them. They fear shame and humiliation. They fear not being considered worthy of their families, and of the money spent on their educations.

'Twenty-four,' James says, in a quiet voice. Or, 'Thirty,' rather more loudly. Or, 'Thirty with *lode*.' With merit. With honour. He says *lode* with a smile of congratulation and immediately writes down the result in the student's *libretto*. But when the mark is lower, he does not write it. He looks up at the student and waits. Because a student is not bound to accept the mark the professor gives them. The student will have an idea of the result they want, the result they are *willing to accept*, and might very well say, No, I'm not going to accept twenty-two. No, I don't want twenty-four, thank you very much. The more ambitious students may even refuse a twenty-eight. 'Ask me another question,' they say. 'Please, Prof. I have studied hard for this exam. Ask me something else.'

Now the professor faces a quandary. He can ask another question. In which case it's understood that if the student does well the mark will be raised. But if this happens, it will encourage other students to follow the same strategy. And if the student answers badly, or can't answer at all, shouldn't the teacher perhaps lower the mark? Will he have the courage to be so unkind? And if he refuses to ask another question, but simply insists that when he said twenty-four he meant twenty-four, will the student now accept it after all, or have the courage to reject it?

So, subtly, each exam result becomes an object of negotiation. It is bad enough having to examine hundreds of students who are not expected to say much more than, Yes, I am, No, she wouldn't, but what if, after each conversation, the student rejects the result and comes back another time? Theoretically, there is no limit to the number of times a student can take an exam. And of course, once James knows that if he gives a student twenty-two she is likely to repeat an exam while if he gives her twenty-four she isn't, why not give her twenty-four? Why not save oneself the chore of asking her once again whether her family lives in a flat or a house, where she went for last year's holiday, or if she prefers barbecued meat to a regular kitchen grill? In other words, is the pass level really eighteen, or is it, in practice, twenty-four? And the answer is, *it depends*. Many students will accept a twenty-two, or even an eighteen, but many will not.

What are the determining factors? At the end of his or her university career, the student will get a grade based on the average of all their exams. A twenty-two might seriously lower that average. But some exams have to be passed before others can be undertaken – obviously you can't take English 2 until you've passed English 1, and maybe you can't take Accountancy until you've passed Statistics – hence to reject an exam result in one subject could lead to a student's falling behind in others. Many students will ask if they can have half an hour, or even more, to go away and reflect on whether to accept the mark or not. They will phone their parents, their brothers and sisters, their friends. They will come back and ask if there isn't something that could be done to raise their result, *just a little*. A twenty-six would be enough to keep their average on track.

One student tells James her boyfriend's dog died the night before the exam. Awake into the early hours and overcome with grief, how could she be expected to perform?

At the beginning, James was bewildered by these goings-on and woefully innocent. His only plan, as far as he had a plan, was to give the grade that the student deserved and that was that. No other course of action occurred, or could have occurred, to him. And at the very first *appello* he was involved in, meaning the first chance his students had had to do the exam, we see him trying to do just that. He conducts conversation after conversation and gives a mark. The main difficulty, he thinks, will be concentration. Concentrating entirely on each new student. Sometimes he can't rightly remember exactly how the young man or woman he is about to give a grade to has really performed. After twenty or thirty different students, each a sovereign individual of course, yet in many ways uncannily alike, the Chiaras and the Silvias, the Stefanos and the Paolos, he finds himself mixing up this one with the one before, Beatrice with Alessia, Nunzia with Eleonora. He confuses Giacomo who couldn't distinguish between the present perfect and the simple past, with Giuseppe who didn't know how to use auxiliary verbs, Cesare who preferred the seaside to the mountains, and Corrado who rated a pizza *quattro stagioni* over a pizza *quattro formaggi*. By now he has heard so many stories about the families that students stayed with when they went to English language schools, how untidy the houses were, how bad the food was, that even to ask a question in this area has a soporific effect. Every conversation is the same conversation. On two or three occasions, in the late afternoon, he panics because he realises he has fallen into a kind of trance and has no idea at all what mark he is about to give. Then he asks another question. How long have you lived in your present house? The young man looks perplexed. 'You are already asking me that, Prof.'

Case closed.

Sometimes he's aware of not wanting to be unkind to a student who has been present at all his lessons, respectful and diligent, but has performed awfully, or again he realises that he would like to use this occasion to punish a student who has been disruptive and unpleasant all year. On occasion, he isn't aware of this conditioning until he has already announced the result.

'If in doubt, aim high,' observes Jerry. 'Think of the future *appelli*.'

Their course is taught from October through to May. There are three *appelli*, three chances, that is, to take the exam at the first 'session' which runs from May through to July, then two further *appelli* in the September/October session, and two more in January and February. In all, seven rolls of the dice. Certain faces will become familiar. Perhaps it is a war of attrition. How many times are you going to tell a student that they have twenty-three when you know they want twenty five? In the event it's a relief when you simply have to fail someone, when no amount of cavilling could ever convince you to pass this person who can't speak a word of English.

The fact that the exam is public is useful in this regard. What will the students think if I pass this girl after the complete hash she has made of it? After they have become good friends, Jerry tells James the story of when he had a so-called mature student in his class and began an affair with her. She was in her mid-thirties. It was a highly passionate *avventura*. She was married, but reckless. Or perhaps reckless because married. Married and childless. But however imaginative and experienced in bed, Jerry grinned, she had no talent for languages. 'I simply had to fail her.' He shook his head. 'I couldn't see any way I could justify to others who were there why I would be passing her.'

'So you do have some principles, Jerry.'

'Alas.'

'She was upset.'

'Not at all. She said it would give her an excuse to go on seeing me.'

'And when she came back? At the next *appello*?'

Jerry had been worried about that. He had been planning, he said, to get his colleague to do the exam – he would be sick on the day or something. Unfortunately, or perhaps fortunately, in the meantime the husband had begun to suspect. The woman realised she was being followed. Incredible but true. Every time she got out of her car, the same car pulled in right behind her. She confronted her husband and he admitted he had set a private detective on her. Touchingly, this only made her even more passionate about Jerry; she was up for anything. Perhaps to punish the husband. Jerry smiled. 'But not me.' He had bailed out at once. 'Enough is enough.'

'And the exam?'

Her husband, who was extremely well off, had now forbidden his wife – as part of their reconciliation deal – to go on with the degree. Perhaps her studying late in the day was just a symptom of the marriage crisis. She got pregnant and stayed at home. Just once, in the third or fourth month of pregnancy, she had come to his flat and said she couldn't bear it. She would suffocate and die living with her husband and his ageing mother. She wanted to make love.

'And.'

'I was implacable,' Jerry said. 'She called up from the street on the intercom. I didn't even let her in the building.'

'Shut her out. Cruel.'

'I didn't escape South Africa to be gunned down in Italy,' Jerry observed.

FUORI CORSO

Although nobody is gunned down at Italian universities, the police do get involved in academic proceedings from time to time, and on one of these occasions James was in the picture and the object of their investigations was exams. His exams.

But not the first-year variety. As we have said James had not been working long for Professor Volpato when the man asked him to teach the third-year course as well. Here the textbook invited students to imagine they were planning a sociological study of football fans in different countries; they must also learn how to read articles from the foreign press that their teacher photocopied and brought to lessons. The exam was first written then oral, the problem being that many would leave this ordeal until the end of their university careers, hoping to pass immediately before their final graduation. For again, an Italian university is not like an Anglo-Saxon institution that demands one do an exam at a certain precise moment in one's course of studies. An element of choice is involved. The students might concentrate on their sociology exams, pass them all and even write the required thesis, be all ready, in short, to collect their degrees, only to find that learning English to the level required to pass English 3 was a serious obstacle. And the obstacle within the obstacle was *lo scritto*, the written exam, since students were not able to take the much easier oral exam before they had done the written part.

Nothing is simple in Italy, and people's characters are formed by the way they react to the complications. Recognisable types emerge: the student who will never accept any result less than thirty and so in a degree requiring, say, twenty-five exams will only take two or three a year, or rather take and retake two or three until the required result is achieved, thus protracting the degree for anything up to ten years, rather than the prescribed four, or, after 1997, three.

Over time James will notice that students like this very likely occupy a particular position in their families. They are simultaneously super-protected and uncritically admired. They are considered extremely intelligent, but delicate and sensitive, in constant need of positive feedback. And how is such feedback to be given, how can the admiration of admiring parents be guaranteed, if they don't always get the top grade? So a charmed infancy, playing the role of adored and coddled genius, is extended into your late twenties, if not early thirties. The parents are happy to keep this son or daughter under their wings, at university, postponing a promising future and paying the larger fees that students who are, as the Italians say, *fuori corso*, out of course, behind with their exams, are obliged to pay. Again everything is understood in terms of in and out: *in corso, fuori corso*.

In stark contrast, there is the more common phenomenon of the student who, knowing that every exam can be repeated and that there are no long-term consequences for today's particular failure, simply takes a punt at each opportunity, studying just one book when there are three on the programme, perhaps in the twenty-four hours prior to the exam, or just borrowing a friend's notes and glancing through them, utterly careless of the final grade. *Get it done*, is the imperative here. I never really wanted to do a degree in the first place. I'm only here to please my parents. At the end of the day Papà will give me a job in his textile company, his advertising agency, his design firm. This student doesn't *need* a good result. He's stamping a ticket. His life lies elsewhere. It's just that, unfortunately, the world he moves in requires that he have a degree, in much the same way that it requires that he have a baptism certificate and wear good shoes.

In between these extremes, there are the astute tacticians, students who study both the programme and the teacher, calculating, for each exam, exactly how much work is required to achieve the maximum result with the minimum effort. James finds these students rather admirable. They have understood that education is as much a question of understanding how society works as grasping this or that fact or equation.

Much rarer are the students who are genuinely passionate about the object of their studies, people who, from time to time, actually read a book or two outside the programme. They are not always the students who get the best results. Perhaps they get a 30 *e lode* where an exam interests them, then risk failure in subjects whose use and pertinence they can't understand. Such courses are all too frequent, since many degree programmes are planned more with an eye to the professors on the payroll than the actual requirements of this or that discipline.

Finally, there are the sad cases, who, to prove their worth to mother and father, absolutely have to finish their degree not only *in corso* but at the earliest possible moment, meaning June of the last year of their pro-gramme. Unfortunately, this is a task for the masochist or the genius. Very few achieve it and many students who believed themselves invin-cible and were quite sure they would bring the trophy home to receive their parents' gloating approval, will fall into a deep depression as it gradually dawns on them, usually at the beginning of their final year, that despite herculean efforts, there is no way they are going to make it. University achievement alters one's status in the family and status in the family is very largely what Italian life is about. At which point such students may very well change attitude quite drastically and simply stop doing their exams altogether. They may become extremely angry. James will know students who, despite good grades over three and more years and almost all their exams completed, will suddenly and furiously aban-don everything, go abroad, get a job, plunge into mental illness. One girl becomes coeliac. Another starts to slice up her arms with a razor.

Why? What are these young people so angry about?

The truth is that the possibility of repeating exams ad infinitum, combined with a lack of control over the numbers of students enrolling in universities, affects the psychology of the professors as much as that of the students. Some are so overwhelmed by the numbers that they pass even the worst students, simply so as not to have to re-examine them a score of times. They may use the same multiple-choice exam at all seven of the year's *appelli* and hardly concern themselves that photos of this exam are circulating on the Internet.

But in every degree course there will be one professor, at least one, who believes it is his or her duty to set the bar high, to guarantee, single-handedly, that this degree is really worth something, that it is at the same level as degrees from the best universities of Germany and America (about which he or she will have a perversely inflated opinion). In the degree course that James was involved with, this role, of standard bearer, or persecutor, fell to the professor of Economia Applicata, Applied Economics, a woman whose written exam would notoriously fail at least 90 per cent of those who took it, time after time. At the oral exam, for those lucky enough to have passed the written paper, she would ask students one question based on her book. Perhaps taken from a footnote on page 435: 'Which sociologist developed a theory based on consumer preferences for beet sugar and cane sugar?' Get your answer wrong and you were *bocciato*. There was no second question. After all, you could take the exam again. But to take it again you now had to repeat the written exam, which you might very likely fail. And so on. One hardly need turn to this or that fable to imagine an implacable dragon defending the narrow mountain pass that leads to a sane future, each aspirant stumbling towards the fatal ordeal over the corpses of the defeated who came before. Around 60 per cent of Italians never finish the degrees they start.

As he slowly becomes aware of what seems to him a bizarre state of affairs, but which to native citizens of his adopted country seems absolutely normal, James is determined not to become an ogre for his students or a curse on their young lives. On the other hand, as the twentieth century draws to a close, the English language is rapidly growing in importance for professionals of every kind and Professor Volpato is eager that his course be taken seriously and receive proper financing. In short, this isolated, energetic man is determined that the third-year exam be tough. To give himself a little importance perhaps. And though it is Volpato's assistants – Jerry, James, and a couple of others – who do most of the teaching and most of the examining, it is Volpato who presides over the three-man commission at the final oral exam and Volpato who signs all the registers at all levels. Officially, *legally*, these are his, Volpato's, exams. He is responsible, even when he doesn't actually do the first- and second-year exams and isn't even present.

All over Italy, professors sign registers authorising exam results without ever having been present at the exams or having much idea how they were set or marked. Because only a proper professor is authorised to give an exam and assign a result. This is not a job for riff-raff. Especially not foreign riff-raff. But in practical terms the universities simply can't afford enough professors to do all the exams required for all the degrees they offer. And, of course, being a powerful group, the professors wouldn't like their numbers to be artificially inflated to meet this demand, just as taxi-drivers don't want the number of taxi-driver licences to be increased merely because there are a lot of people out there looking for cabs. They too have their concerns about riff-raff from abroad.

To sum up, the assistants do the exams and the professors sign the registers and take the responsibility and the prestige. When necessary they can write on their CV that they have been president of this or that exam commission for many years. The assistant cannot make this claim. He set and marked the exam, but was not President of the Commission, not one of the in-crowd.

LO SCRITTO

But to get back to the third-year English exam where we have promised the drama of police intervention. For five years James will be responsible for writing this exam at all seven of the year's *appelli*. Caught between the desire to be serious, and the determination not to be a capricious obstacle to the students' legitimate aspirations, he works out a system that allows the smart student to get thirty and the weaker student to sneak by answering only the easier questions. He feels he has it about right.

At each *appello*, when he arrives in the exam room at the appointed time, the first problem is to organise the students in some sensible way. Having arrived early, they are all crowded high up in the back rows, as far as possible from the teacher. James invites them to spread across the room, to keep copying to a minimum. They don't move. They want to sit next to their friends. Calling their names out one by one from the roll, James tells each student where to sit. There are a hundred and more. It takes a while.

'And please, place an ID card, open at the photograph, on the desk beside you.'

As soon as the students start to write, he and Jerry move along the rows inspecting ID cards, checking that the photo corresponds to the face of the student writing and the name to the name written on the exam paper. Is this what one went to Oxford and Yale for?

All the same, some students manage to cheat. There are so many ways. They could very easily ask for more paper and put someone else's name on the new sheet, hence do the exam for them. And when a student gets up to go to the bathroom, who knows if the person who returns is the same person? There are so many people in here. When a boy who has failed the exam four or five times suddenly gets twenty-eight, Jerry suggests, out of mere curiosity, that they check the handwriting on the old exams. It is quite different. Today's paper is not his work.

What happens to a student like this? Nothing much. He is forbidden to take the exam again for the next couple of *appelli*. No one knows who actually took the exam in his place. No one tries to find out. Whoever it was had pretty good English.

As the *appelli* go by and the years, James notes two names in particular. There are two girls who take his exam at every single *appello*, never scoring the minimum required, hence never being admitted to the oral exam. With the best will in the world one cannot pass these two. One can't even explain to them what their problems are, since they never come to lessons or office hours.

James begins to recognise them when he goes round to check everyone's ID at each *appello*. They are two cheerful, sensibly dressed girls, who always sit as near to each other as possible, quietly doing and failing their exams together, seeking no contact with teachers or authorities, never complaining about their results. The circumstance is so curious that James begins to feel a desire to talk to them, to understand. He scrutinises their papers, full of empty spaces and crossings-out. There is no sign of copying. No sign of urgency. What are they doing? They keep each other company in their incompetence perhaps. It is a bond between them.

Finally, after some three years, both girls pass. At the same *appello*. One with a twenty-three, one with a twenty-five. Immediately, James phones Jerry. 'I feel so insecure,' Jerry laments, 'when the old certainties collapse.' Together they check through the exam papers for copying. Nothing. The two students have got different answers right and different answers wrong. The teachers go to the cupboards where the old exams are stacked away in groaning piles. The handwriting is the same! No cheating. After a score of tries there has been a dramatic improvement in these girls' English.

'Wish I could credit it to my teaching,' Jerry remarks.

'Why?' James asks the two, when he sees them in the queue for the oral exam.

'Why what?'

'You both failed so many times. Then you both pass!'

'We studied,' one says.

'Yeah, we always study together,' the other says.

James knows by now that the students often study in twos, threes and even fours. Some do their degrees, as it were, in little groups, families almost, taking notes for each other, doing the same exams at the same times as their friends. In a joint effort.

'We needed to pass this exam now,' one observes with a certain gravity. 'Otherwise it would have begun to hold us up.'

'By now we were familiar with the kind of exam it is.'

Everything they say is in the first-person plural. James finds it charming and decides not to complain about the hours wasted correcting any number of papers for which the students had not bothered to study.

The oral exam is held in Volpato's office. This is a small modern cube on the second floor of a large modern cube sandwiched between two rather noble Renaissance palazzi. It is cramped. Behind Volpato's metal-topped table, are Volpato, in the middle, with Jerry on one side and James on the other. Like guardian angels, James says. Bodyguards, Jerry corrects. In any event, this is the so-called exam commission. The students, milling in the corridor, come in one by one and sit opposite. The door is left ajar, as a sop to the notion that exams must be public. In reality it is impossible at this exam for the students to listen to their companions' performance. Nobody complains. Volpato greets the students in Italian, then invites his assistants to ask questions, in English, based on the study of football fans as described in their textbook. Apparently he is anxious about exposing his now rather rusty and affected English to student derision. At the end he will ask a grammar question or two, in Italian, then invite the student to go outside while his or her grade is discussed by the commission. Jerry and James look at the result for the written exams, consider the student's oral performance and propose a mark.

'Twenty-six.'

Volpato says: *'Bene. Avanti!'*

Or he says, 'I really didn't like his attitude. Twenty-four.'

Or he says, 'Breasts to die for, my friends, twenty-eight!'

DIAVOLO INCARNATO

One day a *lettore* who teaches in the Literature Department, hence has nothing to do with their exams, phones James and warns him that she has gone to the police. She has reported Volpato for alleged corruption, supposedly taking money to falsify exam results. Asking for sex in return for results.

'I named you as someone *informato dei fatti*' – someone who knows the facts. 'Be ready!'

Context is all. It is not any old colleague who has phoned James. It is a Welsh woman who for years has been leading a campaign for the recognition of the rights of the *lettori*. Since the university language teachers are responsible for setting and marking exams, this woman claims, and since, at least in her department, they teach real literature lessons, doing the same work as the professors, they should and must enjoy the same rights as professors, the same salaries. And she plays a very Italian card: the foreign-language teachers are wrongfully *excluded*, she says, because foreign. This is discrimination. As a result a legal case, underwritten by twenty and more *lettori*, has been under way for years.

We'll leave aside the complex legal niceties of the case and merely record its progress. The petition was initially won at local level, where it was known that the judges in the labour section of the court were historically opposed to the authority of the local university. The

56

victory was a foregone conclusion, to the point that the university's lawyer didn't bother to turn up for the hearing.

But no Italian court case ends with a first decision. There is always an appeal, heard in a different court, in a different town. So, in our case, after a year or so's wait, in Venice, the university won the appeal. This too had been foreseen. The *lettori*'s lawyer had warned that the university would win the case in Venice where the judges had a low opinion of the provincial court where the university was based.

But few Italian court cases end with the court of the appeal, especially if it does not confirm the sentence of the lower level. After the appeal, there is the Cassazione, presided over by the top judges, in Rome. These wise, experienced men don't hear new evidence but simply examine the work of the other courts. Ominously, or promisingly, the verb *cassare*, from which *cassazione* is derived, means 'to annul'. The Annulment Court. And indeed, in the case of the foreign-language teachers, the Cassazione decided that both the appeal court and the local court hadn't done their work properly, there were *vizi di forma*, procedural flaws. The whole process would have to be started again, this time at another court in another town.

Frustrated by this endless legal process, the Welsh woman, Megan Hughes, announces an appeal to the European Parliament and unleashes a series of political and legal attacks inside the university. Volpato, isolated among the English professors, soon becomes one of the staunchest defenders of the professional and bureaucratic abyss between professors and *lettori*, language-teaching assistants.

'A *lettore* is a nobody,' Volpato tells James. 'With respect.' People employed off the street, he says, for no other reason than that they speak the language. *Col cazzo* these riff-raff are going to have the same rights as me!

Perhaps Volpato, James thinks, by defending professorial privilege so staunchly, wants to find his way back into the good graces of his peers. He means to show them that despite never doing any meaningful research, he does have useful qualities. In retaliation, Megan Hughes has gone to the police and reported Volpato for allegedly taking bribes. The scam, she tells James in a conspiratorial voice over the phone, is this: when a student who has repeatedly failed the exam goes to see him in his office hours, Volpato tells them that the best thing to do is to go to a certain *lettore* for private lessons. People who take lessons from this assistant, ten lessons that is, always pass. The students go to this colleague of theirs, and Megan named the man, an Australian – Howard – who then charges them an exorbitant 100,000 lire an hour, about three times the going rate for private lessons.

'Half of which is trousered by Volpato,' Hughes says. Howard, not unusually in a drunken state, has told her so.

James draws a deep breath. The fact is that when he receives this phone call the university is only days away from its long summer break. He already has a train ticket to join his family on an Adriatic beach three hundred miles away. In his head, he is on holiday.

'And so?'

'So Volpato must have some way of making sure these students pass the exam, right? Fixing the written results so they get to the oral.'

'I have no awareness of this.'

'You could do some checking.'

'You're asking me to start spying on my professor.'

'He's poison.'

The Italians have a proverb, *inglese italianizzato diavolo incarnato* – an 'Italianised' Englishman is the devil incarnate. Or rather, the outsider who comes inside takes the worst of our traits, becomes more Italian than an Italian, in the negative. Which is an excellent reason for never letting anyone in.

James calls his pal Jerry and they try to remember examination anomalies. Out of pure curiosity, they check through a pile of old exam papers and find two cases where the mark they had given appears to have been altered. A seventeen transformed into a twenty-seven, a fourteen into a twenty-four. Intriguing, but hardly a sign of systematic corruption. And why, Jerry pointed out, would Volpato do something like that, when theoretically, having control of the registers, he could just write in a final mark there, and in the student's *libretto*, without anyone else ever being aware, without there being any trace at all?

Or did Volpato want the student to believe that he or she, after doing the famous ten lessons, had passed the exam *legitimately*, so that he, Volpato, couldn't at some future point be blackmailed by them for having fixed it?

When you start thinking in these terms, there is no end.

'Glad to be the detective for once, though,' Jerry laughed, 'rather than the object of investigation.'

But Jerry has spoken too soon. They *were* an object of investigation. For what the policeman made clear, when three days later, and only twenty-four hours before his departure for the beach, James was questioned, was that the accusing report he had received spoke of possible collusion on the part of the professor's assistants, James and Jerry.

Clearly Megan hadn't told James everything he needed to know.

L'INTERROGATORIO

The meeting took place on a miserably hot afternoon in a nondescript office in the *questura*, in the heart of the old town. One heavy-breathing policeman, in his early forties, sat behind piles of papers that stirred intermittently with the back and forth of a big electric fan. Another man faced the wall, clacking away at an electric typewriter. This was the early nineties. There was no air conditioning.

'So I must caution you that your own position may be under consideration.'

James was immediately anxious.

'Should I ask to be assisted by a lawyer?' he said, falling into the kind of legal jargon one hears on cop shows.

'If you were formally under investigation you would have received an *informazione di garanzia*,' the policeman told him. It wasn't clear to James whether this was reassuring or not.

'Has Volpato received an *informazione di garanzia*?' he asked.

The policeman said no, not yet. It was important, for the moment, that Volpato know nothing. So he couldn't cover his tracks. Always assuming he had done anything. This *interrogatorio* must remain strictly confidential and James would have to sign a statement guaranteeing this confidentiality.

'No problem,' James said.

The policeman now began to speak about the legal status of a university degree, something of which James was only vaguely aware. Since a degree is a necessary prerequisite for applying for a huge range of state jobs it has a legal value, like a marriage certificate. Or a driving licence. When awarded, the pronouncement is made *nel nome della legge*, in the name of the law.

'So it is a serious crime to obtain a degree by false means.'

James began to feel more and more anxious. The policeman loomed so physically large behind his big desk, he breathed so deeply and was so assertive in his uniform, so complacent in his capacity to make life easy or difficult for others, that it really began to seem one might end up in goal. The papers on the desk in front of him, of various bureaucratic pastels, the occasional phone call, his whispered asides to his younger colleague doing the typing, gave the impression of a considerable authority. Even his politeness was menacing.

'Have a glass of water,' the policeman offered. 'We'll be here a while.'

James took him at his word and accepted. Even so he would never have imagined he would be there three and a half hours. The policeman wanted to understand every aspect of his work at the university, how he had got the job, how it was performed, and, above all, what kind of man Volpato was. Did he have sexual relationships with students? Did he seem worried about money?

James did all he could to keep the conversation generic and innocuous. He spoke of a sense of discouragement among professors when one saw so many people in a classroom. He used the word *deresponsabilizzante*, a situation that makes you feel less responsible. 'Because you can't teach everyone, you see.' It was an atmosphere, James observed, in which all kinds of neglect might occur. He spoke of the fact that students never complained when there were obvious breaches of regulations because they feared that they might be discriminated against. 'It is not an atmosphere where an individual feels safe to speak out,' he said.

The policeman was unimpressed.

But the truth was this was exactly how James felt here, now, in the police station. Insecure. Volpato was well placed in local society. His wife came from one of the most powerful old families in town. It was likely there would be a chain of connections between the professor and the police, such that one day Volpato would get a chance to see what his English assistant had said about him in this *interrogatorio*. So James did not mention the extra marks awarded for fine breasts, or the general feeling that Volpato was a ladies' man, which, after all, is hardly a crime. He did not mention the two results apparently altered in the pile of exams that he and Jerry had looked through. In particular, he did not mention the Australian, Howard, with his debts and his drinking problem.

'Many of the professors,' James went on, 'are connected with language schools outside the university.'

The policeman, he thought, would already know this.

'And so?'

'Well, I suppose someone could argue that they benefit from the fact that the institution they work in is incapable of providing the teaching that would allow students to pass the exams they set.'

The policeman wasn't interested.

'Do people put pressure on you to pass students who should fail?'

'Only the students themselves,' James laughed. 'And occasionally their parents.' He explained how, on a dozen occasions, he had been astonished, keeping his office hours, to find people in their forties and fifties coming into his room, begging him to let their children pass his exam.

'Do they offer anything in return?'

'I would never let them get to that point,' James said.

'And Volpato?'

'I've no idea.'

The policeman breathed deeply. He seemed in no more hurry than a shrink waiting for his client to come up with a dream worth analysing.

James didn't oblige.

'Have you been aware of exams being "fixed"?'

'I have not,' James said.

'If you were aware of exams being fixed, what would you do?'

'I have no idea.'

'You wouldn't report it at once?'

'I'm not sure whom I would report it to.'

'In what sense?'

'Well, my Head of Faculty would be the appropriate person, I suppose, but I would have to understand his relationship with the eventual culprit.'

The policeman threw him a shrewd look. Later James would reflect that, question after question, this long hot afternoon had been an extended test of his Italianisation, a process of self-discovery even. He had become the person who knew to answer in this way.

'You wouldn't report the matter to the police?'

'Working for the university for some years now, I feel a certain loyalty to the institution.'

At this point James actually used the expression *lavare i panni sporchi in famiglia*, one should keep the dirty washing at home. 'As when we catch someone cheating,' he added, 'we don't go to the police. We sort it out ourselves.'

The policeman repeated that a degree was a legal document and that tampering with the process of acquiring it was a crime. At the same time, he had begun to show a grudging respect for James's caution.

'If someone wished to uncover eventual corruption in this area, how would he go about it, do you think?'

'I suppose one would have to look at the concrete evidence, written exams, registers and so on.'

'You have never noticed any anomalies in these areas?'

'I haven't looked for any,' James lied.

The policeman wanted to know where the old exams and registers were kept. James described the dusty files piled in the old gunmetal cupboards in the institute. *Appello* after *appello* after *appello*, hundreds upon thousands of exam papers stacked on the shelves of the cupboard in big grey files. It was disturbing just to think of all the energy and anxiety that had gone into them.

The policeman raised a wry eyebrow. 'You are a philosopher?'

'Whenever I see piles of paper' – James gestured to the policeman's desk – 'I have a sort of horror of futility.'

'On the contrary,' the policeman remarked, 'these papers are extremely useful. Used properly, they can mean guilt or innocence. They can right a wrong.'

James shrugged.

Another half an hour and at long last he was given a statement to sign. 'I the undersigned, born January 1955, in Highbury, Londra, Regno Unito ... on this day of June ... in the presence of ... cognisant of my responsibility before the law, etc., etc.' Reading through it, James could not help feeling that the whole rigamarole was proving an extraordinary waste of time and public funds. Wouldn't the police have done better to have gone straight to Howard, straight to Volpato? As soon as he was back home, he phoned Megan Hughes and told her what he thought of her. What was the point of stirring up trouble like this if you didn't have any solid evidence?

The Welsh woman chuckled. 'Perhaps there is stuff that you don't know about and the policeman didn't mention.'

James set off the following morning to join his family at the seaside. Four or five days into his holiday he was just beginning to relax when it occurred to him to give Jerry a call and ask if he too had been interviewed by the police.

'Thank God,' Jerry said. 'I've been trying to get hold of you. Did you see the *gazzetta*, Saturday?'

This was the local newspaper, open on the tables of every café and bar in the province.

'You had the main front-page headline, my friend,' Jerry told him.

This headline announced that a British language teacher who had studied at the prestigious universities of Oxford and Yale had gone to the police to accuse his professor, Massimo Volpato, of corruption.

'They gave it the whole page. You told the police there was a girl ready to testify that she had sex with Volpato to pass her exam.'

During his five hours on the train that same day, leaving his family and heading back home at once, it occurred to James that Megan had never really wanted Volpato in court; she had created a situation where the professor's reputation could be damaged by telling the press that the man had been formally accused by someone who worked closely with him. That was much faster than any legal process. Naturally, the police would assume it was he, James, who had spoken to journalists.

As soon as he was back in town, James called Volpato.

'Not a word of that article is true. There will be a letter of denial in the paper the day after tomorrow. I've told them I'll sue if they don't publish.'

'I never imagined it was true,' Volpato said coolly. 'Why would you have done something like that?'

They spoke for a few minutes, but the old friendliness had gone.

James called the number the policeman had given him.

'It wasn't me who went to the press.'

'We are extremely disappointed,' the policeman said.

'I don't know anyone at the local newspaper. It's not the kind of thing I do.'

'But evidently you did tell someone that you had spoken to the police.'

This was true. Megan. For weeks afterwards, James wondered if the police would pursue him for this breach of confidence. But the whole thing blew over. In the end it was just a front page in a local newspaper. Nothing had actually *happened*.

'Except that my name has been *infangato*,' Volpato observed at the beginning of the new term. *Fango*, mud. *Infangato*, muddied, sullied. His authority had been undermined. Yet the professor never spoke of suing the newspaper, or James, or Megan. And this is something James would begin to notice over the years. That all kinds of extraordinary accusations can be made, publicly, but at the end of the day things will usually go on very much as they always did.

It was shortly after this episode that James started writing to other universities, looking for a career-track position elsewhere.

PART TWO

Milano

GUELFI E GHIBELLINI

One of the hardest parts of Italian history to get your mind round is the business of the Guelfs and the Ghibellines. On the plus side, if you do manage to grasp the phenomenon in all its longevity and infernal complexity, you're a long way to understanding Italy *tout court*. Or to understanding that it is beyond understanding.

Put aside any illusion that the names themselves have anything useful to tell you. They apparently originated in opposing battle cries – Welf! Wibellingen! – used in the Siege of Weinsberg in 1140, though they were not much heard in Italy until the mid-1200s, a full century later. The background to the division that these very German names came to represent was the struggle between the Papacy in Rome and the Holy Roman Empire, which had its centre of power in Germany. What was at stake was the political control of northern and central Italy and parts of Germany and France. Essentially, the Guelfs supported the Pope, and the Ghibellines the Holy Roman Emperor, though in special circumstances it could also happen that the opposite was the case.

It was not that the Pope or the Emperor ever supposed they could exercise power *directly* in, say, Florence or Bologna, Milan or Venice, not to mention Genoa, Verona, Padua, Vicenza, Brescia, Ferrara, Ravenna, etc. Rather, they were competing for the allegiance of scores of feudal lords, republican assemblies, or simply wealthy families, who held power on the ground. Conversely, the lords, republicans and wealthy patricians were not as a rule Guelf or Ghibelline out of any profound ideological conviction, but as a matter of convenience. That is, the Guelfs, the Church party, tended to dominate where the ruling elite felt they had more to fear from the Empire than the Papacy. And vice versa. This was largely a geographical consideration, but it might also be a question of the kind of social organisation that was most congenial. For example, since the Holy Roman Empire had a strictly feudal structure, it appealed to the old patrician families and nobles, the landed gentry, while the *nouveau riche*, the bankers and merchants, who had an interest in the formation of a looser, less hierarchically rigid society, felt that the Church offered more flexibility, or simply intervened less often. On the other hand, if these forward-looking folk found themselves uncomfortably close to the Papal States, which the Pope was always seeking to expand, even they would very likely be Ghibelline. Equally, a feudal lord might well go Guelf if his territory became the object of imperial ambitions.

But this is still reductive. The fact is that allegiance was collective rather than individual, tribal even. Families, corporations, whole cities declared their loyalty *as a group*. And if a large city was Guelf, very likely the smaller cities around it would be Ghibelline, with an implicit appeal for protection from afar. And vice versa of course, all in the general determination to preserve local sovereignty. Nor did either party, Guelf or Ghibelline, have a stable hold on a group's identity. Some internal division in a family or town could easily lead to part of that town switching from Ghibelline to Guelf. In short, the existence of two parties across the peninsula meant there was always another side to turn to if you fell out with the status quo.

We still haven't exhausted the options that this division gave rise to. For there was also the possibility that both sides might go on being Guelf, but find some other term to establish what *kind* of Guelfs they were. Or Ghibellines. After decades of fighting between Guelfs and

Ghibellines within Florence, when the matter was finally settled in 1289 with the defeat and mass expulsion of the Ghibellines, the victorious Guelfs lost little time in dividing themselves into Black Guelfs and White Guelfs, who would then fight each other with the same intensity and ferocity that they had previously fought, and where necessary would continue to fight the Ghibellines. The terms black and white here, it should be understood, had no significance at all. They were simply borrowed from the town of Pistoia where a similar schism had occurred.

To hold any position of power, then, or simply to receive any concessions or favours, it was important to be a member of a group, a faction. And hence to be Ghibelline or Guelf. On the other hand it could be extremely dangerous to be a member of a faction, particularly a prominent member. Because Guelfs and Ghibellines were, by definition, in conflict, and the conflicts of the time were unspeakably cruel. Enemies were imprisoned and tortured on the slightest pretext. Exiled, their land was confiscated and their houses, even in the centre of town, razed to the ground. Tongues were cut out and hands amputated. People were left in dungeons to starve or they were disembowelled and dragged through the streets, or burned at the stake before jeering crowds; nor is there any indication that one party was morally superior to the other when it came to violence and vengeance. You had to choose your group well, that is, choose the winning group, and make sure you didn't fall foul of the other, or worst of all, find yourself identified as a traitor. In which case torture was inevitable.

If this all sounds a lot like Dante's *Inferno*, that is because it is exactly the world that Dante was writing from. In fact, one way to get a sense of what it meant to be Guelf or Ghibelline is to take a look at Dante's career. This has the advantage of killing two birds with one stone, since all Italians have studied Dante and have some version of his biography, however idealised, imprinted in their brains, with the result that quoting Dante is a way of declaring your Italianness. The more Dante you can quote the more Italian you are. Dante-quoting one-upmanship, as James soon discovered, is a wearily common phenomenon and shows no signs of abating. Not to realise that a person you're talking to is quoting Dante is a serious gaucherie, while spotting it at once, as a foreigner, is to put in a robust claim for honorary citizenship. Certainly, Valeria knows her Dante, which she studied both at the *scuola media* and the *liceo classico*, and indeed will have to go on studying, even for a degree in Communications and Media. James's two children, who attend quite different kinds of schools, will both study Dante inside out.

And what is it that they learn? Essentially, that Dante started as an insider, a Guelf where Guelfs were successful, then became an outsider when his party split and he found himself, in 1301, on the wrong side of the divide, condemned to death and forced into exile until his death in 1321. The *Inferno*, then, is a poem that was written from exile, and very largely about exile, since most of the damned whom the poet meets in hell will be Florentine and seem to suffer more for being away from Florence than for being dead or in hell. They talk to Dante in the hope that he has news from Florence. They beg him to mention them in Florence, to keep their names alive as it were, in his poetry. That is the power he has. Otherwise being dead and being exiled are really rather similar conditions, the latter differing only in so far as a living person might one day return from exile. Much of Dante's poetry was written with the idea that by praising and blaming the right people back in Florence he might encourage them to overturn his death sentence and invite him back from exile. Something that never happened.

But what on earth has any of this got to do with our heroes Valeria and James? We are looking, I suppose, for a key to help us read the events that will unfold in the coming chapters, not to mention the very particular emotions, positive and negative, that will attach to them. Always keeping in mind the risk of being reductive, let's posit the following hypotheses:

That power in Italy is above all the power to include or exclude others. The power of the *padrino*.

That fear in Italy is the fear of being expelled. *Days of Abandonment.*

That courage in Italy is the courage to walk out, to make a bid for independence. *Jack Frusciante è uscito dal gruppo* was the title of one hugely successful youth novel of the 1990s. *Jack Frusciante Has Left the Group.* What courage!

That cowardice in Italy is accepting any conditions, however humiliating, for the privilege of retaining the protection of whatever boss, or Head of Faculty, or Fascist *gerarch*, is running the show.

That goodness in Italy is the willingness to reach out to others as the Church reaches out and, being a Catholic Church, includes *everyone*. Except those it excommunicates.

Hence, finally …

That unhappiness in Italy is exclusion, abandonment.

LE VOCI DELLA SERA

'You will be as lonely as a dog,' Valeria's mother again warns her daughter when the girl sets off to Milan. She has done harm to herself, Carmela insists, not signing up for Don Gabriele's offer of accommodation with other students from her home town. What would it have cost her, to go to Mass on Sunday? Nothing. However, when the two say goodbye, it is clearly the older woman who feels abandoned. She wants all her children round her. She feels lost without them.

As it turns out, Valeria is rarely alone in Milan because she has to share a room with a girl from Piacenza. At the very last minute she was awarded a place in her university's only dormitory. A huge stroke of luck. With all their love of communities, Italians have little interest in the campus university, the idea of a place where students really live and study and play together. When your children already enjoy the comforts of family and Church why invest in a more open, broader form of association notoriously prone to ideologies and drunkenness? This particular university, for example, has no debating clubs or sports teams, no orchestra or dramatic society. The three impressive modern buildings that make up its hub open at 8.30 a.m. and close at 7.30 p.m. There are cafés and a canteen, but they are all shut by 6.00, when lessons end. There is nowhere to get together in the evening. Nowhere to kick a ball around. No volleyball net or tennis court. It is a school, not a living space, and although pleasant enough, the large plaza outside the main building, with its four fountains, two statues, and many proud plaques bearing the names of founders and benefactors, is clearly not a place for fun.

So the university's one dormitory with its mere fifty rooms feels like something of an anomaly. The idea is that in a private institution, perceived as expensive, this handful of rooms offers succour to the worthy poor, or less well-off, rather, since no one really poor could afford to come here. The rooms are all doubles, which is not so good, but they are affordable. Applicants, who outnumber places available by many times, must show that their families have low incomes and live at least ninety minutes by train from Milan's central station. Beyond easy commuting, that is. So it's surprising to Valeria to find that her room-mate is from Piacenza, which is only about an hour away, depending on what kind of train you catch. Valeria will later meet someone in the dormitory whose father is a judge and it seems unlikely that a judge would be on a low income. One learns not to ask too many questions.

In any event, Valeria loves her room, which picks up the sunlight in the afternoon and has a tiny balcony. She doesn't mind that the place feels rather isolated in the evenings, that there is nowhere to go without heading for the metro. During the day it's full of life, and wonderfully easy for getting to lessons. She loves reading with the windows open to the sounds of the large courtyard where other students mill around a café or lie on the grass and smoke. She loves smoking a cigarette herself on the balcony, alternately looking down at it all and then back to the pages of her book. She is happy with her literature course and begins to wish she had studied literature or even languages, rather than Communications and Marketing. But at the end of her studies she will need to get a job. Unlike the two protagonists of the novel she is presently finishing.

It's called *Le voci della sera* (*Voices in the Evening*) by Natalia Ginzburg, was published in 1961 and is in that part of her reading list described as 'optional', which means she'll be one of the very few students to read it. The plot is simple enough. Elsa lives with her mother and father in a small village near a large town. Very likely Turin. It's a family of modest middle-class background and wealth. Meantime the village as a whole is dominated by a large textile factory run by a family with any number of aunts and uncles, brothers and sisters and cousins. Everybody in the village knows this family's history for generations back. They are the only important people around. And Elsa is dating one of the family's younger generation and eventual heirs, Tommasino.

Secretly. Tommasino doesn't want their relationship to be known. Not that the reciprocal families would have any objections, just that he feels he isn't the marrying kind; and their families wouldn't understand a relationship without marriage. So once a week Elsa takes the bus to town, ostensibly to exchange library books; in fact she heads for a room that Tommasino has rented and the two make love. They are happy, in a cautious sort of way.

This goes on for a while. The two talk about their problems. Tommasino feels trapped in his family history, the factory and so on. He loves to imagine a life in some foreign country where he is absolutely independent and the past does not weigh on him. On the other hand, the life offered to him by the family business is so obvious and easy; every day he goes to the factory where he has an office of his own, though no well-defined role or responsibilities. He sits around and dabbles in whatever research takes his fancy. Really, he is only there because he has no idea what else he would like to do. He's marooned.

Elsa begins to weary of it all. She loves Tommasino, but what's the point of a man who keeps you hidden and sees no future for himself? She is having to act like a girl who never has boyfriends, a woman whose life can't be explained. His being marooned, is marooning her. Finally, she refuses to go to the famous room and make love. It's over, she says.

Or maybe not. Out of the blue Tommasino comes to her house, speaks to her father, says he wants to marry her. Elsa is delighted.

So are Elsa's parents. Her daughter is marrying into the richest family in the area. Reciprocal visits begin, evenings spent in company with relatives. Elsa's mother busies herself with the wedding arrangements, the furnishing of a new home. There is so much to buy, so much to decide. Meanwhile everyone in the village is talking about the lucky *fidanzati*. Everybody knows them, congratulates them. Until, all too soon, the couple feel overwhelmed. And if Elsa can just about handle it, because she loves her man, Tommasino can't. 'I wish I'd left home and met you in some foreign place,' he says. 'A girl I'd never seen before, not a childhood friend.'

Elsa bails out. She doesn't want a man whose affection is so easily discouraged. She returns the engagement ring, which needless to say had been in Tommasino's family for generations. The novel ends with Elsa's mother complaining what a blow it has been to her and her husband that the marriage is not to be. They feel so humiliated that they have decided to move away from their village and live somewhere else for a while. Very likely Tommasino is homosexual, her mother suggests. Elsa says nothing in reply. Her opinion doesn't seem to matter.

This novel, read in the early months of her university career, makes a big impression on Valeria. She knows *exactly* what Natalia Ginzburg is talking about. Every day she speaks to her parents, or at least her mother, on the phone, usually just after lunch or just before going to bed. But she never tells them anything intimate, anything that matters, since if she did it would immediately do the rounds of all the relatives. There would be phone calls from aunts and uncles and cousins. Zia Lella in particular. In her convent. There would be criticism, approval, gossip. The fact is, Valeria is presently going out with someone from her home town, Giancarlo, a boy who went to her same school, though in the year above her, and is studying at another university in Milan. Altogether there are about a dozen of her old school friends in the city. Giancarlo studies Computer Science, plays a lot of volleyball and holds strong political opinions quite different from Valeria's own. There's something urgent and defensive about him, handsome but brittle.

They argue. And she understands they are together mostly because they come from the same town. She has a vague intuition that this is not her destiny. She must be careful; to take Giancarlo home and tell her mother about the relationship would be to set a ball rolling she might not be able to stop. Her mother would be so glad that he was a local boy. Fortunately, Giancarlo seems to view things the same way because he hasn't yet invited her to his home either.

All the same, it's good to have a boyfriend, someone you can travel with, back and forth, on those long journeys south for holidays and occasional weekends, someone who understands the difficulties of living, as it were, in two places at once. Giancarlo talks to his parents even more often than Valeria to hers. Three or four times a day. A constant conversation, mostly about other members of the family, or what he is eating, or the cold he is bound to catch if he doesn't dress warmly. His father gives him large bottles of labelless wine to carry north in his trolley bag, a local red he buys wholesale and bottles himself. At the weekends, when Valeria's room-mate goes home to Piacenza, the two Lucani lie in bed eating her mother's *taralli* and drinking his father's wine.

The room-mate is called Costanza. She is tall, blonde, and irritatingly competitive. Studying for the same degree, she keeps asking Valeria what grades she got in this or that exam and is evidently unhappy if they're higher than her own. She didn't get a thirty, she explains of one exam, because the professor asked her a question that wasn't in the course book. They're not supposed to do that. It's unacceptable. If she gets a better mark than Valeria, she offers her condolences. It's all a question of your performance on the day, she concedes.

Costanza's clothes are always a little more fashionable than Valeria's, her make-up a little sharper. She spends serious time in front of the mirror and has more handbags than there is space to store. But when, on this sunny autumn afternoon, Valeria comes in from the balcony and starts talking excitedly about Ginzburg's novel, Costanza grows thoughtful; she pouts, sighs, kicks a sock across the floor, sits down hard on her bed. Her boyfriend Massimo, she says, works for her father. The family has a small company that makes fashion handbags and other accessories. 'That's why I have so many!' Her father is a fantastic, charismatic figure, so busy he's hardly ever in the house. A whirlwind. Her mother's a bit of a bore, a bit of a nag, always afraid some disaster is about to happen. Then there are two sisters, Anna and Elena, both older. Anyway, her father, who really is a brilliant businessman – 'You should meet him,' she assures Valeria – built up the whole company himself, from scratch. Then he got Anna, the eldest, to study Economics, so now she is doing the company accounts; and later Elena, the second, to study Fashion, so she has taken over the design of new products. She's doing pretty well. Their husbands are involved too. One in warehousing. One in administration. The company is growing.

Costanza stares at her fingernails. 'And now he's got me to do Communications and Marketing. With two languages.'

'So you can promote sales.'

'I'm supposed to build up an export market. For future world domination.'

Valeria can't quite see where this is going. Costanza has something moody and troubled about her. She stands and opens the wardrobe door to study the mirror, turning her head from side to side.

'He's always saying what a shame it is that the brightest child is the youngest. He's trying to persuade Anna and Elena to let me run the business, in the future, if they will agree.'

'Great!' Valeria congratulates. 'You'll never have to look for a job.'

'It's just that I feel a bit like the guy in your novel,' Costanza observes. 'I mean, why do you think I wanted a miserable double room in a dorm, when I could easily commute? Piacenza is a bore.'

Valeria doesn't find the room miserable at all.

'What about the boyfriend?' she asks.

'Max? Max is *bellissimo*. Want to see?'

She has photos on her laptop. Hundreds. The young man is solid and beefy, but with a boyish face. His grin is broad. He's handsome and at ease with life. Just the kind of boyfriend you'd want to show photos of.

'*Figo*,' Valeria agrees. Hell of a guy.

'He's doing an apprenticeship in production.' Costanza shakes her head. 'Papà likes him a lot. He's a fantastic dancer. But you can't really talk to him.'

Valeria is sitting on her bed, watching as the other girl arranges and rearranges her hair.

'See the earrings he got me?' She cocks her head to show three rubies at the bottom of a twig of gold.

'What can't you talk about?'

Costanza shrugs. 'Wanting to be a million miles away.'

Valeria spends a lot of time thinking about her room-mate. The girl is obsessive about being the best in every subject she studies; at the same time she is only studying to please her father. She seems besotted with the man. There are long phone calls. The girl goes out on the balcony and talks in a low voice. Perhaps the boyfriend, Valeria thinks, is mainly there to keep daughter and father together. He's not the kind who would take her away.

When Valeria shares these thoughts with Giancarlo, he says, 'Can I meet her?'

'She'll flirt with you, to compete with me.'

'Sounds good,' Giancarlo laughs. 'Maybe she'll give me a job in her dad's company.'

A month or so after that talk, when an afternoon lesson is cancelled at the last minute because the professor is unwell, Valeria returns to her room and surprises Costanza having sex with a man who is clearly not her boyfriend. He's too old. His head is shaven and he has a tattoo on his neck. It's an embarrassing scene. The two are standing in the bathroom, Costanza gripping the sink, the man behind her with his chin on her shoulder. Both are looking into the mirror as they move.

No sooner has she registered what is going on than Valeria retreats, shutting the door hard behind her. She feels upset.

'Sorry about that,' Costanza excuses herself later. 'But how could I know you'd be back so soon?'

'You couldn't,' Valeria agrees.

'So why the long face? You use the place when I'm away. Accidents happen.'

For Valeria, the problem is not the sex, but the betrayal. She feels the bathroom has been contaminated. She feels her room-mate might bring in anyone. The fallout from this episode is that the two girls stop talking to each other about anything beyond immediate practicalities. Both feel the hostility has something to do with the difference between north and south, or at least the different communities they grew up in. Both feel their own world is immeasurably superior.

LA COMPAGNIA STORICA

Aside from this minor unpleasantness with her room-mate, Valeria's life is fruitfully uneventful. She enjoys the teaching at the university. She has learned to ignore what other students say about this or that exam. It's hell. It's too hard. Too easy. It's a joke. She realises this is compulsive chatter, to play the victim or show off. Whatever the subject, she studies all the books on the programme. She goes to all the lessons. Plus any extras: seminars, reading groups, films. There is always time, if you're organised. When a teacher plods or lacks charisma, she focuses on the content. There is always something to get your teeth into, even when that something makes you wish you'd studied something else. It's a process of discovery. When exam time comes around, she chooses her *appelli* carefully, the ones where there will be fewer students, where the teachers will be more relaxed. And in the main the grades she gets are fair, she thinks, the teachers impartial, or as impartial as anyone ever can be in an oral exam. She loves the idea of *meritocracy*, of being rewarded because you are good at something, without needing to ask a favour of anyone, without needing a magic charm, or an influential friend. This is why it was smart to come north. Whatever the pretensions and vanity of someone like Costanza, Milan seems the sort of place where they give you what you deserve, where they want you because you're serious. Valeria is quietly determined to deserve the best. By the end of the second year she has eight thirties and three *lodi*. Quite a haul.

As for a social life, since most of the students rush off to their homes when lessons are over, some commuting far more than the famous ninety minutes, Valeria goes out almost exclusively with her circle from the south, a dozen Lucani who all come from the two or three schools within a stone's throw of Piazza Santa Rita and Don Gabriele's office. They all know each other and their parents know each other, or at least are acquainted, and when anyone new arrives, or just comes north for a few days, for a holiday or a job interview, they are invited along. The tam-tam never fails.

Giancarlo is living in his great-aunt's big old house to the north of Milan. She has allowed him to bring his best friend, Flavio, who is studying engineering. They have their own rooms on the top floor. But since the old lady, Signora Rosa, is in her eighties and needs looking after, there is a granddaughter in the house too, Chiara, who has the bedroom beside hers on the first floor. She's from the northeast, because Rosa's only daughter, Giancarlo's father's cousin, married in Udine. Chiara has signed on at the state university to study Nutrition, but actually spends most of the time cleaning up after the old lady and taking her to the shops or the park. This saves her parents the need either to bring Rosa to Udine, or to pay for a carer, one of the many Filipino or Sri Lankan men and women you see all over the north arm in arm with decrepit Italians. In a space of weeks, Flavio, the southern boy, hits it off with this northern girl and the two are soon inseparable.

So now Chiara becomes part of this long-established group of friends, the so-called *compagnia storica*. She joins them at pizzerias and picnics in the park and Sunday *spaghettate* in their various lodgings. When Valeria asks her how her studies are going, she grimaces. Chiara doesn't say much at their get-togethers. Rarely made up, always in jeans and T-shirt, she eats mechanically. Her hands are pale and fleshy. When she does speak, she is aggressively feminist. Women get

83

a bad deal, because they are powerless. For a few minutes she takes over the conversation. Her accent and manner are a million miles from theirs. Laws must be made guaranteeing equality, she says, guaranteeing equal wages, punishing all discrimination. She stabs at her pasta. It's a disgrace. Aside from these sudden forays, she spends the time mothering Flavio. Always at his side, she likes to whisper in his curly hair. She takes care he doesn't drink too much. Dark and wiry beside her ample pallor, he cracks tacky jokes and talks football with Giancarlo. The men never seem to realise how childish they sound, Valeria reflects, arguing about referees and TV rights. She tells Chiara that in her family, the women are always boss. Even Zia Lella is a sister superior. The men tend to end up on the margins. Aside, that is, from her father's uncle in Rome. And he, of course, never married.

Men have been bossing women for centuries, Chiara objects. And Italy is years behind the other European countries. Especially the south. 'Look at all the men who kill their wives and girlfriends when they try to leave them.' Everybody chuckles at this. 'Flavio's already seen off three,' Giancarlo assures her. 'He's a passionate guy.' Valeria realises that Chiara doesn't want to talk about her university courses because instead of going to lessons she is having to deal with her grandmother's incontinence. She is cleaning the old woman's shit while the two boys prepare for their exams. But who is making her do that? Valeria wonders. I never would.

Or would she? As yet her family loyalty has not been tested.

Giancarlo is annoyed that Flavio and Chiara have become so close. His friendship with Flavio is flagging. He comes to see Valeria more often now, lying on her bed reading comics and checking the volleyball results. Costanza seems a nice person, he decides, after they finally meet. A million times prettier than Chiara, anyway. He's fed up of feminism. 'She should lose weight,' he says. He's dogmatic and restless. Valeria says she's surprised Flavio doesn't help Chiara a bit with the grandmother, to give her more time to study.

'Chiara doesn't want to be helped,' Giancarlo says. 'She likes running the show.'

Towards the end of spring term, Valeria makes a first attempt to leave Giancarlo. They hardly make love at all now, just hang around talking about their families and friends and exams. She tells him she feels the need to be alone a bit and think things through. Life at the university is changing them, she muses, they are becoming different people. 'Don't you think?'

Giancarlo can't see what she's getting at. He finds his girlfriend dreamy and overly solemn. What he likes is when they're both agreed in criticising someone else. Making fun of them. His mother, for example, who has just called to remind him not to forget to wish his cousin happy birthday. Or those northerners who think you're dumb when they hear your southern accent. That ironic smile they smile. It's incredible. 'With some professors the accent definitely affects the exam result,' he says. He sends his cousin a birthday message with an emoticon showing a glass of *spumante*. Afterwards she realises it hasn't even crossed his mind that she might really want to leave him. Yet Giancarlo's far from stupid. He's a star student. Why can't he see what she is trying to say? Does he think that what they have between them is love?

Valeria's best friend of old, Paola, the girl she used to study with as a child when her parents were fighting, has not come north with the others. She is studying law in Bari on the Adriatic coast, just an hour from home. As is her brother. They share an apartment. Her father and mother are both lawyers. Likewise her grandfather on her mother's side. They didn't want their children to be too far away. The family spends every weekend together in a second house by the sea, near Castellaneta Marina in the Bay of Taranto to the south. It's a happy family. The house has a spacious terrace looking down on the beach and there is even a small yacht anchored in the bay. You can sunbathe. You can scuba-dive. Why would anyone want to leave? Valeria misses her friend.

85

But Paola's boyfriend is here in Milan. And her boyfriend's older brother. They are living with a third friend in a western suburb of town. Come to think of it, almost all of Valeria's group are either living with a distant relative or sharing rented accommodation with brothers, sisters or cousins. Valeria is the only one in a dormitory, though there is a girl called Maria Pia who has a room in a convent, where the nuns lock her in every night at 10 p.m. sharp. But Pia likes it that way. She's a swot. She wants to study here, but without really living in Milan at all.

Paola travels north once a month to see her boyfriend Paolo. The two have almost the same name, a cause of endless comments. They are childhood sweethearts and this is the first time they've been apart since primary school. Paolo reciprocates, travelling south once a month. If you book far enough ahead you can afford to fly. There are airports in Bari and Brindisi. None alas in Basilicata itself. The train takes eight hours. There's an overnight bus if you're desperate. Even the car if you have the energy. The couple have taken on this back-and-forth phlegmatically – with philosophy, as Italians say – as if it were a kind of job. It's the price you pay for being southern. They will have to go on doing this for many years if they are to stay together long-term and marry. Paolo is studying Economics. There will be the three-year basic degree, then a two-year specialist degree. You can't get anywhere without the specialist degree. And what will happen then? Five years hence. Will he find decent work in the south? Will she decide to come north? Meanwhile, these frequent trips are disorienting. The north and south are such different worlds. The effort is taking its toll. When Valeria asks Paola how it's going, she doesn't want to talk about it. She wants to talk old times.

Another girl, Letizia, whose father works in the same business as Valeria's father, is sharing a flat with her older brother, but the boy is skiving off all his lessons, simply using the northern university as an excuse for being away. All the same, he goes home twice a month to see his old friends at the stadium, where the local team play in Serie D.

Letizia is distressed because Mario is smoking so much dope and spending so much of their parents' money. She can't decide whether to talk to their father about it. She doesn't want to be mean to her brother. They're very close. On the other hand she feels she's letting her parents down. 'Should I tell?' she asks Valeria. The problem is that if her parents bring Mario home, they'll bring her home too. They'll never give her the money to stay in Milan alone. She doesn't have any other family here. She doesn't have a boyfriend. They won't trust her in the city on her own. They're obsessed with the idea that Milan is dangerous. In their eyes her brother is a bodyguard. Instead he's a liability.

'Don't they ask to see his *libretto*?' Valeria asks.

Letizia says she thinks her mother has guessed what's going on, but her mother is crazy about Mario and would never say anything bad about him to her father. 'She's dreaming he'll turn out fine in the end.'

Valeria doesn't know what to say. She talks to Paola about it, and Paola to Paolo. She talks to Giancarlo and Giancarlo to Flavio and Flavio to Chiara. Only Chiara has a clear idea. Tell the parents at once! But Chiara's northern opinion hardly counts beside the uncertainty of the southerners. How can you decide whether to be more loyal to a brother or a parent? When Mario starts asking Letizia for loans the situation grows tense. Letizia is nervous. She can't concentrate on her studies. Mario spends all day listening to rap, playing slot machines. Who with? No one knows. He no longer joins the others on their southern evenings together. 'He yells at me,' Letizia tells Valeria, 'when I'm out of money. Then he gets sheepish. It's scary.'

'You have to tell your parents,' Valeria decides. 'They won't stop you studying, just because your brother's lost it.'

Letizia doesn't tell. She's hoping the problem will sort itself out over the summer.

Valeria realises that this move north is revealing things about them all. And their families. They are no longer children. They are growing up faster than the local northern students, or their friends who stayed home, still in their old bedrooms with the soft toys on the shelves. She realises she is lucky in a way that her parents are always so busy arguing with each other, even years after their divorce, that they don't have the energy to try to impose on her. She is lucky she is alone here. She is lucky she doesn't have a boyfriend back home. Paola's relationship with Paolo is embalmed, she realises. No one can imagine them apart, but it's hard to see how they can go on like this, hypnotised in the back-and-forth between Basilicata and Lombardy. Two days together then two weeks apart. Valeria worries for Paola. They were such good friends as kids. They still are. Even when Paolo goes home in the summer, she reflects, the two can't really be a couple, because the parents don't let them sleep together. But then they don't *ask* to sleep together. It's not something children do where she is from, though she sees that everybody in the north does it. When Costanza is in Piacenza she sleeps with Max, in her father's house. And her parents are OK with it. That's why she wanted to come to the dorm. To be away from Max. Where Valeria is from, everybody sort of knows you must be having sex, it's just never part of the conversation. Not with your parents. Until a person is married they are still a child and children don't have sex. Valeria would never spend a night with Giancarlo back in their home town. At her mother's or his house. This seemed quite normal to Valeria in the past, but it's beginning to seem less so now. Paola and Paolo sleep together in Milan two nights a month, but not at home, the whole summer. They make love when their parents are out for the day, at work or at the beach. They mustn't be *caught*. But they never have been caught. And nobody's trying to catch them. They are still children. Smart children. With smart parents. Everything seems decided between them for the future, as if they were married, but nothing has been said.

'I tried to leave Giancarlo and he didn't even notice,' Valeria tells Paola. The two always find an hour or two together when Paola comes north. They're drinking espresso together at a table by a busy road. Paola always radiates a wise calm.

'Time will sort it out,' she smiles.

One accepts the verdict of time. Is that the difference between the north and the south? Valeria wonders. Northerners are pushing things on and southerners letting things flow. That famous southern fatalism.

CUCINA LUCANA

Certainly no one seems to care too much about punctuality when the Lucani arrange a place to meet in the evenings. All through the day, text messages fly back and forth. Someone has found a restaurant that makes great lasagne, but there is another that has good fish. The service is slow, though. Valeria turns her phone off during lessons. When she turns it on again, on the stairs between one classroom and the next, there are twenty messages. A Burrata here. A Scamorza there. Friendly atmosphere. TV for the game. If there's a game, the boys will have to see it. Valeria worries because she has less money than the others. It mustn't be too expensive, she texts Letizia. Letizia understands.

They agree eight o'clock near Lambrate. There's a trattoria with *cucina lucana*. Valeria arrives at ten past and no one is there. At half past they begin to arrive. Giancarlo is always the last. He's been to volleyball practice. If she complains, he says, 'Who's becoming a little northerner, then?'

'You make it on time to the cinema.'

'Who's obsessed by punctuality?'

When she sees how much oil there is on the pasta, she says nothing. That's another change. She's not sure how much she appreciates olive oil any more. Or not in such quantities. Why is it only she who is becoming less of a southerner? Why must a change of eating habits be interpreted as a betrayal?

This evening they've met to discuss their summer holiday. They are going as a group, of course. Chiara is against it, she wants Flavio to herself, but he can't imagine not being with them. Old Nonna Rosa can go and stay with your parents, he says. Mario has come with Letizia this evening because he will be joining them too. He has lost weight since Valeria last saw him. His wrist moves jerkily around his wine glass.

Are they all agreed about the place? Paolo asks. Paolo tends to be the leader. The same place as last year. It's a campsite on the Gargano peninsula, just south of Vieste, in a wooded valley running down to the Adriatic, isolated but well equipped, with its own beach, its own tennis and basketball courts, volleyball, five-a-side football, restaurant, bar, discotheque, scuba equipment. They will arrive, park the cars, set up their tents and never leave the place for two weeks. The only thing to decide is the dates. They have to book in December, if they want to get places for ten in August.

Maybe eleven, Giancarlo says, if his sister's boyfriend wants to come.

They count the names of four couples and three singles.

The waiter brings salamis and cheeses. He pours from a bottle of Primitivo di Manduria.

Valeria goes along with it all. But she feels less enthusiastic than last year. Last year they were celebrating the end of school. They had been sitting together in class, doing exams together, going to the beach together. There was a sense of conclusion and achievement. This year feels different, more precarious and less exciting. She's glad to go with the group, because she doesn't want to go with Giancarlo alone. She will be able to spend time with Paola. She has applied for an Erasmus next year, in France. That will be the moment to leave him. There's much discussion of logistics. Which people in whose car. Driving from where. 'You have a car, don't you?' Paola asks Valeria. Valeria says officially she owns a car. But actually her sister uses it. 'I pay her fines.' Everybody laughs. Everybody understands these arrangements.

Many of them officially own things that others use – cars, houses, even businesses – or use things that others own. It's a matter of bureaucratic convenience, spreading ownership across the family, keeping taxes down. It ties them together.

'Do you think you'll be able to use it?'

'I'll try,' Valeria says.

Letizia points out that if they go later this year she will miss her grandmother's *onomastico*, her saint's day. She has never not been at home for her grandmother's saint's day. Chiara chuckles. She can't believe it. Why would anyone change their holiday plans for a saint's day!

'Let us know,' Paolo says.

On the TV above their heads, the second half of the game gets under way – Juve Napoli – and Valeria goes out to smoke with Letizia. There's a message on her phone from her mother complaining that her father keeps coming to the house and expecting to be fed. As if they'd never divorced.

'Tell him to do the cooking,' Valeria replies. Her father does an excellent *spaghetti con le cozze*.

'What do you think of Mario?' Letizia asks. Her brother.

'He is shooting up,' Valeria says.

Back in the restaurant, while the boys watch the game, the girls plan their next meetings. There's a concert. Schubert. Student prices. Maria Pia will book the tickets. And the city's *pinacoteca* is free Thursday evenings. There's a Caravaggio show. For once Chiara finds a reason to appreciate her southern friends. They are regular consumers of high culture. Never a week goes by without a play or a concert. They always go together. They always discuss what they've seen afterwards. She can't remember anything of the kind in Udine.

But now Valeria is itching to leave. If she doesn't go now she'll miss the last metro, she says. It's past midnight. She has Statistics at nine tomorrow. 'Flavio will take you home,' Giancarlo says. Flavio has a car. 'We can all leave together.' Chiara is unhappy with this. She needs to get back to Grandmother, she says. And Valeria lives at the other side of town. She whispers in Flavio's ear. He frowns and reaches for the wine. Chiara will have to learn that it is unthinkable not to take your friends home, however far. Her feminism is only emphatic in the abstract, Valeria realises. Chiara is afraid of losing her man.

I BARONI

The following autumn Valeria has her first unsettling experience with a professor. To say that this is a foretaste of trouble to come would be an exaggeration. Nothing serious happens. But it's a wake-up call. She begins to see the university in a different light.

Professor Domenico Galli. teaches Sociology. In his fifties, he's charismatic, entertaining, apparently has a big reputation outside the university. If there's a problem it's that he wastes too much of the lesson talking about himself, his achievements, clever things he said in conversation with famous people. He dresses smartly. Sharp suits, gleaming cufflinks, bright ties. Valeria sits with her pen poised over her notebook, waiting for the next item of real content. She's conscious of waiting too long. The man wants to be liked, but he's beginning to annoy her. He's lonely, she realises. He's letting his private needs seep into his lessons. Still, when he gets back to his subject, Galli is sharp as a razor. She is writing fast now. She likes Sociology. She likes the idea of societies being systems you can analyse and explain.

Word goes around that to get the top grade in this course you have to do a group project. It's not obligatory. It's not officially on the programme. And it's time-consuming. But if you want thirty, you'd better do it. Valeria wants thirty. Even more than that she wants to get as much as she can out of her teachers. She wants to learn. The guy is irritating but she likes him too. He cracks good jokes. She even feels sorry for him. She signs up.

Galli splits them into groups of six or seven. Since he has no time during the day, he says, they'll have to meet in the evening. He names a bar beside one of the *navigli*, the canals, a popular place to chill out. They can get together there, he suggests, and discuss how to proceed. The idea is to do some group research on mutually defining relations and perceptions in some well-defined social unit. A city gym perhaps. Or an orchestra. Or a sports team. They will analyse where everybody involved is coming from, how they regard what they're doing and understand the institution in relation to themselves and others, what mutually sustaining or deconstructing stories are being told.

This sounds fun. The first meeting goes well. They pull three tables together beside the canal, order Spritz Aperol and fetch themselves a plate of food from the buffet inside the bar. It's free with the drink. Though the drink is expensive. Who is going to pay? Valeria wonders. When the waitress brings the tray, she asks for eight euros each.

Progress is slow, partly because Galli talks so much about himself. He orders a second drink, for himself, a strange pink concoction with a stirrer and a straw and sugar round the rim. Nobody can decide which social unit exactly they should investigate. 'Wouldn't it be better if one of us were a member of whatever it is?' Valeria asks. 'To get access.' 'Why not the university itself?' someone suggests. Galli laughs. He leans back on his chair with his hand pushed into his thick hair. He shouldn't say it, he says, but the university is a *letamaio*. A dung heap. If they did an honest study of the university and made it public they'd all be kicked out at once. If not worse.

Now he will have to explain himself, of course. He goes and gets himself a second plate of artichoke pasta. Grilled zucchini. Pepperoni in oil. He speaks between mouthfuls. Essentially there are three factions, he says. He has loosened a yellow tie. Each run by a *barone* who brings in his own buddies in every possible role, academic or administrative. Or his lovers. Didn't they realise the Head of Faculty was having an affair with Dottoressa Randaccio? Galli laughs. And the Rector! He beams at them all. 'How do you think they got the financing for the new television labs? Why do you think one of the psychology researchers is a Minister's son?'

The students are excited to be getting a privileged insight into the university. Valeria has never before stopped to reflect on how power is organised between the faculties. It's all fine, Galli is saying, until a professor wants to bring in a friend and there's really no role for them. Or alternatively when they want to get rid of an enemy who's actually useful. Or when someone who thought they were going to win a *concorso*, thought they were the chosen candidate, doesn't win and cries foul, goes to a lawyer. In any event, he winds up, the only way to get anywhere in the university is to be absolutely loyal to your *barone*.

A brief silence falls round the table. There are four girls and two boys. Each with notebooks open. Almost nothing has been written down. Galli stands up to go. His hand touches the arm of the girl next to him. They walk along the canal for a while towards the centre, even though Valeria should be going in the opposite direction. She senses Galli wants the company. There's a nervous energy around him. She notices he contrives to brush against an elbow here, a shoulder there. When they finally part he salutes the girls with a rapid touch of the cheeks, as if they were friends, equals.

Another appointment is fixed. And another. Valeria is irritated by the expense, and the lack of progress. When will they actually start researching anything? The boys want to study a *curva* at the stadium. Two of the girls a yoga class. 'Anything,' Valeria says, 'so long as we get going.' Galli smiles and tells his anecdotes. He's a handsome man in his way. How he made this or that observation, in this or that department meeting or commission. The point is that the *baroni* can pretty much decide which of their students will publish in reputable academic journals and which will not. You know? And without your quota of publications you have no chance of making a career. Sometimes it seems he's talking to himself more than to them. Like

an actor soliloquising before a full house. There's something polished and mechanical about him. He's said all this a thousand times.
Walking towards the centre, he takes Valeria's elbow and turns her
to a shop window to observe, he says, the subtle messages suggested
by the way the mannequins are gesturing. You see? He still has his
hand inside her elbow. To Valeria the messages don't seem subtle in
the least.

Professor Galli invites them to his home on Saturday morning so
that they can compare the data they've been gathering on different
social groupings, decide which they're going to study and share out
the research involved. Valeria doesn't go. A friend tells her about photos Galli showed of a holiday home in Liguria. He lives with his
mother but she was nowhere to be seen. No final decision was made
about the project. Valeria doesn't go to the next meeting either. She
drops out of the project. It's too creepy, too expensive, too boring.
Above all, there is no mention of projects in the official course programme. The exam is based on Galli's book and Galli's lessons. And
she is always at lessons, where the professor occasionally casts her an
inquisitive glance.

This is a one-semester course. The exam is officially in February,
after the Christmas break, but Galli lets those who've attended regularly do it during the last week of lessons in December. This is standard
behaviour, a so-called *pre-appello*, one of those universally accepted
differences between regulations and reality. Everybody knows the students at the *pre-appello* get better treatment, because they came to all
the lessons. Which is a sign of respect.

On the day, Valeria is confident. She has prepared carefully as
always. There is nothing she can't answer from Galli's book, which she
feels is excellent. She enjoyed it. There is nothing of substance Galli
has said at the lessons that she has not noted down and digested.
Second-last to be called to the front from a group of twenty, she sits
down and answers the professor's questions confidently. Galli is affable
and businesslike. At his most professional. He smiles. He asks if she is

well. And after just five minutes he announces that her mark is twenty-seven and picks up the *libretto* which she has put on the desk.

Twenty-seven is an OK mark. It's not the kind of thing you refuse in order to take an exam again. On the other hand, she has answered perfectly to just three questions. The other students were kept for much longer.

'Can't you ask me another question?' she suggests. 'I've really enjoyed studying the subject and your book. I was hoping for something more.'

Galli is already writing down the result, in words and figures. Something he is not supposed to do. He is signing, and he proffers the register for her to sign. With a smile, as if she hadn't spoken.

Valeria understands. She signs, stands up and leaves without any of the pleasantries of thanks and goodbye one usually offers in these moments. '*Buon natale, signorina,*' he calls after her. All the students who stayed on the project get thirty. Nothing substantial was produced.

FRATELLI E AMANTI

At the time we are speaking of, James had been at this university for some years. In the beginning he had barely more appreciation of the organisation or politics of the place than a student. Teaching on annual contracts he played no part in any decision-making process and was not invited to faculty meetings. He taught an optional course, largely of his own invention, in which he looked at English translations of Italian fiction. He considered Verga's story 'Black Bread'. '*I fratelli*,' the third paragraph begins, '*che erano come le dita della stessa mano finché viveva il padre, ora dovevano pensare ciascuno ai casi propri.*'

How difficult that was to translate! *I fratelli*, the brothers, but it actually includes the sisters too – the brothers and sisters. Italian has one word for both, a familiar, intimate word, quite different from the dry, technical 'sibling'. '*The brothers, who were like the fingers on the same hand as long as their father lived, had now each one to think for himself,*' D. H. Lawrence translated. Forgetting the sisters. But '*the fingers on the same hand*' hardly sounds colloquial in English. It doesn't carry the impact of, say, '*these kids pulled together like five fingers, before their father died, then it was every man for himself*'. Or every man and woman, rather!

He taught Natalia Ginzburg's *Family Lexicon*. '*Noi siamo cinque fratelli*,' the most famous paragraph begins. We are five brothers (and sisters). How simple. But who, in English, would ever say, We are five brothers and sisters? And in parenthesis how irritating that once you

99

have two words they have to be sequenced, man and wife, boy and girl, and since the male usually gets placed before the female there is a sniff of hierarchy – brothers and sisters – or if we start reversing the order – wife and man – of self-consciousness, of needing to avoid a traditional hierarchy. How much nicer to say, as the Italians do, *i coniugi, i fratelli, gli amanti, i ragazzi*. '*My parents had five children*,' is how the most recent published translation solves the problem. The first-person plural has gone, the present has become the past; intimacy turns cold.

Looking back on those lessons years later, James will marvel at what a time of innocence it was. He saw little connection between the books he taught and the lives of his students, or even the lives of his own family, where his father-in-law's death had profoundly altered the relationship between his wife's brothers and sisters. He was entirely focused on the language, on his students' sensibility to it, and their knowledge of English. But one day, during a last lesson before Christmas, he was teaching another story by Verga, 'La lupa', 'The She-Wolf', about a sex-crazed Sicilian peasant woman. '*Le donne si facevano la croce quando la vedevano passare, sola come una cagnaccia, con quell'andare randagio e sospettoso della lupa affamata*.' The women made the sign of the cross when they saw her go by, alone like a stray dog, with that suspect vagabond look of the hungry she-wolf.

The story won't come to life in English. Nothing can give the brutishness of *cagnaccia*, a bad dog. We feel drawn to translate this as 'lonely as a dog'. But the she-wolf isn't lonely, she's alone, on her own, by herself, and she doesn't give a damn. She's not lonely. She's *unnatural*. Because it's unnatural not to care about being alone. Vagabond sounds romantic in English. A Dylan song. But *randagio* has the same sound and feeling as *cagnaccia* and is loaded with negative emotion. Everyone is afraid of a stray dog. Or afraid of becoming a stray dog. The she-wolf falls in love with a young man and gets him to marry her daughter so that she can seduce and enjoy him whenever she wants. It can only end badly.

The lesson was coming to a close. Outside, the December dusk had already fallen. 'Those crazy Sicilians!' Someone shook their head. There was a holiday mood in the room. 'I guess the moral of the story,' one girl remarked, 'is to keep your boyfriend away from your mum.' Everyone laughed. And James asked, wasn't it traditionally the boyfriend's mother who was the biggest problem? Not the girl's. There was a subdued muttering. As usual almost all the students were girls. Such is the way with language courses. They started to swap stories. About the boyfriend's mother who insisted on keeping a key to her son's apartment which was on the floor above hers. 'She keeps barging in when she thinks we might be making love.' The mother who worried whether her son's girlfriend knew how to iron his underwear properly. 'She wants to give me ironing lessons! She presses the iron in the crotch and says, You have to wiggle it like this!' More laughter. 'I always get the feeling,' another girl observed, 'that his parents would rather he was dating his little sister.' '*Già!*' another girl shouted, as if this were some kind of revelation. Right!

Some years into his job James is asked to tutor student theses. For no extra money. Italians are obliged to offer a so-called thesis for every degree. James is not officially qualified to do this, not until they make him a researcher. But he does it anyway, as so many of his colleagues are doing things they are not officially qualified to do, or paid to do. Because if you don't show willingness you will never be promoted. When a thesis he has tutored is discussed before the degree commission on graduation day, the official tutor, or *relatore*, the professor who invited him to the university in the first place, asks the graduating student the questions that James has prepared. When the public retires after the discussion and the commission debates what mark to give, the professor reads out the report James has written.

A thesis student walks into James's office in the hours designated for *ricevimento*, his office hours. This girl is a success. She is on the brink of a top-grade graduation with an excellent translation of an early Barbara Pym novel. She is also lucky. Eager to gain experience of the world she has put her name into the annual US green card lottery and *won*. Amazing. As soon as she graduates, next month, she will be able to start preparing for emigration. Why then has she been crying? Her eyes are red. A teacher can't help noticing these things, even if his duty now is simply to dot the 'i's and cross the 't's on the girl's thesis. Eventually, as she sighs and stutters through their conversation, he is obliged to suggest that maybe this is not a good moment for discussing her bibliography.

She bursts into tears. 'If you feel like telling me,' James says.

Because of the green card, she explains, she and her boyfriend have decided to marry. That is the only way he will be allowed to go to the United States with her. But despite the fact that they have been together three years now her parents are dead set against the marriage.

'What do they object to?'

The boyfriend is Romanian. And unemployed. He does casual work when he can find it. Her mother, who never said anything before, has now gone completely crazy. She is insisting that they don't marry in her home village, near Brescia, because she doesn't want the neighbours to know. It's a *vergogna*. She won't come to the wedding. Her father is refusing to buy the rings, which is what Italian fathers are supposed to do. Even her brother is saying he won't be a witness; he won't sign the register. She feels like a pariah. 'And Mihai feels like shit.'

'But you are going to get married anyway?'

'Yes,' the girl says. They will go to Chicago, and the hell with her family for ever.

A month later, on graduation day, when the student defends her thesis, James sees her family, proud and solemn in the front row. Presumably the boyfriend will be somewhere in the crowd too, though he doesn't appear to be together with them. At the next *ricevimento*, when she comes to his office to offer him the ritual gift of *confetti* (sugared almonds), he asks her why they have chosen to go to Chicago. Why not New York? Or California.

'Because I have an uncle there,' she says.

Sometimes it's the reverse. The parents are *too enthusiastic* about the marriage. Again a girl comes to James's *ricevimento* and begins to cry. There are times when he wonders whether his psychologist father's vocation hasn't rubbed off on him. People are always baring their hearts. Initially, he assumes her tears are a reaction to the unexpectedly poor exam results she has come to discuss. But no, Monica says, she got the low result because she has been so upset about something. A personal problem. She doesn't know what to do.

'If I can help,' James says.

She has broken up with her boyfriend. They had been together eight years.

Eight years is a long time, James agrees, especially when you are only twenty-two. He hesitates. With time, the pain will pass.'

Monica shakes her head. She is happy to have broken up with her boyfriend. It was long overdue.

James fears the worst. 'I hope he isn't making life difficult for you. I mean, if you feel threatened ...'

The girl is puzzled. 'Oh, no!' She realises what he's thinking. 'No, it's not that.' Biagio is completely relaxed about their splitting up. They're from Reggio Calabria. He has a job there. A good job. In the town hall. For three years they've been trying to keep the relationship going, travelling back and forth. But for a year and more they'd both realised their hearts weren't in it. 'He doesn't want to leave Reggio, and I don't see any future for myself down there. We're not in love.'

Now it's James's turn to be puzzled. If both partners are happy, what kind of excuse is this for the poor exam performance?

'It's my mother,' the girl sniffs. Over these eight years, her family and her boyfriend's family had become the best of friends. Her father is a doctor, his father an engineer. They get on really well. They go cycling together. The mothers regularly cook together. Last year they went on holiday together. Her mother just can't accept that the two have split up. She is constantly phoning, begging them to think again.

'But in a week or so,' James says, 'surely ...'

'It's being going on two months already!'

Last week the girl's mother went to see a psychiatrist and was pre-scribed antidepressants. Her older brother phoned, blaming her; he says Mamma is ill with thinking she will never come home to Reggio. 'God knows who you're seeing in Milan,' the brother had said.

'Biagio's parents are convinced I have someone else. They're calling me a *troia*.' A whore.

Suddenly, both James and the unhappy student burst out laughing. This is something he is slowly getting used to; how rapidly people, particularly young people, can pass from tears to laughter, laughter to tears, as if they lived two lives, in different worlds; what happens in the family is absolutely conditioning and terribly solemn; but the moment they manage to see it from outside, it's comical.

James says wryly, 'Perhaps the only thing you could do to make your mother happy would be for you and Biagio to get together again.'

'Right,' she says. 'I'll have to think about it.'

MANGERIE

After winning his *concorso*, as the privileged internal candidate, and becoming a *ricercatore*, meaning that he now has an official, salaried, career-track position at the university, James continues to do exactly what he did before – but with a much increased salary. Up to this point, for seven years, he has been travelling to Milan from the provinces for each lesson, barely breaking even, spending far too much time on Italian railways. Now he has enough cash to stay over in a hotel for a night, sometimes two, cutting out the three-hour journey time, enjoying Milan in the evening, socialising with colleagues, making friends. He becomes aware, for example, of the Milanese obsession with the *aperitivo*, a whole overworked, wired-up citizenship, entirely invested in a northern work ethos, pouring from their offices, studios and workshops into the city's endless bars, along the twilit canals, under imposing old facades, in balmy side streets and gritty thoroughfares, from the majestic centre through the stately inner residential areas, right out along the squealing tramlines to the drab and dirty suburbs, ordering Spritz Aperol in tall elegant goblets, glittering with ice, glowing ruddy orange; there's a twist of fruit, an explosion of chatter, then another glass, *per favore*, and perhaps another again, with plate after plate of *mangerie*, which is to say, tasty snacks, but oddly enough this word also means, as the dictionary explains, 'illicit and regular profits made possible by chaotic and corrupt government'.

There are certainly plenty of those around, James reflects, reading his *Corriere* at a table on the Naviglio Grande. It seems that despite the Tangentopoli scandal, now long past, political parties are still taking cuts from suppliers and builders in return for the award of public contracts. As much as 10 per cent. Some of James's colleagues believe that his own university is involved in this. Professors and researchers sit together over their Spritzes after lessons discussing the matter. If an institution undertakes a major building project, the reasoning goes, applying for building permission and subsidies, then some kind of backhander will doubtless be required. Best not to look too closely into the matter, the more conservative colleagues observe.

James reflects that he has never looked into the question of who owns and runs the institution that employs him, nor of the exact nature of its role in society. He turns up two or three times a week and teaches language and literature. He is happy to do that. He decides that he doesn't really want to know. He doesn't want to give the matter his mental energy.

'The politicians do not steal for themselves,' one apologist tells him. It's Domenico Galli, the professor who teaches Valeria Lasala Sociology. Domenico doesn't drink Spritz Aperol, but something rather sugary, in a champagne glass, called a Pink Lady. 'They steal for the party,' he explains, 'because this is the only way to have sufficient finance for a properly functioning political organisation that can put its case before the electorate. Democracy has to be financed and if the individual politicians didn't ask for kickbacks when in contact with the business world, it would be a form of disloyalty to their party which relies on this income.' It's naive of James, Domenico feels, not to see a moral dilemma here, and a serious problem for the judges when bringing politicians to trial. Stealing for your party, or family, is different from stealing for yourself. 'For example, a man stealing a loaf of bread for his children. As in *Les Misérables*.'

'Are we supposed to feel sorry for these people?' James enquires. He's not drinking Spritz Aperol either. He is drinking beer. The

Aperol is too syrupy and the rush of alcohol it brings makes it impossible to think. Domenico says for the nth time that James, being a Brit, a Brit who continues to drink beer despite twenty years in Italy, can't understand what is involved here, culturally, emotionally, practically. And he starts to trace the complex connections between the founders of the university and various members of political parties at local and national level, and newspapers, and major manufacturers and rotary clubs, and industrial associations.

'And the Freemasons, of course,' says another voice. A mocking voice. Alessio always arrives half an hour after the others, when his *ricevimento* ends. He too orders a beer.

'Does that mean *he* can't understand either?' James ribs Domenico.

'Only Pink Ladies can know the secrets of our town,' Alessio mocks. Alessio always mocks. His face is gently twisted in a cheerful sneer, behind John Lennon glasses, beneath an improbable trilby. Alessio plays the clown. He teaches Media Studies. 'The only way to get on at the university,' he tells James, 'is to be a Freemason. The problem is, which lodge to join?'

'Berlusconi's?' James suggests.

Berlusconi, who of course owns a football team and has founded a political party, is also believed to have set up his own Freemason's lodge, being too important to join anyone else's.

Domenico cannot joke, he has no sense of humour. His face is round and solemn with thin hair falling forward over a creased forehead. He talks earnestly about the various lodges that the Rector and the Head of Faculty and certain members of the Board of Directors are involved in. Their political affiliations. Their connections with major newspapers. How does he know all this? James wonders.

'Isn't membership of a Freemason's lodge supposed to be secret?'

'Oh, he knows, he knows,' Alessio mocks, 'and their mistresses and call boys. And who likes licking arse and who likes sucking cock.'

Domenico smiles wanly. 'Indeed I do know,' he says. 'And so do you.'

Returning to his hotel, James asks himself what he would do if he were ever to discover that he was really part of some criminal organisation. Would he take a moral stance, would he inform the police, or would he go on as he always has? There is no word in Italian for 'whistle-blower'. On the rare occasion that someone does assume this arduous role, the English word is used.

In the hotel the receptionist takes James's ID card to copy down his particulars. 'If we don't fax the police a list of our guests every night, we would be liable to criminal charges,' he explains. It is the hundredth time James has heard this from a hotel receptionist. But after he has been there a few times he notices that there are occasions when they don't ask for his ID card and don't give him a receipt. Does that mean he has become a trusted friend?

Perhaps eighteen months after winning his *concorso* and receiving his superior salary, James takes a phone call from the Rector's secretary. The Rector wishes to speak to him. The secretary names the day and hour of the appointment.

'In his office?' James can hardly conceal his surprise.

No. The Rector will not be coming to the university that day. 'He can see you in his home.' She gives directions, counsels punctuality. Somehow it feels as if James had asked the Rector for an audience. In any event he's excited. This can only mean promotion. Are they going to propose him as the internal candidate in a *concorso per professore*? It does seem a bit soon. On the other hand, the Rector was only appointed a few months ago and is perhaps looking to establish some kind of inner circle.

On the day, he finds himself outside a well-appointed eighteenth-century palazzo in the centre of Milan. Buzzed through the main door, there is a charmingly ancient lift barely big enough for two. Its doors have to be opened and closed manually. The lift climbs through the well of a splendid stone staircase that spirals voluptuously upward with elaborate ironwork railings and a polished wooden banister. Who would not wish to live here? James is admitted into a spacious apartment by a smiling Filipino man and guided into a large room where thick white rugs are spread on dark parquet. The teak desk to his right is topped with leather, scattered with books and paper. On the wall opposite, above a low modern sofa, is a life-size reclining portrait of a woman who is no longer young, but certainly not old. Nude. Voluptuous as the spiral stairs, she is recognisably the Rector's wife, who teaches in the Marketing Department. The Rector's third wife.

The important man enters. He is welcoming and affable. He is ready to flatter. He has heard good things about James, he says. He has heard he won a prize for one of his translations. Many congratulations! He opens his arms as if embracing the air. The university is proud to have him as a teacher.

James says thanks. He's pleased. He's glad if it helps the university's image.

'I would like you to translate my book,' the Rector announces. He is sitting on the grand executive chair behind the desk, smiling benevolently, as if he has just offered a young man a huge opportunity.

But James is past forty now and not so easily impressed. Suddenly he feels he's walking on eggshells. The Rector is in his late sixties, wispy white hair carefully combed across a pale scalp. He swivels his big chair to a shelf where every dusted volume bears his name. He is a philosopher. He writes popular philosophy, omniscient, paternal and reassuring. James has never got past page 10 of any of the man's books.

'This treatise,' the Rector is saying, holding up a thick volume and waving it, as if at a promotional event, 'has been a bestseller in seven countries.' He names them. France and Spain, among others. Sweden, Norway, Bulgaria perhaps. 'But it is not even published in the USA or the UK. I need an English translation.'

'Those are difficult markets,' James observes. 'Everyone wants to publish in English.' He simultaneously wishes to have the Rector's gratitude and all that this would mean for his career, while knowing instinctively that he does not want to translate this book which looks at least three hundred pages long. Is he expected to do it for free? 'Perhaps they have writers of their own covering this kind of territory,' he adds.

The Rector shakes his head. He is wearing a pale blue polo neck under green tweed, a curious mix of would-be youthful and musty academic. 'Clearly you haven't read my work,' he tells James. The book is in a territory all its own. It has an entirely innovative approach to the nature of happiness and the best way to achieve and sustain it. Reviewers in countries as distant as Korea and Finland have observed this and admired it. Its lavish use of case studies and its intimate approach have been much appreciated. It has already sold half a million copies worldwide.

James is a born fool. 'One hardly judges a book by its sales,' he laughs, and immediately bites his tongue.

The Rector sighs, the corner of his mouth raised in an ironic smile. 'Read it and you'll see what I mean.' He passes the book across the desk, so that James has to reach and take it. The older man falls silent and watches, as if ready to savour the inevitable admiration of one lucky enough to find such a masterpiece in his hands.

'With pleasure,' James says.

'I fear,' the Rector goes on, 'that they don't have anyone who can read Italian properly. Once you've translated it and they can see what they're getting, the book will soon find a publisher.'

James turns to the last page which is numbered 437.

'Naturally, I will help you with the technical terms, which need to be accurate and consistent throughout. I can't stress that enough. My writing is deceptive, you know – it appears to be relaxed and personal, but actually the terminology is precise to the tiniest nuance. It would be easy to make mistakes.'

'Let me read it first,' James says. 'I have a little personal rule that I never agree to translate something without reading it all first. It could be out of my range,' he observes. 'I might not be the right person for the job.'

Two weeks later he writes to the Rector complimenting him fulsomely on his remarkable achievement but regretting that he really does not feel that this is a style to which he would be able to do justice. He names two other translators who, he feels, are better equipped for this sort of project. No reply is received and there will be no further communication between the two either before or after the moment, three years later, when the Rector is ousted in an academic *coup d'état* and left out in the cold writing ferocious letters to the press accusing his colleagues of every kind of shameful corruption and *mangeria*.

However, shortly after that one meeting with greatness, at a conference in Florence, James describes the Rector's proposition to a prestigious English academic, Italophile and pioneer of translation studies. This grande dame laughs and explains to him that she herself left Italy, where she had once worked as a young researcher, because she could not contemplate life in a system that demanded she be at the beck and call of someone more powerful than herself, someone to whom she would have to be eternally grateful for every advancement. 'You should leave,' she tells James. 'There is no future here for an academic who refuses to translate his Rector's book.'

Taking advantage of being in Florence, James boards the train for Rome where he plans to hand in two copies each of four books he has translated at the Ministry of Culture which administers a lucrative translation prize. This was still some years before the advent of high-speed trains, and sharing a compartment with three others all speaking on their phones, he has time to contemplate the landscape and think about the older woman's disturbing remarks and advice. Certainly he wants a future in the university. But equally certainly he doesn't want to have to leave Italy to achieve it. Or rather, because it does not seem to be a question of wanting and not wanting, he has no plans to leave. Nothing moves him in that direction.

Why not? Is it because he loves the country, for its sunlight, and landscape – the gracious slopes of Tuscany growing starker and sharper as they move south into Lazio – or for its art, its cuisine, a certain ease some Italians have with life? No. He does enjoy these things, of course, Italy's undeniable delights. But this is not why he stays. Is it because of his wife and family? Because over twenty years Italy has become home? No. His wife often talks of her desire to go abroad and homes can be rebuilt. It might even be exciting to start again.

Why then? Because he is stubborn? Because he is the kind of person who hangs on, the kind who wants to get what he wants, and get it the way he wants, despite being advised by everyone that this is impossible? No doubt that's part of the story. But not all. *Why am I here?* Listening to a woman across the compartment who keeps trying and failing, with extraordinary patience, to arrange a hospital appointment, presumably through some kind of automated answering system, James can't find an answer to this question.

RACCOMANDATO

In Rome, James sets out for the Ministero dei Beni Culturali in Via del Collegio Romano. From Stazione Termini it's a pleasant half-hour walk that takes him down Via Cavour, past the majestic Basilica Santa Maria Maggiore, the elegant Villa Aldobrandini. The air is mild, the streets alive with purpose and bustle. Perhaps one needs no other justification for living in Italy than a walk in the centre of Rome. Yet, carrying his bag with the eight heavy books, ambition tells him there must be something more.

He heard about this government translation prize by chance. It is not widely publicised. There is a *bando* – an official proclamation (as in the English word, marriage banns) – in the *Gazzetta Ufficiale*, a newspaper that announces all changes of law and job offers, or awards, in the public sector. But James would never buy the *Gazzetta Ufficiale* on the off chance; the paper is dense with small-print *burocratese* that never seems to be put on the page in a way that might encourage someone unfamiliar with the world of bureaucracy to consult it. Rather he saw, in an academic journal, that a certain translator had been awarded this prize at some point in his career, then he phoned people he knew, consulted colleagues, and eventually discovered that the sums involved were substantial. However, the deadline for application was just days away. And applying wasn't easy. As well as two copies of the translations themselves, one had to provide a CV, income tax code, detailed descriptions of all one's activities, and this had to be written on special *fogli di protocollo*, legally stamped paper, which would set you back a few thousand lire a sheet, then sent by registered letter, which could be notoriously slow, or delivered by hand. It was almost, James thought, as if they didn't want you to apply. But since as good luck would have it he had already arranged to go to the conference in Florence, it wouldn't cost him much, he thought, to go a bit further to Rome and hence be quite sure of getting his application in on time.

Running north–south, Via del Collegio Romano is a narrow street barely two hundred metres long, a kind of canyon between massive brick buildings, in particular the huge Collegio Romano which forms a solid six-floor wall the whole length of the west side. This was built, James remembers, in the sixteenth century to house Ignazio di Loyola's Company of Jesus, better known as the Jesuits, the organisation that more than any other would seek to put the Protestant genie back in the Catholic bottle and return Christendom to obedient conformity. It was here, for example, that Galileo tried to defend his revolutionary ideas. In vain.

The long brick wall, as James walks beside it, looking for a doorway, is dark and dusty, interrupted at regular intervals by window surrounds of deeply pitted travertine. At street level these surprisingly small apertures are blocked with sheets of black metal. At first-floor level they have a criss-cross of thick black bars which have recently been repainted. Between the first and second floors, five or six cables run twisting and sagging along the wall, with here and there a cable branching off to slip into a window or burrow into the wall, here and there a muddled tangle gathered with a few twists of wire. It's a curious combination of the antique and the makeshift. High up, craning, you can see the Italian and EC flags caught up together on white poles, with a thin rope to run them up or down disappearing into a nearby window. They seem quite insignificant beside the brooding corporate power exuded by the big solid building. Beneath the flagpoles is the doorway.

It's the typical big wooden door with a smaller door, barely six feet high, cut into it. Curiously, because this is a government ministry in the end, there is no *carabiniere* defending it, no need to have one's bag inspected. The problem is where to go once inside. Corridors and staircases lead this way and that, cavernous or crabbed. James pokes his head into a room where cheap metal desks are lost in oceans of sixteenth-century space, wires exposed on grainy grey walls, cast-iron radiators incongruous beside antique panelling.

'Does anyone know where I might go to hand in an application for the translation prize?' James asks of three dusty occupants. They don't. They weren't even aware there was a translation prize. Though they don't seem surprised to hear that there are prizes of which they are unaware. Eventually, after three or four such attempts, he is directed to the post room, since that would be, he is told, where applications of whatever kind must surely arrive.

Here they do know about the prize. James lifts his bag of books onto a wooden counter and takes out the A4 envelope with his application. The state employee shakes his head. No one brings applications by hand, he says. Something in his manner, its combination of shabby resignation to a dull job and truculent assertion, reminds James of the man who tried to reject his application for *equipollenza* several years ago.

'I have filled in the form,' he says, 'I have met all the conditions stipulated in the *bando*, I have affixed a *marca da bollo* of the correct value.'

The man continues to shake his head, looking at the bag. He wears an old suit, without a tie. He shaved two or three days ago. His glasses are greasy.

'You have to be *raccomandato*.' A woman has stood up from her desk behind him and comes to explain. 'Recommended, invited,' she says. 'Otherwise it's not worth applying.'

'There is nothing about needing endorsements in the regulations,' James replies.

The two state employees glance at each other. 'We can take the application, of course,' the man says, 'but the truth is you're just throwing away these nice books. They won't be considered.'

'They're famous names,' James insists. 'The jury can't fail to sit up when they see them.'

To prove his point he pulls the first three books from the bag and places them on the counter in such a way that the two can see the celebrated names.

They are unimpressed.

'It seems a shame,' the man says drily, replacing the books in the bag and accepting the application envelope from James.

'I'd appreciate a receipt,' James says.

'Of course.' The woman writes a few squiggles on a torn piece of paper while the man takes the books away towards the dark shelves behind, stacked with brown packages and files.

'*Buona sera, signore,*' she says, handing the paper over.

Out in the narrow street, blessed by a beam of sunlight, divested of his bag of books, the weight of his ambition, James feels light and cheerful, and decides to walk back via the Trevi Fountain and Piazza di Spagna to take in the Roman air. All around, the traffic presses through the streets, whether narrow or broad, the tourists amble, the locals make haste, the scooters weave between pedestrians and cars. One can feel pleasantly lost in the flow, happily awed by the magnificence of the city's monuments, agreeably dwarfed by this great thing that goes on and on, century after inexorable century.

All at once, at the corner of Via del Corso and Via Condotti, sirens have the traffic parting, the pedestrians staring. A buzz of blue-and-white police bikes are escorting three long, sleek and very black vehicles to some important destination. It is impossible to see through the darkened windows as they pass. The blast of noise pushes the crowd back. Other cars move aside. And as the sirens fade and greatness moves on, James is aware that he knew all along that some kind of recommendation would be needed to apply for this prize. The word is on everyone's mouth: *raccomandazione*. Everyone accuses each other of having their positions only because *raccomandati*. And at the same time everyone seeks *raccomandazioni*. Didn't he himself phone Professor Lonardi years ago? So that he would speak in his favour for the *equipollenza*? Wasn't he also *raccomandato* by his professoressa protectress? Then of course those who have power love to show it by offering *raccomandazioni*. Do you want me to put in a word for you? If ever you need my help, just ask. He recalls his first meeting with his father-in-law, when the man produced a stack of business cards, influential people, and said, 'If you need an introduction to any of these people, just ask.'

He knew all this. Does he really imagine that the mere fact that he has done a few passable translations of celebrated authors would put him in a position to win a large pot of money that the authorities do everything possible not to publicise? How ingenuous can you be? He should have thanked the gloomy pair in the post room and taken the books back, steamed off the expensive *marchi da bollo* from the application form so he could use them on some other occasion. He *knew* this. So his only reason for applying for the prize was to experience the injustice of not being considered for it. Is that possible? That he has gone towards this defeat *on purpose*. To savour his outsideness. His not having made the right friends, not having even sought to make them. And with outsideness, a sense of virtue. Wounded virtue. As when Dante claimed, 'Exile brings me honour.' The only thing left to the person who is on the outside is an enhanced sense of virtue. I did not sink to asking for a *raccomandazione*. Official honour is dishonour, in Italy. That's the logic of it. You were *raccomandato*. How else would you have got where you have? James is suddenly awed by the thought that he now moves wholly inside this mindset. Could it be that this is why he stays here, to feel the rush of identity, virtuous identity, that comes with exposing the gap between the official version of events and the more squalid reality? What kind of future will that offer him? Perhaps it really is time to make an important friend or two.

Back at Termini, strangely happy despite these disturbing thoughts, he idles away the last half-hour before his train leaves in the station's bookshop. Perhaps the important thing is just to feel that you are involved in life, however successfully or unsuccessfully. At the front of the shops, where bestsellers are stacked by the cash desks, all the authors are famous journalists or TV presenters – Enzo Siciliano, Giorgio Bocca, Bruno Vespa – and they are all writing about corruption, political stalemate, the Mafia, and in general the special nature of Italian life. *Italiani strana gente*, is one title. *Italians, Weird Folk.* They love it, James realises. We all love feeling that we are a special mystery, a conundrum among conundrums.

But James is tired of thinking about these things. Needing an easy read for the journey back he picks up a cheap copy of an early Verga he doesn't know, a short novel, *Storia di una capinera – Story of a Black-cap*, meaning a nun. A love story, presumably. This should offer some pleasant evasion for the six-hour trip home.

Earplugs in place, ensconced in a corner seat of his compartment, he settles down to this story published nine years after the unification of Italy but set seven years before it, in 1854. We're in the Sicilian town of Catania and the nineteen-year-old Maria is preparing to take her vows as nun when the town is hit by a cholera epidemic. The convent is evacuated for the duration and Maria returns to the family she left at seven, when her mother died. In the meantime her father has remarried and had two other children, a girl and boy. How wonderfully happy Maria is to be welcomed into the family by her younger half-brother and -sister, what a joy this domestic life, what fun meeting all the other families and children who have fled the epidemic, running and dancing with other kids her age, including the handsome Nino, first son of the rich Valentini family. Verga really makes you feel how marvellous life can be when things are going well.

And of course Maria falls in love. With Nino. Which is a problem, since her destiny, as a poor girl without a dowry, is to return to the convent and become a bride of Christ. Unusually for someone in love, she falls into depression. She is not worthy of her high religious calling, because she is thinking of boys and kisses, and simultaneously she is excluded from the ordinary destiny of loving and marrying. She is neither one thing nor another. When she discovers that Nino reciprocates her love and wants her to abandon the convent, things are almost worse, for she senses their love can never be.

She's right, James thinks. He's reading fast as the train races through the tunnels north of Florence, absolutely hooked and absolutely certain things will end badly.

Sure enough, Maria's stepmother, whose concerns are all for her own children and hence wants her daughter to marry the rich Nino, smells out the budding passion and forbids Maria to go out with the others. She must stay locked in her room and prepare for her return to the convent as soon as the cholera epidemic is over. Torn between guilt and desire, the girl falls ill. Why, James thinks, oh, why doesn't Nino now assume the role of hero and carry his girl off, free her from the miserable social prison she is trapped in?

Verga's answer? Because Nino is trapped in that prison too. Boy and girl both have impulses that might prompt them to oppose society, but they do not possess a strong sense of themselves outside the models society provides for them. The 'story' of rebellion just isn't available to them. Departing the village, now that it's safe to go back to town, Nino does no more than leave a rose on Maria's windowsill.

I hate tear-jerkers, James thinks. I hate books about the impossibility of being happy. On the other hand, this is a wonderful book.

A year later, back in the convent, it doesn't help Maria to hear that Nino has indeed married her half-sister, her stepmother's daughter. It won't help when the two come to see her at the ceremony where she take her vows of chastity, or again when she discovers that from the convent's belvedere she can just make out the couple's bedroom window in the town. How contrived can a writer get! James protests. Why torture us like this? Obviously the more intensely Maria yearns for the earthly love of that distant bedroom, the more terrifying the prospect of eternal damnation for her duplicity becomes.

At this point James would really like to throw the book out of the window and spend the last half-hour of his journey staring into the foggy night of the Po Valley. But there are only a few pages left now and Verga is far too persuasive a presence to let him go at this late stage.

There is a cell, James reads, in the convent known as *la cella dei matti*, the mad cell. This is where any nun who loses her mind gets locked up, alone. Excluded. Right now a certain Sister Agata is in that cell, but she is at death's door, the only door that offers a way out of there. The 'sane' nuns, meantime, smelling Sister Agata's end, take a perverse pleasure in the superstition that there must always be someone in the mad cell, always someone outside their community, which is itself segregated from the main community beyond the convent walls. Someone more outside than these outsiders. Maria realises she is soon to be that someone. Fortunately, after a failed attempt to escape the convent to see Nino, she dies in a delirium of disappointed love before they can wall her up for ever.

Why, James thinks, finding his car in the car park at the station, are so many Italian narratives surrounded by this tremendous sense of resignation, the same resignation the students show when faced with a professor who is misbehaving? Society *always* wins. Power *always* crushes. The struggles of the vulnerable individual are rarely more than a pathos whose sad sweetness the wiser conformists consume in the pages of fiction, or on the screen at the cinema, content that they have chosen well to conform, that they have been *raccomandati*.

You have been well warned, James reflects. *Grazie*, Verga.

UNA SCELTA OBBLIGATA

Some eight years after leaving those eight books in Via del Collegio Romano, James will receive a letter from the Ministry of Culture. It is not a belated reappraisal of his translation credentials, but an invitation to become himself one of the jury that awards the prize. It seems recognition can be won without prizes. Feeling honoured – has someone recommended him? – he flies to Rome and takes part in a meeting where thirty or so men and women, but mostly men, sit around a huge table beneath a massive chandelier in a chilly room lined with antique furniture in various states of repair. The stone floor is decidedly cold, the windows at the far end of the room huge. The papers he is given announcing preliminary deliberations for this year's awards are written in a bureaucratese that would challenge the finest minds. The chairman invites this or that person to talk about possible winners for this or that prize, for there are many: a prize for the best translator from a foreign language into Italian, a prize for the publisher who has published the best translations from abroad, a prize for the best foreign translator of Italian works, a prize for the foreign publisher who has published the best Italian works, a prize for lifetime achievement. The jurists' answers are long and reflective, naming many names, but rarely referring to books read and never giving actual examples of translation.

James had imagined that he had been invited to join the jury in order to give his opinion on the quality of translations from the English, or into English. But this does not appear to be the case. On arrival at the ministry, he is neither greeted nor briefed. At no point is he invited to speak. At no point is it suggested that he read this or that book, nor is he asked what he has read, or if he has anyone to recommend. Since there have been no general introductions and since most people seem to know each other and call each other by their first names, he has difficulty knowing who is speaking. He is not an initiate. But not a gatecrasher either. Looking at a list of those present, he is aware that many are prestigious members of Italy's cultural elite, but since he rarely pays attention to such things he has no idea who is who.

His first task, then, he decides, must be to mingle with this group, to talk to people, to form friendships, to find out what is really going on. Participate. When a coffee break is announced and espressos are brought on a silver tray he tries to do this, without success. Everyone is networking but for the moment he is not on anyone's checklist. He stands, coffee cup in hand, watching, listening to other people's conversations. And he notes that everybody he hears speaking seems to be Italian; so how extraordinary that he, an Englishman, was invited, but again, how odd that having been invited he is not welcomed in any way. He catches a return flight in the evening and discovers over the coming month that it is far from easy to get one's travel expenses reimbursed.

They still haven't been paid when he returns to Rome for the decisive meeting at which the prizes are to be assigned six months later. The scene is much the same as at the previous meeting with the one positive exception that this time he sees across the table at some distance to his right a face he knows, a poet, critic and professor he has met at various conferences. At least there will be someone to talk to at the coffee break. The chairman begins by announcing that the under-secretary to the Minister of Culture will address the jury at the end of the meeting when the prizes have been decided; then he invites one of those present to offer a general reflection on the applications that have been received. An elderly man speaks for some ten minutes lamenting a dearth of applications and that perhaps something more should be done to ensure that the awards are properly publicised.

James raises a hand. He would like to speak. Mildly surprised, the chairman gives him a nod. 'I should introduce myself,' he says and does so. He feels nervous, but determined. 'On the question of applications for the prize, I thought it might be useful for you if I recount my experience of some years ago.' And he does. When he reaches the word '*raccomandato*' in the mouth of the lady in the post room – 'There is no point in leaving your books, if you are not *raccomandato*' – there are some murmurs of protest. 'Thank you,' the chairman says, and moves the meeting on to the best foreign publisher prize. There is no further debate on the matter.

There is no debate at all. For each prize, a delegate speaks for some fifteen minutes before proposing a name. There is no discussion. They will vote after the coffee break. 'I know,' says James's poet acquaintance when they are standing together with coffees in their hands, 'that it might all seem a little frustrating and formal and mysterious, but it is worth getting involved. I assure you. Over the years you'll see there are advantages to be had. The moment will come when you can promote the person you want to, or when your own work will be considered. It's worth hanging on.'

Only at this point does James appreciate that the jury is *permanent*. He has been invited to be a member of the Ministry of Culture's translation prize *for life*. Not merely for this year's edition. He had thought that this was to be a fascinating but brief experience, a window on how a certain kind of world worked; instead he is to be part of that world, travelling to Rome three or four times a year, sitting around this long table, networking with people who have power in the world of culture. Immediately he is anxious. With a sense of real fear he sees the endless hours of wasted time stretching off into the future. His poet friend has gone off to speak to someone else and James stands alone watching people chatting in groups, moving knowingly from one to another, affable, relaxed, conspiratorial. It dawns on him that of course the jury would be permanent. One forms a group and then one belongs to it. It takes time. One becomes a team player, furthering one's own interests through the group. In a spirit of give and take. Why does such a prospect fill him with horror?

When it comes to voting, the chairman goes round the table person by person. Everyone must vote individually by repeating out loud the name of the person or publisher proposed for the prize, or, presumably, by announcing another name, or by abstaining perhaps. But no one announces another name. No other names have been proposed. And no one abstains. Everyone votes for the person proposed for each prize. Out loud. Saying the name. Again and again. Perhaps James should have been ready for this because the prize regulations state clearly that the 'commission reaches a unanimous final decision ...' as if one could predict that decisions of taste would be unanimous.

It's odd. The buck passes round the table with each member announcing the proposed name quickly but firmly. And James pronounces it too. Not knowing the person the name refers to, not knowing the work of the translator from this or that language, not knowing the foreign publisher who has excelled in publishing works from Italian. He knows nothing, but nevertheless says out loud the name the others have said. It's a strange feeling, as if one were swearing loyalty, putting one's own credibility in the hands of others.

But when it comes to the last round of voting, James again intervenes. It's the prize for lifetime achievement. A name has been proposed that he doesn't know. Someone who has translated scores of books, from the French. James raises his hand. He admits that he hasn't read these translations and supposes that the others have and are better informed. He begs to be forgiven his ignorance. But with reference to the number of books translated he does know that there is a tendency in the translation world for a depressing inertia to set in, an inertia associated with celebrity. A translator translates a book that is famous and successful, gets a name and then is given far more work than he or she can possibly do well. And he just wonders, he says, if they shouldn't talk more about the quality of the work than the amount done, if they shouldn't perhaps read out loud a passage or two and discuss it. Or perhaps they could make a shortlist and all read the same few books and then vote.

The chairman thanks James for this interesting intervention, but then reflects that as far as this prize is concerned, the name proposed this year really is a *scelta obbligata*.

How to translate this ominous expression? Literally? A *scelta*, choice, that is *obbligata*, obligatory? Or more loosely? A clear choice? An unavoidable choice? The voting process moves round the table. When the time comes for him to pronounce the only name in the hat, James observes that a *scelta obbligata* is no choice at all. So there is hardly much point in his voting.

Finally he gets a reaction. 'That is a ridiculous and distasteful insinuation,' the chairman says curtly. 'Nor is it clear what can be gained by making it.'

The following day James resigns. To do so involves losing half an hour to walk to the post office and mail a registered letter. He receives no reply. He does not go back to Rome for the prize awards. He is not proud of his behaviour. Italy makes it too easy for someone who doesn't want to play ball to do some righteous posturing. 'Those who insist on their moral purity,' observes Antonio, in Vitaliano Brancati's wonderful novel *Il Bell'Antonio*, 'are always the losers. Their righteous indignation is the merest compensation.'

Perhaps I should have hung on, James reflects, as his poet friend had suggested. Perhaps in the long run it would indeed have been worth it. But a little pharse comes to his aid: *Non è da me*. It's just not me. He can't be that person, sitting with the others round the big table, voting for names he has never heard of. In which case, the question is what place *can* he occupy in Italy? He doesn't want to be for ever the guy screaming from the sidelines.

It was not long after these events that the ex-comedian turned dem-agogue, Beppe Grillo, organised an event called V-Day, short for Vaffanculo Day, Fuck Off Day, where the people being invited to Fuck Off were those politicians and businessmen who, whatever their apparent credos, always seem to come to cosy agreements behind the public's back. Vaffanculo Day attracted huge crowds of people who presumably felt something like James did on the jury for the transla-tion prize. But he did not join them.

PASTA CON LE COZZE

'Here I go, my beautiful Naples, I'm leaving you!'

So says a character in one of Basile's fables. He has carelessly injured the King's son in a stone-throwing fight and has to get out of town fast. Leaving his identical twin behind him and riding away on his father's enchanted horse, Cienzo turns back for one last look at the city gates and asks:

'Who knows if I'll ever be able to see you again, bricks of sugar and walls of sweet pastry, where the stones are manna in your stomach, the rafters are sugarcane, the doors and windows puff pastry? Alas! ... I feel my soul split in two! ... Farewell, carrots and chard; farewell, fritters and cakes; farewell, broccoli and pickled tuna; farewell, tripe and giblets; farewell, stews and casseroles! Farewell, flower of cities, glory of Italy, painted egg of Europe, mirror of the world! ... I leave you to become a widower of your vegetable soups; driven out of this dear village, O my cabbage stalks, I must leave you behind!'

Valeria's small town in Basilicata could hardly be called the painted egg of Europe, but nothing can beat it when it comes to vegetable soups and casseroles. All Valeria's aunts and uncles, parents, cousins, sister, brother, wonder how she can survive on the kind of fruit and veg they sell in miserable Milan. It is the subject of interminable phone conversations. The dire Lombard bread. The supposed dearth of fresh fish. The exorbitant prices. 'Let me send you a crate of oranges.' 'Let me send you a box of dried tomatoes.' Letizia's brother Mario, constantly back and forth between north and south to watch his local football team, reconciles his parents to his dope-hazed disorientation by taking back suitcases of southern food for his diligent sister and indeed the whole *confraternità lucana* as these youngsters sometimes jokingly call themselves. Paola and Paolo's comings and goings also bring regular deliveries of home produce. Returning from a cousin's wedding, Flavio manages to transport two boxes of persimmons. Any trip by any member of the group nourishes a collective umbilical cord.

Yet the burden of Basile's fable, all his fables, is that it is only outside his home town and away from the protection of his family, not to mention the pickled tuna, that a hero like Cienzo can show his worth and really become someone. Only away from family and fritters can a man find a treasure, save a fairy from being raped, kill an ogre or a dragon with seven heads and marry a splendid princess. And when his twin brother turns up, as turn up he must – otherwise why would we have a story with a hero who has a twin? – Cienzo immediately supposes he has exploited their likeness to bed his wife while he was away, and cuts his head off. The old family from beloved Naples is encroaching on his new life, so he destroys it. Fortunately, after the princess wife explains that although the twin, pleading tiredness, slept in the marriage bed, he did nothing, a repentant Cienzo is able to use a magic herb to put his brother's head back on. So the story ends with the twins bringing their father from Naples to join them in their new life. The family is together again, but rather than the old absorbing the young into their world, the young have taken the initiative and brought the old into their new abode. Perfect.

Valeria does not feel that she has found any treasures in what are now her three years in Milan, and although dumping Giancarlo was a big relief, he was hardly an ogre and she was far from courageous. During a six-month Erasmus exchange in Norwich she wrote to tell him enough was enough and the following summer on another group holiday on the Gargano coast she met Michele, a friend of Flavio's, who was actually in the class below her at their school. Michele, a very serious boy, is studying Archaeology in Naples, lodges in a religious community and is not someone likely to throw stones or pronounce eulogies to puff pastry; they write constantly and see each other rarely, and she is happy with that for the moment. She is happy too that Giancarlo has a new girlfriend, a taciturn creature from Trento who never says a word at their collective dinners but looks very blonde and rather pretty. So Valeria needn't feel guilty about leaving him.

No, Valeria's only problem right now, on this third Sunday of a blistering June, is that the day after tomorrow she has to present her thesis, the final requirement of her degree, and this afternoon her parents are arriving. Both of them. Separately. And her brother and sister. And her Zia Lella. They will all be present in the great Aula Magna together with scores of other students and relatives when she steps up on the podium and takes her place behind the desk with the microphone, facing the eight professors of the thesis commission who will examine her work. It is unnerving. And doubly unnerving to think that her family will be watching, judging, criticising, understanding nothing.

She meets them off the train at Stazione Centrale and in the metro Zia Lella asks her niece if she has been to Mass yet and when Valeria says no, she still has a lot to study, the nun says if she doesn't go to Mass she will make her *nonna*, who looks down on her from heaven, cry. Zia Lella has been saying this to the children all their lives. Meantime Carmela, Valeria's mother, is talking about the dress she will be wearing for the great event on Tuesday, something she picked up cheap because it supposedly has a defect that she hasn't as yet identified. Terribly excited to be in Milan beside a daughter who is really going to graduate, an absolute novelty, she wants to get the dress out and show it to them all in the metro, it was such a bargain, in lime-green crêpe with a very unusual neckline, but Carlo, Valeria's younger brother, is squirming. It's so embarrassing, he complains, to be pulling open suitcases in the train; you'd think they were gypsies. Their older sister, or rather half-sister, Vanessa has folded her arms and is looking intently at the other passengers as if they came from a different planet. 'There is always a Mass at six,' Zia Lella insists. 'We still have time.'

Valeria's room-mate Costanza more or less lives with her lover in Milan these days, while nevertheless remaining the long-term *fidan-zata* of Massimo who has now risen to junior production manager in her father's firm in Piacenza. In any event, she has let Valeria take over their shared room for these forty-eight hours so that tonight and Monday night Carmela and Zia Lella and Vanessa will be sleeping in the university residence, while Carlo, whom she feels closest to, will be staying in a hotel with her father. But first they must go to Mass, Zia Lella repeats. She won't hear no. And then dinner, Carmela reminds them. They must book a restaurant that does decent food, if such a place exists in Milan, and woe betide your father if he doesn't pay.

Valeria understands that Lella is anxious that if she, Valeria, doesn't go to Mass the Sunday before her graduation exam God might punish her for it, causing her to get a low grade. So she goes off with her aunt to the nearest church and sits in a sparse congregation, her mind churning over aspects of the EC's film-funding policy, the subject of her thesis, as the priest intones the *Ave Maria* and her aunt joins in the responses. Later, rather too late in fact, over fish, in a place that boasts traditional cooking from Basilicata, her mother reminds the company for the thousandth time of that little girl who years ago answered the enquiry after her father by saying, 'We've split up.' And the message – that children always identify with Mamma rather than Papà – is clearly meant for her ex-husband who is sitting at the head of the table. He, Marcello, is in every way smaller and some years younger than Carmela and cultivates, behind a neat grey moustache, an expression at once long-suffering and smug. He will not rise to the bait. He does not want another argument with the wife who once got a court order that stopped him seeing the children for a full five years. He clearly enjoys sitting together with his family, but at the same time relishes his independence, driving up from the south on his own, stopping to see friends and relatives in Rome and Bologna. He is both a father and a loner. And our family is a matriarchy, Valeria thinks. Mamma calls the shots.

'You could see that lovely little girl would never abandon her mother,' Carmela insists, draining a third glass of wine, 'even if her parents had fallen apart.'

'But you're both here together,' Vanessa, her oldest child, objects. Vanessa is the fruit of a short-lived, teenage marriage and has always resented Valeria's father, a man who came into her life when she was ten, upsetting what she would for ever look back on as an idyllic mother–daughter relationship.

'*Grazie a Dio!*' chimes Zia Lella.

'God's got nothing to do with it,' Marcello observes drily. 'We're talking the patience of Job.'

'We're talking someone not capable of making a life of his own,' Carmela snaps.

Suddenly she pushes her plate aside. Restaurant food, she declares, is never as good as what you can cook at home. She can't understand why people go out to eat. But she does pour herself another glass of wine. Thank God I didn't invite Michele, Valeria reflects. Her boyfriend will be arriving from Rome tomorrow, but they are delaying a meeting with the family until after the thesis commission. So as not to add to the stress.

That night, in the small hours, Valeria sits at her desk. The room is three metres by three. Her mother and Zia Lella are in Costanza's bed, back to back, a tight fit, both snoring. Vanessa is sharing her own. The TV is on low showing some old Western. When Valeria tried to turn it off Vanessa protested she couldn't sleep without the TV. Silence makes her panicky. Valeria managed to sleep an hour or so but was woken by a nightmare. It was an exam in her old school classroom. Ancient Greek. The text was incomprehensible. Paola, though, had a crib. *All the others* had a crib! But they wouldn't give it to her. Paola was smiling slyly, but she wouldn't help. Valeria must fail on her own. She had been kicked out of her circle of friends.

Cristo! Waking in a sweat, she goes to her desk, turns on the lamp and leafs through her thesis for the nth time, muttering facts and figures through the small hours.

It would be the same the following night after another hot June day of family friction that included a trip to find shoes for Vanessa, an animated discussion about buying or not buying a *bomboniera*, a fancily packaged gift of sweets, for Valeria's thesis tutor, and an interminable search for decent *cozze*, mussels, so that her father could cook his party piece – *pasta con le cozze* – in the tiny residence kitchen, with the other students, mainly southerners, wandering in at intervals to sniff the odorous air and enthuse about the joys of home cooking. 'Give 'em hell, *figlia mia*,' her father repeats every time Valeria says she needs to study. 'Go out and show them what's what. I know you can do it.' Then over their excellent lunch: 'I left school at fifteen,' he reminds the company. 'And it never held me back.'

'They're driving me insane,' Valeria texts Michele.

When her father goes out on the balcony to smoke after lunch is over, Valeria would love to join him, she's dying for a cigarette, and maybe for a moment of intimacy with her father, whom she feels sorry for, but she doesn't go because officially, for her mother, she doesn't smoke. Of course Vanessa has long since told Carmela that Valeria smokes, but it has never been brought out in the open. Mother and daughter both pretend she doesn't. Why don't I just do what I want? Valeria wonders. Why is it so hard for her to disappoint *officially* when it's clear her mother is already disappointed unofficially?

These dramas are distracting and as the second sleepless night before the biggest day of her life drags on Valeria is in tears with the stupidity of it all and sneaks out onto the balcony for a cigarette on her own. Since the day has been so hot, the French windows are open in the hope of fresh air. She has to lean far out into the mothy night to stop the smoke from wafting back in to where her mother and aunt are snoring and another mindless movie is preventing Vanessa from waking up to panic. One by one, she goes through the names of the professors on the thesis commission, remembering their specialisations and the kind of things she has decided to say that might please them in the event of their asking questions. There will be her tutor, Dr Rubio, Alessio Rubio, who is hopefully on her side. The commission chairman is the pompous Head of Department, he who hurries away at the end of lectures announcing that his niece is waiting to be taken for a spin in his Porsche. There's a guy with an English name who's presumably there to ask a couple of questions in English. He will be her teacher next year if she decides to go on to the higher-level degree. Then a young French researcher who seems rather severe for the questions in French. The thought of speaking those foreign languages in her parents' presence is unnerving. There will be Professoressa Modesto, pedantic, but innocuous, she thinks. And of course the creepy Professor Galli. Does he still resent her dropping out of that famous project? If only she had some magic herb, some fairy accomplice to get her through the next twelve hours.

SANTA PAZIENZA

For James the thesis commission is the most onerous and useless part of his university work. It is also the part that simply cannot be avoided. It is a legal obligation for a researcher or professor to be present at a thesis commission.

The scene is a large lecture theatre. For the students and their relatives milling in foyer and corridors, dressed to the nines, it is a moment of exciting tension and celebration. For the professors who will sit up on the dais for three or more hours without a break, it is a time to arm yourself with *santa pazienza*.

James pushes his way through the chattering crowd and into the hall just two minutes before the event is due to kick off. He knows others will be later. A mobile frame for hanging academic gowns has been wheeled against the wall. All the professors must wear gowns with the right colours for their faculty. Black with a green slash, or a blue, or a pink. There will be photographs, of course. The *bella figura* consolidates a sense of occasion. Bored to death, one is paid to cut a figure.

Yet there is an unusual buzz among the professors today. Antonio, a young French teacher, is asking James who he's going to vote for in the election. The young man is in earnest. Who would make the best Rector? Alessio joins them. And a certain Federica, James's closest ally these days. They speak in low voices. To discuss such matters is to conspire; the proper behaviour is simply to vote for the person your protector has told you to vote for. Ottone, Federica says. We must vote Ottone, who is Head of Department – the government has just abolished faculties and transformed them into departments – and also president of today's thesis commission. *Più porco ma meno pirla*, Alessio agrees. More of a pig but less of a prick. A pig *and* a prick, but on our side, Federica insists. What's more, he has the ear of the Minister for Education. He can bring big money. Looking out of the window, James sees the great man himself drawing up in his Porsche at the university gates. His shadow, Professoressa Modesto, is beside him.

'He's on his way up,' he announces.

The law requires a commission of eight, but there are twelve of them. The long desk on the dais ordinarily has space for nine seats. Ottone, who exudes the goodwill of the warrior who wins every battle, takes his own especially large seat, a kind of armchair on wheels, and invites everyone else to squeeze up tight.

An usher now asks if they are ready to let the public in. The president glances left and right along the faces of his colleagues and nods, the usher turns and opens the big double doors on the foyer where Valeria and her family are waiting with nine other candidates and all their families. The show can begin.

But no. Ottone had not noticed the feeble gestures coming from a junior researcher at the other end of the dais. 'Professor Galli has not arrived.' Her professor. And he has tutored the first thesis. Ottone is irritated. One of the privileges of being the great man is to be the last to arrive, never to have to wait. The researcher phones Professor Galli, who says he has been delayed by heavy traffic. Theoretically, they could alter the order in which the students are to present their theses and begin without him. But Ottone is already standing up and has moved to a corner of the hall with his mobile glued to his ear. Phoning the Minister of Education perhaps. The others keep their chatter subdued so as not to disturb. Meantime, let's take advantage of the delay to explore some background to this great event; otherwise it might not be clear what is at stake.

Italy, some will be surprised to hear, is perpetually involved in a process of simplification. People understand that the present tangle of rules in every walk of life is time-consuming and counter-productive. One Berlusconi government even established a Ministry for Simplification. So when, in the early noughties, the traditional four-year degree was scrapped for a three-year version, the Laurea Breve so-called, there was great enthusiasm. The problems with the four-year degree were evident enough. There was a high dropout rate, and when students didn't actually abandon their studies, many were taking ten years rather than four to complete them.

To top it all, there was the thesis. To graduate, every student had to produce a work of a hundred to two hundred pages involving, hopefully, original research. This might have been feasible when universities were restricted to a privileged elite, but became a headache and even a nightmare when they expanded to involve tens of thousands of students with a quite inadequate number of professors. Not only did huge quantities of paper have to be filled with words and smartly bound, as if what had been written there were important; not only did they have to be read, or at least leafed through, and their student authors guided and tutored, or given the impression of being so; they also had to be presented before a commission in an occasion open to the public, open above all to the student's parents and extended family, all eager to see their young genius perform and then to celebrate afterwards. For the mark given for the thesis after its discussion was immediately added to the overall mark achieved in four years of exams so that the President of the Commission could solemnly and publicly pronounce 'in the name of the law and with the powers conferred upon me by the Magnificent Rector' the student's final graduation grade. It was a moment of resolution, the young scholar leaving the room no longer a mere undergraduate but a real *dottore*, a crown of laurel crammed on his head and a glass of *spumante* pressed into his hand. Or hers.

Needless to say, all this took an inordinate amount of time, for how could a thesis of two hundred pages be presented, discussed and defended before a dozen or so gowned professors in less than, say, fifteen minutes? So when the four-year degree was abolished it was widely assumed and urgently hoped that the thesis would be abolished with it. The government's new regulations for the Laurea Breve, everyone noted, did not *require* the thesis. It could legally be dropped and forgotten. However, they didn't *exclude* the thesis either. It became optional, a choice, not for each student, but for each university. Each academic institution could require the students to write and defend a thesis, or not. The key idea behind the reform, it should be said, was that after this first three-year degree, students who wanted to go on and specialise could do a further two-year, higher-level degree and *that* would be the occasion for a proper thesis, a truly serious thesis, an obligatory thesis, which, since there would be fewer students, and these few would be better motivated, could be more carefully tutored.

At the time, James was delighted. Italy is changing, he told himself. The future will be better than the past. Alas, no. When push came to shove, despite the possibility of dumping the thesis, most universities decided to keep it, in some form or other. Why? Why dream for years of liberation, then not walk out of your cell when the door is opened?

Clearly there was something deeper going on with the thesis than a mere academic requirement; a rite of passage was required, some awesome task that would mark the student's passage from youth to adulthood, a dragon slain, a monster tamed. The business of stepping up before family and friends, expensively bound thesis in hand, to face an inquisition of professors while a photographer 'immortalised' the moment from various angles was the perfect solution.

It further has to be said that this famous reform – the three-year degree – was introduced at a moment of intense competition between the universities, competition not for excellence, but for student enrolments, since the more students a university attracts the more fees it receives and the more government subsidies can be claimed. Not that there aren't genuine and even successful attempts to improve excellence, just that the number of enrolments is more urgent. For with falling numbers of enrolments some universities were facing closure, and you can hardly be excellent if you're not open for business.

In this climate the thesis and in particular the thesis-commission experience was identified as a big attraction to students, and above all to students' parents, who, at the moment of their child's graduation, are given a spectacle of what they have paid for, of how worthwhile it has all been. A university would have to be mad to abolish this theatre of achievement, merely because, in educational terms, it is close to pointless, seriously disrupts the year's teaching calendar, and imposes hours of crushing boredom on the university's employees.

So despite reducing the degree to three years, the thesis was retained. What's more, the higher-level two-year degree, the so-called Laurea Magistrale, rather than being a matter for an elite few, quickly became the inevitable next step for about 60 per cent of those who had struggled through their first degree. Because the three-year degree, despite its retention of the thesis, was never considered quite as serious as the four-year degree; youth unemployment was growing at an alarming rate, employers needed a more qualified workforce, etc., etc. What could a student do but go on? Go on being a student, that is.

And of course the Laurea Magistrale required a second thesis, a second ordeal, and a second celebration. Two anxiety-inducing deadlines. Two family trips from Puglia or Palermo, two expensive dresses, two drunken parties. For the professors, the hours of boredom were doubled, or almost, the morass of bad faith deepened and the sense of futility wonderfully intensified. In short, initial simplification led to massive complication.

NON VI È PEGGIOR BURLA CHE LA VERA

But that is only the macro-analytic point of view. The micro-analytic – each single thesis or thesis commission taken on its own – opens a whole new can of spaghetti. James had sat through no more than three or four commissions before he realised that some professors considered it a matter of pride that the students they had tutored got the best results. This was the case even when these professors had not personally done the work with the student or more than leafed through the thesis. Their name was printed (in gold) on the cover, and that was enough.

Equally, there were professors determined that the students of rival professors did *not* get the best results. To show that your students always get the best results is to show you have power, the power to protect, to further a career, to gather a clan. And the person who exercises such power is eager to make sure that others are not able to exercise it, or only exercise it *on sufferance*, my sufferance.

Unbeknown to themselves, then, the students become pawns in games played out between their elders. Not all the time, for there are professors without megalomaniac tendencies, but often, remarkably often. During the commission, but also at department meetings, the *barone*, the great and powerful scholar, almost always a man, will put a positive spin on student–professor relationships, declaring himself the *allievo*, the pupil, but the word might equally well mean disciple, of this or that *maestro*, some older and by now quite mythical *barone*, a truly great scholar, everyone agrees, retired of course, and hence beyond envying or competing with. Or even dead, in which case even more fondly admired and complacently exploited.

'As my *maestro* used to say,' the *barone* will let slip, apropos of almost anything, 'the distinguished but admirably unassuming Brizzi,' he may add for anyone ignorant enough not to know who his *maestro* was, 'when we were together in Rome in the seventies,' he goes on, warming to the moment, enjoying the attention everyone is obliged to pay him, 'or was it Bologna in the eighties? My alma mater, you know?' And then, lowering his voice, as though in condescending parenthesis for those too young to be aware, 'That was when I was editing *Testi Millenari* for him,' or, 'That was when we were organising the memorable conference on Derrida,' or again, 'That was when I was teaching a module of his renowned course on post-structuralism and socialist semantics, one of the great honours of my early career.' The *barone* shakes his head. 'You've no idea what astonishing attention to detail Brizzi had! We will not see his like again.'

But at this point the great man pauses, for he has forgotten what it was his *maestro* used to say, or what he had been planning to say that his *maestro* used to say. He purses his lips, frowns. But it hardly matters. The spotlight is on him and this is always a pleasure. 'As my renowned *maestro* used to say,' he repeats, and then comes out, more or less at random, with something quite banal: '*A buon cavalier non manca lancia*' – a good knight always has his spear – or '*Nell'eternità si arriva sempre in tempo*' – you can't be late for eternity. If his audience have trouble relating this profound reflection to the matter in hand, they don't show it. Or, '*Non vi è peggior burla che la vera*,' the *barone* announces – no worse trick than the truth. All these are ordinary proverbs anyone might say, or attribute at convenient moments to their mothers or grandmothers. Again it hardly matters. The only important thing is that amid avuncular smiles and a generous air of nostalgia for a nobler past, to which the *barone* had the great privilege to belong, everyone understands that he, the *barone*, has the power to grant admission, or not, to this magnificent dynasty, the same way a bishop might claim the right to pass on the sanctity of apostolic succession; but *only if he so desires*, only if the supplicant is worthy, where worthiness refers, yes, to an extent, to being a good Christian, in the bishop's case, or to being a talented academic, in the *barone*'s, but more, far more, to the question of loyalty, absolute loyalty to the *barone*, or the bishop, who is considering extending a little grace in the miserable supplicant's direction.

Loyalty is everything. And loyalty, to return to the present thesis commission, is Antonio's problem. For the young researcher – actually in his mid-thirties – has not been absolutely loyal to his *maestro*, or rather *maestra*, Professoressa Modesto, who is herself the ferociously loyal *allieva* of Ottone, Giuseppe Ottone, to give him his full name. Beppe to those in his clan.

In what way has Antonio let his protectress down? Antonio has declined to take part in a research project which Professoressa Modesto proposed. He declined because he was already engaged in another project proposed by another professor and more in line with his interests. He has assumed, that is, that he has the right to decide for himself what he studies, a right actually enshrined in the constitution of all universities. But, all the same, what presumption! Especially because this other professor, whose project Antonio signed up to without asking the permission of Modesto, is none other than Domenico Galli, who, if not exactly a sworn enemy of Modesto's, is very definitely in the camp of Professor Tedeschi, Galli's *maestro* and the candidate opposing Professor Ottone, Modesto's *maestro*, in the Rectorship elections. Hence the two disciples must be enemies even if they have no desire to be so and actually barely know each other.

But Antonio's effrontery does not end with his wish to study the things he feels he has some affinity for. The fact is that, commuting from faraway Padua, the young academic has twice failed to present himself for conferences organised by Modesto, occasions when it was important for the professoressa to show others that she could command a certain respect and attract a good crowd and was not merely an underling of the mighty Ottone. Which is how she tends to be seen.

Why is Antonio behaving in this foolish way? Perhaps because the conferences in question promised to be dull and trivial. Perhaps because he believes that being a Category B researcher, so-called, with excellent publications to his name, he is already in *una botta di ferro*, an iron cask. Already home and dry. Which actually he is not, because although it may be unheard of to deny someone with a Category B contract a permanent position at the end of their three years, the unheard-of is all too often heard in academic circles, and heard rather loudly.

The deeper problem is that Antonio has a strong sense of personal dignity and a genuine passion for the literature of francophone Africa, object of all his studies. James has noticed with pleasure that such people do exist in Italian universities and he finds himself attracted to them. He enjoys their conversation, he learns from them. But he has also noticed that to be absorbed in one's studies, or even worse in one's teaching, is about as great a mistake as an academic can make, an academic who wants a career, that is. And really there is no way an academic can be an academic without a university career, since no one else is going to give you money for knowing about the literature of francophone Africa. No, to be entirely focused on one's studies is comparable to the footballer who takes his eye off the ball. Because the ball is politics. And the people whose whole focus is on politics always win out over the people who are interested in what politics, or power, is supposed to be *for*. As Machiavelli tells us in *The Prince*, to be and remain in a position of power one's supreme and overriding priority must be to be and remain in a position of power. Any other consideration is a dangerous waste of energy. Unfortunately, to be warned of this state of affairs is hardly a help, since those who have a passion for their studies will find it as impossible to concentrate entirely on politics as those primarily interested in politics will find it impossible to concentrate, even occasionally, on their studies. Antonio needs to watch out.

James too is experiencing issues of loyalty. The kind lady who brought him into the university and has guided his career ever since is a curiously hybrid creature. She can never quite decide, or at least so it seems to James, whether her first priority is her studies, in sixteenth-century English poetry, or the Arts Department which she helped to build up from scratch many years before, or indeed the power game outside the department for control of the university. And what has floored James is that this astute and intelligent woman – Professoressa Ventura – has announced her support for Professor Tedeschi – from the Economics Faculty – in the Rectorship race. But James and all his friends are convinced that Tedeschi is the wrong candidate, from the wrong faculty. They can't understand what could have induced Professoressa Ventura to make this odd decision. Hasn't Professor Tedeschi spoken of winding down the Arts Department, and in particular languages? All kinds of unsavoury conjectures are in the air.

In any event, James is planning to betray his protectress and vote for Ottone, and this not so long after Professoressa Ventura was instrumental in converting his research position into a professorship, another long, complicated story which for brevity's sake we must pass over. However, James has never construed loyalty as something absolute and to her credit Professoressa Ventura has never tried to bind him in any way, merely suggested what she thinks it would be convenient for him to do. The election is tomorrow, the day after the thesis commission. Unofficial headcounts suggest it is going to be a tight race. The ballot will be secret, but prevailing opinion holds that precisely where there's a perceived need for secrecy it is unlikely to be guaranteed. Many professors are convinced that their university email is monitored and some do not rule out the idea that staff offices are bugged. It's that sort of place.

GRAZIE PER LA VOSTRA ATTENZIONE!

At last Professor Galli has arrived. He slips off a sharp blue linen jacket, dons a gown boasting a pink slash and, with much flashing of gold cufflinks, takes his seat on the tightly packed dais, demoting a researcher to floor level. Twenty-five minutes late, the commission can begin its work.

'Style and Journalism: the Case of *La Repubblica*,' Ottone reads from the programme. 'Candidate, Laura Tresoldi. Tutor, Professor Domenico Galli.'

The morning's candidates are sitting in the front row, six girls and four boys. Laura Tresoldi gets to her feet and walks to the right side of the dais where two steps bring her up to professorial level. She moves carefully, for her heels are the height that a good girl only uses on special occasions. Her body sways awkwardly; her black dress is tight with a low neckline. The custodian, or attendant, who watches over these occasions, moves fast to stop a member of the public taking photographs. The girl's proud boyfriend perhaps. For the official photographer is already at work, clicking away as Signorina Tresoldi settles herself on her swivel seat behind a low desk facing the commission. She turns on her microphone and fiddles with a computer to open a PowerPoint on a large screen above and behind the professors' heads and likewise on a line of screens in front of them. High tech is good publicity for the university.

'*Buon giorno*,' the candidate says to the commission.

'*Buon giorno, signorina*,' says Ottone with an indulgent smile.

Galli, who has rather unusually tutored this thesis himself, because the girl is smart as well as pretty, makes some general remarks about style and journalism and the particular circumstances in which the newspaper *La Repubblica* came into being in the mid-seventies. He is showing off for Ottone, whom he is not supporting in the Rectorship election, but nevertheless needs to impress, in case he wins.

'But I won't steal any more time from our candidate,' Galli announces and invites her to present her work.

James knows exactly what will happen next. These things are regular as clockwork. First the girl thanks her professor for his generous introduction, then goes on to repeat it more or less word for word. But whereas Galli had spoken with relaxed conviction, the nervous young woman launches into her spiel at high speed, as if afraid she might not finish before some gong sounds and her time is up. Preamble over, she ploughs on, speaking faster all the time. If for a moment she hesitates, the PowerPoint comes to her aid. She glances at the text, changes slide, sees what she was supposed to be saying and races off again.

The official purpose of the PowerPoint is to help the professors and public understand the structure of her thesis, but its real utility is as a crib to get the student through. The trick of the thesis commission, Alessio once explained to James, is that while it must appear as an ordeal to the student and her family, and indeed be experienced as an ordeal, and so in a sense really *is* an ordeal, it must on no account be so truly challenging that any student actually fails to get through it. What kind of *festa* would that be?

So rather than being engaged in a real discussion, the students must be allowed to parrot. And since parroting for a whole fifteen minutes, or even twenty, can be tough, there is the PowerPoint to help you through. In the past it was photocopies distributed to the members of the commission, then the overhead projector with its makeshift transparencies. The PowerPoint, however, offering scope for fades and animations, bulleted paragraphs and elaborate bar charts rising one after the other in different colours on the screen, is far superior; now the crib can masquerade as a demonstration of expertise in exposition. So as she speaks, Laura Tresoldi brings up text after text from *La Repubblica*, homing in on this or that word to illustrate this or that rhetorical ploy, until finally the longed-for slide, '*Grazie per la vostra attenzione!*', appears. Thank you for your attention. In truth, Ottone has been scrolling through his text messages throughout.

It now remains for someone to ask one question in English, to prove that Laura can meet her language requirement, and the 'discussion' is over. She knows what the question is, since this has been agreed beforehand. James asks it: 'How would you characterise the difference between Italian and English journalistic rhetoric?' The girl answers: 'The Italian tends to be a little more elaborate and roundabout, the articles rather longer.'

'We consider the discussion sufficient,' Galli informs Ottone with a satisfied flick of his cufflinks. Ottone looks to right and left along the faces of his colleagues and asks if anyone else on the commission has any further question for the candidate. His voice is sufficiently discouraging to guarantee there are no further questions. The show can move on to the next candidate.

Only nine to go.

How to get through these three or four hours? When he has a few students of his own, students whose theses he has tutored, that is, James can feel he is usefully employed. On a day like today, when he merely has to ask a question or two in English, the thesis commission experience is beyond boring, as if one were invited to hold tedium in one's hands and caress it there like a cuddly little animal for hours on end.

The students come and go. The themes. Comic cinema. Gentrification as a global phenomenon. The Photoshop revolution. While each candidate talks, a document is passed along the row of professors so that they can sign off on the grade that they haven't yet given, thus saving themselves the time and trouble of signing after it is given. Looking at the paper in front of him, James savours the minor pleasure of studying his colleagues' signatures, wondering why some feel the need to write their names carefully in full – Elisabetta Angela Modesto, Domenico Secondo Galli – while others favour squiggled illegibility. Alessio's is a baroque rose of self-mockery. Spiralling curlicues of silliness. What a strange and charming man he is.

Occasionally, as one topic follows another, something interesting gets said. Mostly, though, the presentations are flagrantly superficial and invariably delivered in a vaguely self-righteous, self-congratulatory tone. 'This issue is highly relevant today.' 'This subject warrants further study.' 'This wrong urgently needs to be set right.' As if the students were engaged in a TV talk show rather than an academic endeavour. Perhaps that is the only model of public debate they are familiar with. From the floor below the dais, Federica passes James a note: *Modesto, che pirla!* – what a prick! This as Ottone's protégé introduces with the utmost solemnity a thesis on the achievements of Italians abroad, complimenting her student on 'a work of profound and original research'.

While the boy, the fifth candidate of the morning, does his stuff, James turns to look at the woman who will no doubt be a force to be reckoned with should Ottone win the election for Rector. Bettina Modesto is in her early forties, younger than himself by several years, and somehow contrives to be both very feminine, yet masculine too. She has lipstick and nail varnish of the same mauvish colour, she wears dresses for preference – today's is silver grey – and doesn't hide her curves; yet her movements are wooden in the way only a certain kind of man can be wooden, and her voice has a distinctly male depth to it.

For the thousandth time James ponders over the relationship between Modesto and Ottone. It has been the talk of the university ever since Ottone arrived, from Puglia, and brought his supposedly brilliant *allieva* in his wake. For the truth, as everyone soon realised, is that she is far from brilliant. Her lips purse with apparent concentration as she leans into a discussion, pen in outstretched hand. The air fills with expectation. And when she starts to speak her voice is clear and strong. But what she actually says is the merest jargon-ridden fluff, like this ridiculous praise for a student now parroting his reflections on Italian expat communities.

Why has she praised the boy so extravagantly? James wonders. There is nothing in his presentation that couldn't be found in ten minutes on the Internet. He's a handsome lad, for sure, tall and bearded, in a dark suit and bright tie, but he doesn't have an idea in his head. 'This is a thesis that should be read by all our embassies abroad,' Modesto applauds when the last slide goes up.

'*Bravo*,' Ottone concurs.

Again *why*? What does Ottone see in Modesto? He's not a ladies' man. In his mid-sixties and respectably married to a woman some years older than himself, the *barone* would appear to be content with his lot. James doesn't get it. If you were looking for a lover to cheer yourself up – there are rumours Signora Ottone is a bit of a shrew – who would choose Bettina Modesto? With all the pretty young academic staff there are around. True she's single, she's free, but you sense at once that this is only because there's something cold about her. And punctilious. You can see it in the way she dresses and the attention she pays to everything said, how careful and formal her emails are. You can never really *talk* to her. It's more like engaging with the tax office. The idea of going out for a drink with the woman would be surreal.

'I have a question.' Alessio wakes everyone up.

Ottone looks at his watch and sighs. 'Go ahead, Dottor Rubio.'

There is irony gleaming behind the researcher's spectacles.

'You have been telling us' – Alessio smiles affably at Modesto's handsome young student – 'of the achievements of Italian ex-patriates worldwide; I was just wondering whether, in the course of your research, you had considered recent claims that William Shakespeare was in fact an Italian. This would offer further proof that it is only

148

outside our sometimes difficult country that a certain kind of Italian talent can flourish.'

James smiles. This is pure mockery. At a loss, the student stretches his neck in a starched collar and looks enquiringly at his tutor. The question wasn't in the script.

'You'll be aware, no doubt,' Alessio goes on, 'of Lamberto Tassinari's breakthrough monograph, *The Man Who was Shakespeare*, in which he argues that the bard was none other than John Florio, son of Michelangelo Florio, exiled from the Grand Duchy of Tuscany.'

The student is evidently not aware of the book, nor is there any reason why he should be. But he doesn't know that. Modesto hurries to his aid: 'The candidate was firmly advised,' she says drily, 'to circumscribe his studies to the post-war period.'

'Ah,' Alessio breathes. 'Circumscription.'

'*Caro* Dottor Rubio,' Ottone interrupts, mildly amused. 'We mustn't be taking Shakespeare away from the poor English, must we? What on earth would be left them?'

'Beyond our co-nationals in flight ...' Alessio laughs.

Modesto's face is a picture of indignant puzzlement. She loathes Alessio. The curious thing, James thinks, is how while Ottone protects Modesto, protects her modest intellect, he doesn't seem to mind others making fun of her from time to time. As if being able to promote a nobody like this, for no particular reason, or none that anybody has worked out as yet, were a gratifying sign of his own growing power.

After the fifth candidate, the President of the Commission invites the public to leave the room while the professors assess the theses so far presented. It's time for the bargaining to begin ...

110 E LODE

The final grade for an Italian degree is expressed in one hundred and tenths. That is, a mark out of one hundred and ten. Why on earth? Because, just as normal exams began as a mark out of thirty, there being three examiners each giving a mark out of ten, so originally the thesis commission was made up of eleven members, each with ten marks to give. This is also, perhaps, why marks are referred to as *voti*, votes. Each examiner offered a vote for the candidate, like the judges at a boxing match. But once again while the expression of the result remains the same, the means of arriving at it has radically changed. These days, the average of the student's many examination results throughout the degree is first multiplied by a hundred and ten, then divided by thirty to give a result expressed in one hundred and tenths. This average is then taken as the mark that the student 'starts from' before some extra points are added for the thesis, directly after the presentation. These may range from as little as one to as many as ten, thus giving extraordinary weight to a piece of work that may very well have been read, cursorily, by only one person, and in some cases not at all.

Look at the system closely and you can't help but be struck by its combination of complex computation and extraordinary vagueness, something not unlike the bizarre mix of mathematics and mysticism in the calculation of a sinner's years in purgatory. In a comparative analysis of various European systems for establishing degree grades, the Italian Law Students' Union observed that the major difference between the Italian system and others is the large percentage of marks that remain absolutely at the professors' discretion.

But to the matter in hand. Laura Tresoldi starts from a *media*, an average, of 101.3. Is that the *media ponderata*, someone asks, or the *media normale*? That is, does the *media* take into account the number of credits each course offers in relation to the exam result achieved (*media ponderata*), or is it just a straight average of all the results (*media normale*) regardless of the credits for each exam? The two can give quite different results. Ottone says it is the *media ponderata*, but he is happy to accept whichever average is higher. There is a pause while the young man to the right of Ottone, a researcher whom James does not know, looks through the student's documents to find the *media normale* which turns out to be 101.6, meaning Laura Tresoldi can be rounded up to 102 rather than down to 101, before the mark for her thesis is added to arrive at her final degree grade.

The debate begins. Domenico Galli, her tutor, observes that the girl has worked hard. There are some interesting ideas in her thesis. Seven points, he feels, would be in order. Professor Modesto frowns; that would bring the girl to 109 and this is a result one simply doesn't give. The same way one doesn't give 29 out of 30. Perhaps the feeling is that the 9 result is a kind of mockery, *una beffa* is the word. As if it drew more attention to what had not been given than to what had. Galli turns to James. 'How was the student's English?'

James knows perfectly well the card Domenico is playing. If he says the girl's English was exceptional, this affirmation will be used to ask the commission to have her arrive at the maximum 110 rather than round her down to 108. Needless to say, Laura Tresoldi will have done all kinds of English exams through her university career, written and oral, and the commission has a printout of her results available and could perfectly well check how she scored. All the same, extraordinary weight is now going to be given to the very few words she spoke in English in this tense situation in front of the gowned professors sitting behind their long desk like so many old crows. James observes that the girl spoke fluently but made a few typical errors. In short, he passes the buck.

A professor of Comparative Literature sitting just beyond Alessio observes that he felt the girl rather confused issues of rhetoric and organisation of content. 'Of course, the two can't be entirely separated, but nor should they be altogether conflated,' this middle-aged woman observes. Ottone confirms that he too had the same impression. Everyone immediately understands that the mark will be rounded down, not up. Modesto is thus free to comment that the bibliography did not seem as *nutrita*, literally, 'well fed', as one might expect for an analysis of this kind, meaning the candidate hasn't pretended to have read a huge number of books. Modesto is particularly surprised, she says, to notice the absence of any works of semiotics.

'Ah, semiotics,' Alessio breathes. 'How did we manage without them?'

Seeing which way the wind is blowing, Galli says he will be more than happy if the commission gives the student 6 points, taking her to 108. Quite possibly, James reflects, that was all he was aiming for in the first place and the whole suggestion that the girl might arrive at 110 was just a way of conditioning the commission to feel that they'd thwarted him by giving 108. Ottone asks if the commission is now agreed, but in such a way as to indicate that since he himself agrees the case is closed. And so it is. Laura Tresoldi will for ever remember this day as the one when she graduated with 108 out of 110. The only member of the commission who has read anything of the girl's thesis is Galli, and there is no way the others will ever know how much exactly he did or didn't read.

And so on for the next four students. When it comes to the last, the boy who wrote about Italians abroad, Antonio, the young French researcher, is quizzed by Modesto as to the quality of the candidate's French and dutifully tells his protectress that it was admirably fluent. The student is awarded 9 points to reach 110. 'This is such a remarkable thesis and such a resourceful student,' Modesto says with grave formality, 'that I am duty-bound to ask my colleagues if they would be so generous as to grant a *lode* in this case. Of course, I'm aware that this decision has to be unanimous.'

There is probably no one at the table who agrees with Professor Modesto's assessment of the thesis. But Ottone is the man of the moment, the power in waiting. Everyone can feel it. And Modesto is his beloved disciple.

'After long reflection,' Alessio says, making no attempt to keep a straight face, 'I have . . . no objection.'

The boy's family will be delighted.

Discussions over, the menial goes to the door to call back the students, their families and friends. About eighty people troop in, tense with expectation. It's the climactic moment of three years' work. What grades are they going to get? The photographer is on hand. Ottone stands up in the centre of the thirteen professors. His gown has the white fur of the Head of Department. Seen from the floor of the hall, the cameo might appear a parody of some old religious painting, a *Last Supper* perhaps; the great man is about to perform the transubstantiation.

'Laura Tresoldi.'

One by one the students are called. Again they show off their smart clothes and youthful nerves as they climb the dais, this time to stand face to face with the President of the Commission across the long table. 'Signorina Tresoldi,' Ottone begins, with his strong Pugliese accent, 'the commission has discussed your thesis and considered your university curriculum, and now, in the name of the law and with the powers conferred upon me by the Magnificent Rector of this academy, I proclaim you doctor in Communications and Management, with marks of one hundred and eight out of one hundred and ten. With many congratulations and all best wishes for the future.'

The girl's face breaks into a smile of relief, as she reaches across the table to shake Ottone's extended hand. The crowd erupts in applause.

Taking a copy of her thesis from Ottone, the girl moves behind the table along the line of professors, shaking everyone's hand. Everyone mutters *complimenti,* or *brava,* or even *bravissima.* James finds her slim fingers damp with sweat. As she steps off the dais her proud father is there with a laurel crown held high.

'Dottoressa!'

Onward. The ritual is repeated for student after student until, as Ottone calls the name of the last, the boy Modesto has tutored, the whole commission of thirteen professors rises to its collective feet. It is a token of respect for one who has been granted *la lode,* or perhaps for the professor who has persuaded the commission to give that *lode.* The public immediately understands the significance of the move and there are subdued oohs of expectation. The boy's mother raises a tissue to her eyes. Ottone's smile is particularly indulgent as he announces, 'with the addition and honour of *la lode'.* The room explodes in cheers.

And the cheers continue as the five new doctors and half the public hurry out for their celebrations. No sooner are they through the door than polite applause morphs into wild shouts, then the familiar chant echoing along the corridor: '*Dottore, dottore, dottore del buco del cul, vaffancul vaffancul!*' Doctor of arseholery, up your arse, up your arse!

All this is more than audible as Ottone calls the next candidate to present his thesis, so that the poor boy kicking off the second half of the morning has to launch into his discussion of European legislation regarding low-cost airlines while his friends are yelling jolly obscenities outside. No one seems remotely upset by this. No one intervenes or goes out of the room to quieten the celebrations. Looking at the candidates remaining in the front row, two girls and two boys, James feels a quiet admiration for the way the students handle this sort of situation. One of those four will be the last; he or she will have to climb up on the dais after a wait of almost four hours, with everybody in the room bored out of their minds, desperate for a pee or a smoke. Yet all look perfectly resigned to their lot. One girl is even smiling as more cries of *vaffanculo* waft in from outside. Invited to ask the present candidate a question in English, James enquires, as agreed, whether Ryanair has altered the social status of tourists coming to Italy and the young man says, 'There is yes certainly the more working-class people on the Adriatic beach nowadays.'

Down on the floor, in the front row of seats, Valeria winces as she hears those mistakes. She will do better, she hopes, when her moment comes, but she knows the tricks that nerves can play. Penultimate in the morning's programme, she is very far from being the calm collected young pro James imagines. It's just that the education system she has come through has inured her to waiting her turn at orals, often for hours at a time. And her strategy is always to go over and over the first things she plans to say. The first sentence, then the second, then the third. Hopefully the rest will follow, like a series of dance steps.

What makes matters more tense today is not so much the thirteen gowned professors, but the presence of her family, and in particular of her mother's admiring, but always critical, gaze. Mamma always made such a big deal of the fact that they were not from the professional classes, that their family did not have the kind of contacts that would make life easy. 'Your father is a nobody,' she told her children time and again. 'He didn't even finish school.' Aren't the family simply waiting for her to screw up and tumble back down to their level? There's a mad hubris in being here, the young southern woman suddenly tells herself, at this solemn occasion, instead of back in Basilicata, working in a shop or post office. A bed-and-breakfast. After it's all over her half-sister will raise mocking eyebrows, as she always does. What if Valeria gets her degree but then can't find a job? The three-year degree is worth nothing without the two-year Magistrale afterwards. What was it all for? Vanessa will ask. All the sacrifices the family has made. Why is she doing this?

LA FANCIULLA LUCANA

'The candidate Valeria Lasala,' the President of the Commission announces, 'presents a thesis entitled, "Help or Hindrance, European Subsidies for the Film Industry: the problem of regional distribution". Tutor, Dottor Alessio Rubio.'

Valeria walks carefully to the dais. 'It's too tight,' her mother had told her at the interval, criticising her choice of dress. Michele is here too – her boyfriend – towards the back somewhere. She sits down and exchanges one glance with Ottone before his eyes drop to his mobile. Alessio takes over in a rather plummy, intellectual voice. 'The candidate has approached her subject,' he observes, 'not so much from the financial and statistical points of view, though she has carried out the necessary research in this regard, but as a question of aesthetics: how is the content and narrative structure of European films altered by financing rules that reward projects set in more than one Community country and featuring characters of various Community nationalities?'

Disoriented, Valeria launches into her spiel. Or rather, her spiel starts up in her mouth, which feels oddly stiff and achy. With every sentence she speaks into the microphone in the big room, it's as if she were more alone, more distant from the people around her. And as she moves from one PowerPoint slide to the next, the words accelerate in response to some pressure she is powerless to control.

'Signorina Lasala.'

What a jolt! Unlike other tutors, Alessio wants a discussion.

'I was wondering if the Film Funding Council had carried out any studies on the consequences of its policies.'

His voice has an ironic ring. Has she said something stupid? Valeria glances along the line of professors. Galli shows no sign of recognising her. Ottone is intent on his phone. Two women are whispering, rather loudly. What will her parents make of this rudeness? How can they understand that this is simply what universities are like? She answers her tutor's question rather brusquely. The council's statute requires that it produce an annual assessment of its own performance for consideration by the European Commission for Culture. However, this is quantitative. They don't analyse the quality or content of the films that meet their funding requirements. She clicks forward her PowerPoint.

'But do you have an example?' Alessio interrupts again. 'Can you tell us about a particular film whose plot was clearly influenced by the funding rules?

'Influenced?' In her nervousness, her retort is almost scathing. 'The plots are *created* to fit in with the funding regulations. There's no question of *influencing* a pre-existing idea. The idea is to get the funds.'

Without pausing she starts to talk about the difficulties of using actors of different mother tongues. 'In certain cases, misunderstandings ...'

'Speaking of which ...' her tutor says.

Apparently it's already time for a question in English. How can that be? She was only halfway through her presentation. And French too. She has opted for two languages.

'Aren't there similar constraints on film financing all over the world?'

The question had been agreed by email, but she has never met or spoken to James, and the way he asks it now in his British accent it sounds as though he were objecting to something she said before. She responds as planned, but the English words feel muddled; there's a stone under her tongue.

'Mademoiselle Lasala.' Antonio is handsome but severe; for some reason he gives her the impression of a well-groomed dog, perhaps it's the neat beard and moustache. '*Vous avez parlé surtout du cinéma française . . .*'

Unexpectedly, he asks a second question, beyond what they had agreed. 'What is the Funding Council's attitude to films dealing with Africa?'

'*Excusez moi?*'

'What is the Funding Council's policy on films featuring African issues?' The researcher appears to be looking at her kindly, intently.

'*Je n'ai pas recherché la question africaine,*' she says. 'However, coverage of francophone African communities resident in France is rewarded in various ways.'

It's a lame answer.

'*Pouvez vous donner des exemples?*'

Her mind is blank. 'Many films about Moroccan and Algerian families consider the conditions of women in immigrant communities,' she says.

'In your bibliography,' comes a voice from the other end of the table, 'page 213, you cite the book *European Film Industries* by Anne Jackel. Can you tell us how that was useful to your research?'

At first she thought it must be a man's voice, but it's Modesto, another professor she doesn't know. Of linguistics. She tries to remember Jackel's book. 'It gives an interesting account,' she invents, 'of an Austrian film set in the South Tyrol because that setting allowed the producers to say there was both an Italian and an Austrian involvement. However, this caused authenticity problems because of the specificity of Tyrolese dialect.'

Will that do?

'You do realise you've indicated that the book was published in 1904?' Modesto arches a plucked eyebrow. 'I presume you meant 2004.'

Valeria sits through the last student's presentation with a profound sense of shame. Her parents must have realised how poorly she performed. They will commiserate, which is worse than criticism. They will criticise the professors, not realising that it was up to her to defend herself. Looking up, she is struck by Professoressa Modesto's fresh complexion: there is something odd about it, as if it were painted on enamel. Then Professor Ottone invites the public to leave the room while the professors discuss the final results.

Everyone agrees on 110 *e lode* for the boy writing about low-cost airlines. And for the third student, who considered translations for advertising. Certainly the second part of the morning was better than the first. Then it's late for lunch and this creates a sense of common purpose even between enemies. The decisions are coming thick and fast.

'Valeria Lasala,' Ottone reads from his programme. 'The girl who doesn't like film funding.'

'I did not find her very convincing,' Modesto says at once.

'Her English?' Ottone enquires.

'Competent,' says James, 'despite the accent.'

'Lucana!' Ottone chuckles. Being from Puglia, the neighbouring Lucani are forever to be condescended and disparaged.

Unusually, the candidate's tutor, Alessio, who would normally speak first, doesn't comment.

'Her French was excellent,' Antonio puts in rather earnestly.

'Excellent?' Modesto queries.

Galli is consulting an expensive watch. 'What does the *bella fanciulla* start from?' he says briskly.

Bella fanciulla. Pretty young maiden. James shakes his head.

The researcher who is playing secretary to the commission, a self-important clean-shaven fellow constantly paying excessive respect to Ottone – yes, Professor, no, Professor – leafs through the papers in his file.

'One hundred and ... seven,' he announces, and in the brief ensuing silence, '*Media ponderata*.'

'Case closed,' Federica says drily. 107 is such an unusually high mark they will simply have to give the girl 110. Nobody else today has started from over 104.

'And five *lode*,' the secretary adds, almost apologetically.

'So?' Ottone turns to Alessio. It is the tutor who must ask for the final mark. It's now clear why he was in no hurry.

'I'm sorry but I still don't think,' Modesto cuts in, 'that we can give her a *lode* for a thesis like this.'

A marvellously sardonic smile lights up Alessio's face. It's as if he has chosen his rimless glasses precisely to have this long-cultivated smirk glint in their lenses.

'Do go on, Bettina,' he says, knowing how impatient the others are to be done.

Modesto wriggles in her blouse. 'As I said, I did not find this presentation convincing. For a *lode*, as we know, the regulation requires marked originality.'

'As with our man praising Italian expat genius around the globe,' suggests Alessio.

'Exactly. Not someone who gets their dates wrong in her bibliography.'

'Very unoriginal,' Alessio concedes.

'Please,' Galli says. 'It's one forty-five.'

'*Caro* Alessio,' Ottone takes over. 'Could you please tell us what mark you want to ask for our *fanciulla lucana*?'

Alessio sighs. 'It's a good piece of work. The candidate is smart. She's not overawed by institutional rhetoric. She speaks decent French and English, despite obvious nerves. In these circumstances, and with her starting from 107, I cannot imagine a tutor who would not ask for *la lode*.'

'Which requires the commission's unanimous consent,' Ottone reminds his colleagues.

Modesto is shaking her head. 'How can we give a *lode* to someone so careless as to write down the wrong century?'

James is fascinated. A young person's academic career is possibly at stake. It is about to be decided by a dozen people with disparate agendas and rumbling stomachs.

Unusually, Antonio wades in. 'So all those excellent exam results are to count less than a typing error?'

The young man has forgotten that Professor Modesto is his protectress.

'*Lode* and lunch,' Federica says. Everyone murmurs their assent.

Ottone turns his big swivel seat to look at Professor Modesto. Tomorrow is the election, James reflects.

'Bettina, *carissima*,' he says, with indulgent irony, but also, it seems, a genuine affection. 'I must say I enjoy hearing a clever girl with a strong Lucana accent taking on the European culturecrats. *Una ragazza del popolo*,' he smiles, 'who has got herself a fine education thanks to our academy here, the excellent lessons and lectures of all our colleagues, the tutoring of the astute Doctor Rubio. Of course, we all respect your celebrated meticulousness, Bettina, but don't you think, perhaps, you could make a very small exception in this case? We need unanimity for *la lode* and at the moment it seems we are twelve against one. And dying of hunger ...'

Years later, talking this over, James, Antonio, Alessio, Federica and Valeria herself would all marvel at Ottone's cunning in this phase of his university life. It was as if his unpleasantly pedantic ally were there precisely to allow the great man to show his magnanimity, his superior sense of justice.

Seeing the gowned commission rise to their feet for her daughter, Carmela Lasala burst into sobs. 'I nearly died of pride,' she would henceforth say, remembering that famous moment when a member of her family became a Doctor of Communications and Media Studies, with 110 and the honour of the *lode*.

Dottore del buco del cul, vaffancul, vaffancul.

PART THREE

Grandi ambizioni

APPUNTO

How to introduce new blood but stay in control? A king and queen reign contentedly over their extensive territories surrounded by a swarm of complacent courtiers. Everyone is happy, everything is stable. The only possible shadow on the horizon is a terrible ogre who has built himself a castle deep in the forest. Fortunately, neither ogre nor king has reason to cross paths; all is well.

Along comes a charming young man, Corvetto, who attracts the attention of the court. Dazzled, the king starts to show Corvetto all kinds of extravagant favours. His courtiers, dismayed by this change in pecking order, hatch a plot to be rid of the intruder. The ogre, they tell the king, has a wonderful enchanted horse, a horse that can talk, an intelligent horse, a beautiful horse. How happy the king would be if he possessed that splendid animal! Since Corvetto is so smart and courageous, why not send him to the ogre's castle to steal it?

The king observes that no one has ever come back alive from the ogre's castle, but the courtiers point out that Corvetto is no ordinary man. Indeed, he's so amazingly capable it's almost an offence on his part that he hasn't already stolen the horse for his lord and master. The king takes the bait and gives Corvetto his orders. 'Fine,' Corvetto says. He sets off, does the deed with great panache and returns in very short order with the fabulous horse, astounding and infuriating the courtiers.

As in all fables, the stakes are upped twice more. Another false need is created for the king, in order to introduce some instability into the situation and put Corvetto on his mettle. How can a king live, the courtiers are soon asking, without the marvellous tapestries that hang in every room of the monstrous ogre's castle? Corvetto sets off, deploys various clever subterfuges and all too soon is back with the tapestries. But how can a king, the desperate courtiers insist, look himself in the mirror when a mere ogre possesses a castle infinitely more impressive than his own? Once again Corvetto sets off and this time outwits and brutally slaughters the ogre and all his ogre entourage, conquering the castle for the king who now gives the young man his daughter in marriage. Corvetto has joined the family.

This is a benign version of events. The courtiers' world has been turned upside down, but the king, who has behaved foolishly throughout, not only remains on his throne but greatly extends his power. It's not hard to see that all this depends on the unlikely combination of Corvetto's unparalleled prowess and unflinching loyalty. He is the perfect son-in-law.

Alas, perfection is rare, especially when it comes to in-laws. Another of Basile's tales tells of a king so self-obsessed that he cultivates his own fleas and lice. Nothing else interests him, not his handsome wife, not his beautiful daughter. He does nothing but breed parasites from his own body, encouraging them to grow to greater and greater sizes. Finally, in secret, he produces a flea as big as a pig. Meantime, his gorgeous daughter is desperate to leave the family's isolated castle and marry. When the enormous flea dies, the distraught king has it skinned, hangs up the hide, emblem of his self-centredness, and announces that his daughter will marry the first suitor to identify the animal it came from. Unfortunately, none of the charming young men queueing up for royal bliss can work out what on earth this strange pelt is. But an atrocious, filthy, savage ogre is all too familiar with that old flea smell and after a couple of sniffs and a grunt of 'common flea', carries off the terrified daughter and sets her up in a freezing cave in a remote mountain gorge. She will have to survive all kinds of blood-chilling vicissitudes before she manages to slit her massive husband's throat and return home. But now she is no longer the sweet and obedient maiden everyone knew before; gruesome experience has transformed her into a determined outsider. She pushes her ineffectual parents aside and takes over the kingdom for herself.

Again and again, whether it's fables or novels or films or simply news stories, there's the sense that the family, the group, the institution, however apparently stable and happy, nevertheless lacks something crucial, some energy or charisma essential to its future, hence is simply obliged to invite a stranger in, at enormous risk to both the insiders themselves and the new arrival. In *The Garden of the Finzi-Continis*, the young narrator is lured into the reclusive Finzi-Contini family by the beautiful daughter, sucked dry over a period of a year or so, then coldly expelled, an experience that leaves him deeply traumatised. Meantime another outsider, the marvellously ambiguous Giampiero Malnate, seems to have wormed his way into a position of powerful influence in the family and is possibly the lover of both brother and sister.

In Pasolini's film *Theorem*, an attractive young intellectual seduces his way into the household of a rich Milanese industrialist, has sex with more or less everyone – servants, daughter, son, even the industrialist himself – then walks off scot-free, leaving the family in tatters. More often, though, the outsider has no intention of walking off; he takes over. In Moravia's *Time of Indifference*, Leo Merumeci first seduces the widowed mother of Michele and Carla, then the daughter Carla, then survives Michele's half-hearted attempt to murder him, then proposes marriage to Carla in order to take possession of the family villa at the expense of the mother who originally drew him into the family group.

All this by way of gentle preamble to suggest that the story of how Professors Beppe Ottone and Bettina Modesto arrived one fine day from Puglia to insinuate themselves into and eventually take over the northern academic community in which James was rather desultorily trying to put together some kind of university career, is a typically Italian story. All Italian Rectors will at some point refer to their university as a family – it's an irresistible analogy – and all families are susceptible to this kind of infiltration.

But how did these two, at once so different in character and so oddly united in purpose, get into the university in the first place and in particular why did a majority of presumably intelligent professors vote a man like Ottone into a position of power? James and his friends will be pondering these questions for many unhappy years to come. One answer might be that it is in the Italian character to commit this kind of collective suicide from time to time. 'How can one help becoming a master in a country of slaves?' Mussolini famously excused himself for becoming Italy's dictator. The idea was hardly his. Even some of the most fervently patriotic Italians have referred disparagingly to their countrymen as slaves in search of a master, or so afraid of life as to be forever craving the protection of a boss. But James is wary of stereotypes. Can these observations really be any truer of the Italians than, say, the English or the French?

Let us think back to how it was before Ottone and Modesto took control, before Valeria began her second, higher-level degree, and then her PhD, before Antonio was forced to heed the warnings of his friends, before the ambitious international conference that Federica dreamed up and James delivered, the great event that brought disaster on them all.

The university back then, in the nineties, the early noughties, was certainly a quarrelsome place, sometimes a childish place and always a frustrating place, but, in the end, functional, in the end, benign. If learning did not flourish quite as one might have hoped, still it wasn't altogether blighted or systematically sabotaged. The limitations were those of ordinary people jockeying for position within the framework of a national system apparently designed to make everything as difficult as possible for everyone and in every regard. Rectors and Heads of Department were regularly elected or not elected and generally accepted the verdicts of their peers. Hiring was never strictly merito-cratic, but nor did it entirely ignore merit. Gripe as you might, you could think of this place as your home, your family, albeit a slightly dysfunctional one.

Take the *consigli di dipartimento*, the department or, earlier, faculty meetings where much of the university business was done. Held once a month and invariably beginning fifteen minutes late, these gather-ings were a shameful waste of time. All kinds of suspicious things went on, with the most surprising allocations of funds and teaching posts slipping into the minutes in befuddling swirls of bureaucratese that the more powerful professors, the *ordinari*, who always seemed to have stitched up every decision among themselves before the meetings began, generated with enviable ease. So the junior professors and researchers might find themselves called on to vote for the creation of a professorship in, say, archaeology in a university with no archaeol-ogy courses, no ancient history, indeed nothing even remotely akin to archaeology. In that particular case the young man appointed to the post turned out to be the nephew of a government Minister. Or again they might be invited to award an Honorary Degree in Aesthetics to a particularly brainless rock star, this just as the year's enrolment cam-paign was heating up. The rock star was invited to give a (brief) talk, posters were put up all over town, the local youth flocked to see their idol. And hopefully enrolled.

Etc. You get the idea. But at least there were debates. At least people could disagree. The ageing professor of Spanish, for example, Samuele Scilli, was apt to grow dangerously excited, literally bouncing on his seat, vigorously rubbing his spectacles with his shirt tails eagerly stut-tering his opposition to almost everything. '*Appunto!*' he yelled. '*Ap-p-punto!*' Precisely. Exactly. The more excited he became the more he repeated this favourite word. '*Questo è ap-p-punto uno sc-scandalo.*' This is exactly a scandal. '*Perché come, appunto, il nostro collega, appunto Professor Galli, ha appunto spiegato*' – because as our colleague Galli has exactly explained – '*non c'è appunto nessuna, ma appunto nessuna, logica in un corso di archeologia.*' There is exactly no, but exactly no, logic in an archaeology course. '*Punto e basta.*' And that's that!

The *consiglio* was a fine place to observe speech tics, James discovered, and to wonder at the ability of his colleagues to field pompous vocabulary in the most humdrum circumstances – *imprescindibile, anteriorità, ottemperanza* – and then to mix these sonorous Latinisms with marvellously mispronounced and oddly concocted Anglicisms – *steykoldas, mixato, hackeraggio, impreenting, opinion mekers* – all in extended sentences of wonderful syntactical complexity and profound subjunctive incertitude. Sometimes he took notes. And with the passing years he would occasionally intervene himself. He too had begun to feel he belonged; he had reached the point where he could wax indignant when someone unworthy was introduced into their community, and even more so when someone worthy found their contract had not been renewed, some young researcher, full of talent and goodwill; but not related to a Minister.

Invariably, when James spoke, those he opposed would hint that as a foreigner he could not really understand how things were done in Italy. However many years one lived here, however effectively one had worked the system oneself to arrive at this or that position, nevertheless a foreigner remained a foreigner, and by definition naive.

So James's occasional interventions cut little ice. Because he was a Brit. He had an accent. And the same went for the French professor Patrice, and the Swiss-German researcher Jakob. Their objections were largely ignored. How could these outsiders understand a situation where law after law is invented to make nepotism and favouritism impossible, but in such a way that nepotism and favouritism thrive?

A rule is introduced to prevent close relatives from working in the university. A Rector or Head of Department cannot employ his or her son. Or daughter. That may be an unfair restriction of their human rights, but it is in the interests of the community. It is forbidden. And so the Rector of one university employs the son of another Rector who then returns the compliment by preparing a *concorso per ricercatore* for the first Rector's daughter, or niece or cousin. However, another law says that the commission judging that *concorso* must include professors from other universities so that the favoured internal candidate will not automatically be chosen. This is an excellent idea. In theory. In practice, what professor from outside will oppose this favoured internal fellow if that means that when other professors come to his university they will not allow him to favour his internal candidate?

Is all the interminable travelling, then, of professors up and down the long peninsula, back and forth across the wide North Italian Plain, to sit on the commissions of other universities in order to prevent something from happening that goes on happening just the same, entirely pointless? Well, perhaps occasionally an eyebrow will be raised, as much as to say: The appointment of a complete imbecile to a research post in mathematics just because his father or uncle or grandfather or great-aunt is Rector of this or that other university where your daughter or nephew or younger sister has long held a professorship in Sociology is not a great idea, not likely to improve either the quality of the teaching or the standing of the university in national and international rankings.

That raised eyebrow perhaps is useful. Perhaps next time someone will think twice. But for the moment the matter will end there. Nothing else will be said. As we have already remarked, the Italians don't have a word for whistle-blower. Rather they speak of disloyalty, of greasing. If a foreigner can't understand 'the secret things of our town', we certainly can't understand one of our own who wants to shout those secrets from the rooftops.

'These losers only cry foul,' Domenico Galli remarks over *aperitivi*, commenting on a case that has led to the arrest of six law professors in Rome, 'when they don't get the job they want. It's nothing but sour grapes.'

'The Pink Lady has spoken,' Alessio laughs. Then explaining to James the subtle operation of the anti-nepotism laws, he says it's rather as if the owner of a house built a wall inside the main wall to keep out the rats and then another wall, even further in the house, when that wasn't sufficient, and then another and, why skimp? yet another. All taking up more and more room inside the house. But the rats find the spaces between these warm walls more congenial to their tastes than any habitat they have previously come across. The owner, now trapped in the tiny remaining space cries, 'Look, no rats! Thanks to my wonderful walls.' And the rats cry, 'Right, no rats, we're not rats, we're rodents.'

'It's the same in every country in the world,' Domenico says dismissively. He has taken to using a cigarette holder when he smokes now. The same gold as his cufflinks. 'It's flagrant national stereotyping to say nepotism is worse in Italy.'

'If things are the same as elsewhere,' James objects, 'how is it that a foreigner can't understand?'

But back to the story. The point is, yes, there was some shady stuff going on in those pre-Ottone days. Of course. But there were good decisions too. There were sensible appointments. Above all, people felt free to debate. They felt free to vote against the Head of Department's wishes. They were not living in a climate of fear. Only under Ottone, and more particularly Modesto, would people begin to speak of the value of *unanimity*. 'The department must produce a unanimous decision,' on this or that appointment, Modesto would insist. And only much later, far too late, did James understand that an organisation in which all decisions are unanimous is an organisation whose members live in fear.

GIUSEPPE OTTONE

For a community to invite someone new and powerful into their midst, there must be a perceived need. And when that community is a business, the obvious need is not miraculous horses or tapestries or magnificent castles, but money. In the years we are speaking of, private universities, even more than their public counterparts, had had their government subsidies drastically cut. Some serious fund-raising was in order. But, as with whistle-blower, there is no term for fund-raiser in Italian. An article in *La Repubblica* in 2010, some years after the appointment of Ottone, reports the arrival of '*il* fund-raising' in Italy, a new practice brought back to the old country by Italians returning from the USA, but with limited success, the newspaper observed, due to the lack of any culture or tradition of donating money to educational institutions. In general the figure of the philanthropist is not so common or so visible in Italy as in America.

James has thought about this matter a great deal. He has reached the conclusion, perhaps flawed, but widely corroborated, that American culture gives enormous attention to questions of winning and losing. Stories of success and failure are everywhere in the USA. It's a society that celebrates its billionaires while allowing people without insurance cover to die on the street. These are standard American narratives, making and losing fortunes, rags to riches and back. And the American who succeeds is doubly a winner if he can show that he is also *a good person*, that he has won fairly and is willing to share his winnings. So the American adds to his or her achievements and celebrity with grand gestures of philanthropy.

Things don't work like this in Italy. An Italian family will not allow a poorer member to go hungry on the streets, or not if they can help it. Valeria, for example, has an old school friend, Monica, who never works or studies and has recently had a child out of wedlock, yet insists on living as an unemployed single mother in the centre of Bari. Still, her family pays up and puts up, because on the occasions when they stopped paying, with the intention of encouraging their daughter to become independent, Monica simply went to live, sleep and very likely die on the street. She wouldn't get a job, wouldn't fend for herself. Natalia Ginzburg's novels are full of figures who exploit the Italian family's admirable unwillingness to let a member go to the dogs. Such characters act helpless and hopeless in the sure knowledge that the family will pay their way.

Conversely, when Italians are enormously successful they tend to hide their wealth from the public, rather than show it. High walls conceal luxurious villas and their extensive gardens from public view. A gloomy facade on the public street hides a magnificent courtyard within, a courtyard only the privileged will ever see. Envy is a weed best left unwatered, was one of Cosimo de' Medici's favourite sayings. When rich folk then decide to busy themselves on behalf of others, those others are very often their relatives, or friends, or close associates, or fellow townsfolk, not the bums on the street, not the poor folk of Africa or Asia, and certainly not their old alma mater.

In short, it would be pointless for a university to spend too much money on a fund-raising office of the Anglo-Saxon variety since it would be unlikely that ex-students, however successful, would give. The more logical solution, then, is to bring into the university people who have the kind of contacts and friends that will allow them to attract funds from outside.

Ottone was such a man. A Freemason and proud of it, he sat on the boards of a number of banks and insurance companies, had been the Mayor of his village in the hills above Foggia, had taken time out from his professorial role to serve a term in the Senate after getting himself elected for Forza Italia. In those years he had been an undersecretary in the Ministry for Culture, and even after his return to academe was occasionally tipped as a future Minister for Education, or even something grander. Certainly he had charisma. The dark eyes flashed in his long gaunt face as he spoke of ambitious projects for the future, of his pride in working for a free and private university, his belief in Italian youth as second to none, deserving of the most advanced and enlightened education system that money could buy, and conscientious talent deliver.

One says, 'his return to academe', but one mustn't understand by that a return to teaching. An *'ordinario'* who takes a few years away from the university in Parliament, or some government office, will have his place kept warm for him. He – or very occasionally she – will continue to hold the *cattedra* (chair) in Philosophy at this or that university while someone else fills in for him, at a much lower salary. He can come back to it when he likes. Even then he is not obliged to teach. Naturally he will have courses assigned to him, since by law every professor has to work a certain number of hours, but then he will ask 'an assistant', most likely a young researcher, to substitute for him for most of the lessons. The assistant receives his assistant's pay. In her first year at the Magistrale in Publishing and Journalism, Valeria had Ottone as her teacher in the course on Modern Italian Language Usage, but for most lessons the great man was substituted by a charming, rather disorganised young woman who did not encourage the idea that she had a firm grip on her subject. On the two memorable occasions when Ottone came to the classroom – for the first and penultimate lessons – he preferred to speak of what the Italians, remembering Galileo's dialogue on Ptolemaic and Copernican astronomy, call *i massimi sistemi*, the grand scheme of things. That is, he told the students how profoundly Italy, Italian, and in particular the study of the Italian language was changing thanks to people who were his close friends and projects he personally was involved in: dictionaries, encyclopedias, online usage manuals, and so on. The best students present in class, he hinted, might in the future find themselves participating in this change and the earning opportunities that went with it.

To be brutal, we have a situation where a professorship is assigned not because the appointee is involved in valuable research, not because he can teach or even will teach – these are possible side benefits – but because he will bring money into our community. Sponsors. And bringing in money, he will have to be granted a certain power. So it is logical to think that when Ottone was invited to come to James's university, the positions of Head of Department and with it the Vice Rectorship must have been part of the negotiation.

But this is the custom of the town and must not be used to sully the man's reputation or deny his qualities. On first meeting, Giuseppe Ottone was irresistibly affable – You and I are going to be friends, his rather lanky body language said, we are going to do great things together – yet aloof too. And reassuringly authoritative. Ours will be a professional friendship, his manner told you, not a private matter. It would be he who called the tune. And fair enough. Because it was he who knew where the money would be coming from. You would be a willing lieutenant. And you would be rewarded. The plan was expansion. There would be room for everyone, everyone who was willing to muck in and make the university their home, their community. Everyone who was loyal.

All this he got across in a handshake and a smile. It was a generous smile, you felt, a welcoming smile. This man is a natural leader, you thought. He asked where you were from, the area, the town, even the village. He nodded approvingly. He named a famous figure from your part of the world with whom he was on friendly terms. They had spoken only yesterday about some project or other. He did not need to ask for your support; it was taken for granted. When he gave you his hand to hurry off, it was be-ringed and firm, and lingered just that split second longer than is normal, especially for a man in a hurry. Many were convinced the fingers lingered caressingly. Not in an ugly or inappropriate way. Heaven forbid. Rather to convey his deep affection for you, and for the people in his team in general. You are one of us, those lingering fingers said. I know your touch now.

Arriving from Puglia, from Foggia, on the invitation of that same Rector/philosopher who had wanted James as his translator, Ottone was immediately formidable in the *consigli di dipartimento*. Soberly, but never too formally dressed, neat without being natty – it was rumoured that his older wife, from an aristocratic Tuscan family, chose his clothes, his tweed jackets and dark blue ties, even his marvellously purposeful rimless glasses and steel Rolex – he would lay thick folders on the table before him and when the appropriate moment came expound ambitious research projects in great detail and with great emphasis, as if there could be no question but that they would go ahead: an online encyclopedia of Italian art and art criticism absolutely guaranteed to attract funds from the Ministry of Culture; an in-depth survey of the employment aims and education choices of ethnic communities in Lombardy that would doubtless bring in generous sponsorship from the Regional Government. When Head of Department elections came around, the outgoing Professor Ventura, James's protectress, warmly recommended Ottone to her colleagues. And they duly voted for him, James included. Samuele Scilli, who stood against, received three votes to Ottone's thirty. It was three more than expected. Who were those far-sighted rebels? At the very next department meeting Ottone proposed a new professorship, in Applied Linguistics, for a certain Elisabetta Modesto. A winning manager needs his personal team.

Why then did Prof Ventura oppose Ottone in the elections for Rector some eighteen months later? Tedeschi, the other candidate, was a typical northern academic baron, squat, barrel-chested, drily presumptuous, fiercely pragmatic. Rumours began to circulate that being a statistician, Tedeschi, Head of the Department of Communications and Public Relations, was planning to slash positions in the under-performing liberal arts courses.

James phoned Federica, also a protégée of Ventura, and she told him that according to Ventura the outgoing Rector had not resigned of his own accord. Ottone, *l'aveva fatto fuori!* Literally, done him out. Exclusion again. Not, we did him *in*, but we did him *out*. Ottone, Ventura was saying, had discovered something about the philosopher Rector and forced him to resign, on pain of unpleasant revelations. It was blackmail. Which was why Ventura felt morally obliged to support Tedeschi.

Closing this phone call, James was aware of a sense of danger, a premonition perhaps. There was something disturbing about the way Italian life always drew you in to a world of machination and intrigue. What could the philosopher Rector possibly have done that would make it so easy for Ottone to force him to step down? Wouldn't the Rector himself have known things about Ottone that would have allowed him to counter-threaten?

James had separated from his wife now, for better or worse. He was renting a flat some fifteen minutes' walk from the university, living with his youngest son who had just started a course in Fine Art at Brera College, supposedly the best place to study art in Italy. James had accompanied his son the day he went to enrol and witnessed a chaos that made him appreciate the relative efficiency of his own small university. The institution is located in the cavernous ground-floor rooms of the vast palazzo that houses the Brera Pinacoteca, Milan's main art gallery. The place was all cracking plaster, exposed pipes, cobwebs in the corners of high ceilings, barred windows and bare stone floors. Gloomy corridors milled with would-be students, many of them Asians who spoke no Italian and had no idea where to go or what to do. Offices were hopelessly inadequate for the purposes they were supposedly serving. Advice, when you finally reached the front of long and irritatingly undetermined queues, was incoherent at best. You found yourself listening to highly specific technical considerations referring to rules and requirements you had known nothing about. Explanatory brochures failed to explain. Peeking into classrooms, there was such a mismatch of numbers and equipment that dozens of students were on their knees drawing on pieces of paper taped to the floor. Yet James's son was incorrigibly cheerful. '*Tranqui'*, *Papà*,' he told his father. Which is to say, 'Chill. It'll all be fine.'

James hoped he was right. For the most part he loves his Italian life. He loves his morning walk to the café where an extrovert barman from Brindisi makes a cappuccino to die for, swirling ironic designs into the chocolate and foam. He enjoys the streets of Milan, the old greengrocers with their wares spilling out onto the street, the art-deco facades, the squealing trams. He even loves the weather, the windless air, the mists in winter and the summer heat haze. He likes his evening *aperitivi* with Domenico and Alessio and Federica. He enjoys his teaching, the smart students with their easy irony, the earnest students, even the lazy students. He never tires of watching how Italians walk and talk and gesture. And for some reason he has always felt freer in Italy, being an outsider, freer to say what he likes, in a language not his own. Certainly, learning to live in Italian and to allow all his thoughts and memories to fall under the spell of this different tongue, has been a wonderful and liberating experience.

James smiles, eating pasta with his Italian son. Yet he senses this freedom has become more memory than reality. As a university professor who has accepted an administrative role in the coordination of a new postgrad degree in Publishing and Journalism, he must also accept that he can no longer be carefree. He must have plans, ideas, assessments of the situation, and he must be aware how those plans will affect other people. Already he has begun to feel how unwise it would be, in department meetings and PhD commissions, to contest the opinions of Ottone and Modesto. He has observed that one or two people who have spoken against them have been rapidly and quietly sidelined.

Voting for a new Rector is a responsibility.

'*Fregatene, Papà*,' his son says, stacking the plates in the dishwasher. Don't give a shit. 'You have your job. They can't fire you. What do you care who's Rector?'

The boy's right, James thought. One mustn't start to take oneself too seriously. Perhaps Ottone will be an excellent Rector. With power, he will relax and make the whole show work. The following day he cast his vote in the *barone*'s favour.

L'INAUGURAZIONE DELL'ANNO ACADEMICO

The first time Valeria saw Ottone in institutional action, she was hugely impressed. It was the Inauguration of the Academic Year, the second year now of her Magistrale, her higher-level degree. She had never come to this formal event before; it had never seemed to have any relevance to her studies and projects. But the longer she stays at the university, the more she feels involved and grows curious about its various mechanisms. Four years and more have created a sense of belonging. Or perhaps longing is the better word. She feels more and more attracted to the academic life. She would like to be a part of it, to study more deeply, to know the world better. She is also rather attracted to her French teacher, Dottor Antonio Furlan.

Not that there is anything wrong with her relationship with Michele. They spend a weekend together once a month in Milan or Naples and see each other most days back home in summer. Her mother likes Michele, she likes his respectful seriousness and the fact that her daughter is obviously calling the shots. Last Christmas she met the boy's parents and they brought excellent home-made artichoke ravioli; though, being twice divorced herself, she is always suspicious of middle-aged couples pretending to be romantically in love. The only love that counts and lasts, Carmela never tires of repeating, is the love between a mother and her children. Every evening, towards eleven, Valeria takes a phone call first from her mother, then from Michele. Her mother wants to know what she's eaten, if she is dressing warmly, what products she is using for her hair, her period pains. Michele talks about an archaeological dig south of Pompeii and a scandal in the Soprintendenza Archeologia Belle Arti e Paesaggio, the organisation that oversees ancient sites. Somebody had set up a network of private buyers for ancient artefacts that should have been headed for museums. He's definitely going to vote Movimento Cinque Stelle, Michele announces, Beppe Grillo's Five Star Movement, to shake up the world.

Valeria listens and agrees. It's good having a boyfriend, she thinks, closing the call with her head on the pillow. It's not a problem for her that he's far away. She trusts him completely. He's far too focused on his studies to be fooling around with other girls. His father likes her and she knows how eager Michele is to please his father. They are both lovers of routine. They want their parents to be happy with them. It's a perfect fit.

Still, there is something rather special about Antonio Furlan, she reflects, closing her eyes. About his passion for French and for Africa, for literature and translation. The man has grown a small moustache and started brushing his hair back from his forehead. The morning of the Inauguration, on entering the huge space of the Aula Magna, Valeria stops and looks around, but the exciting face is nowhere to be seen in the bustle of hundreds of students, professors and administrative staff trying to settle on the right seat.

The most obvious curiosity of the Inauguration of the Academic Year is that it is not held at the beginning of the academic year, in October, but halfway through the year, in February, or even March. 'With the help of God I declare this academic year open,' the Rector will announce with emphatic solemnity six months after the courses have been up and running. James has noticed how often there is this drastic gap between ceremony and reality in Italian life. Perhaps the point is that ceremony has a reality of its own, deliberately cut off from its supposed referent in order to stress its separate existence and function, which, essentially, is to celebrate the community's existence and the loyalty of all its individual members. For this is one of those moments when a researcher or professor simply *has to be* present, and has to wear his or her academic gown, or *toga* as it is called, a noble form of uniform which makes everyone feel vaguely Roman, or as if part of some ancient religious order. A Freemason perhaps. Not that you actually own the gown. You are lent it for the occasion. In fact, it is when you accept your gown over the counter in the cloakroom that one of the administrative staff will tick off your name on the register. The powers that be are keeping a careful check on who is present and who is not.

On the first occasion that Ottone headed up the Inauguration as Rector, last year that is, James had somehow got it into his head that the ceremony was in the afternoon, turning up at two o'clock when in fact the long affair was just drawing to a close after a ten o'clock start. Professor Ventura, who met him by chance on the stairs, was appalled. Ottone would assume, she said, that as her protégé he, James, was snubbing the baron from Puglia, because she, the Torinese, had supported Tedeschi, the Bolognese, at the Rector's election, and lost. He mustn't feel that we northerners are 'harbouring rancour', she said, and hurried James into the lift and up to the fourth floor to apologise to Ottone in his newly renovated Rector's office. Knocking and waiting some moments before being called in, they found the great man sharing a glass of champagne on blue velvet armchairs with the government Minister who had come to give the keynote speech. The irony being, as James was intensely aware, apologising profusely to the Rector and pleading his age-old tendency to confuse morning and afternoon appointments, that he had in fact voted *for* Ottone, something he had never had the courage to confess to Ventura whose career, as a result of Ottone's victory, was very much on a *binario morto*, a dead railway line, a siding, one that could only lead, James now realised, to the breaker's yard of early retirement.

Yet like someone who just can't and won't believe they are on death row, Ventura seemed to be doing everything possible to make amends to Ottone for having opposed him. On this occasion she complimented Rector and Minister on their wonderful speeches. Her praise was woefully fulsome, James thought. And no sooner had she finished with the compliments than the older woman began to apologise, profusely, for James's absence at the event. It was a just a silly mistake, she said, and perhaps partly her own fault, though it was truly hard to see how this could be the case. The Rector, his face a mask of benign irony, didn't bother to get to his feet to greet them. 'Our resident English gentleman,' he smiled, introducing James to the government Minister. 'He heads our postgraduate degree in Publishing and Journalism and is proposing an ambitious collective project on the internationalisation of journalism within the European Community.'

'How interesting,' the Minister nodded, his voice betraying his Sardinian origin. Like the Rector, he remained firmly on his seat.

'Actually, the project was Professor Motta's idea,' James offered. Meaning his friend Federica.

Champagne was not offered.

'We will leave you to your discussions,' Professor Ventura tried to gloss over the awkwardness.

But the Rector lifted a hand.

'There was a matter I wanted to raise with you,' he addressed James. He turned to the Minister. 'Our Englishman is a celebrated translator and has published articles in a number of prestigious international magazines.'

'My warmest congratulations,' the Minister said coolly.

'However, it has come to my notice,' the Rector went on, 'that the credit line in these publications does not always mention that you are a professor at this university.'

There was a brief silence. The office had the stiff mahogany solemnity of a modern funeral parlour. The large-format books lining the shelves seemed to have nothing personal or *read* about them; they were encyclopedias, dictionaries, learned reviews in black binders. Academic furnishing, James thought.

'Anglo-Saxon cultural magazines,' Professor Ventura hastened to put in, 'are not always in the habit of mentioning the writer's university.'

'It's hard to see what use it is to us' – the Rector turned to the Minister – 'to have our professors publishing in prestigious places, if they will not credit the institute where they are privileged to do their work.'

'It's a question of reciprocity,' the Minister observed.

'I'll make sure it doesn't happen again,' James said.

No sooner was he out of the room than he was furious with himself. Why apologise when you have done nothing wrong? They were turning him into a creep.

Pushing through a crowd into the Aula Magna, Valeria instinctively went to sit in one of the front rows, as she always did at any event, only to find them reserved for the 'authorities', Rectors of other universities, the Vice Mayor, the head of the local police force, the head of the fire brigade. And so on. After which large blocks of seats were set apart for professors from this or that academic department. Retreating then to the more humble seats higher up at the back of the hall, she had the pleasure of seeing Dottor Furlan hurrying to his place at the last minute.

'*Buon giorno*, Valeria,' he smiled as their paths crossed and he raised a sandy eyebrow. 'What are you doing here?'

'Curiosity,' she said. 'It's my university.'

'Let's hope it's rewarded,' he said wryly, and she realised he thought it mad that anyone with anything better to do would come here uncompelled.

Then music blared out. A trumpet. Or a recording of a trumpet. Everyone was on their feet. The national anthem had begun – Fratelli d'Italia – the happy national family. Centre stage, up front, the Rector placed his hand on his heart. His lips began to move. Many, many people moved their lips, yet curiously no sound issued, as if it were important to be seen to sing, to participate, but not to contribute any volume or passion, which might be in poor taste. So hundreds of lips mouthed the climactic lines '*Stringiamci a coorte, siam pronti alla morte*'. Close ranks together, we are ready to die. The idea, Valeria was aware, was beyond absurd.

A pretty girl with a microphone and a skirt well above her knees climbed on stage and announced in the kind of voice presenters use on television, 'Il Magnifico Rettore, Giuseppe Maria Ottone!'

Again there was a burst of music, as when a celebrity guest steps into the enchanted space of a late-evening talk show. Ottone stood up from his seat and walked over to the lectern on the right. Behind him, on straight-backed chairs, like so many sentinels in their black gowns, or crows on a wire, were the Heads of Department and coordinators of the degree courses. Valeria was surprised to make out her English professor among them. He really didn't seem the type for a formal occasion like this. In fact his shoulders were slumped and he was staring disconsolately at his hands. But now, after some leisurely adjustment to the height of the microphones, the Rector had begun to speak.

'*Onorevole presidente,*' he began, turning to the man who had been sitting beside him – the Speaker of the Italian Senate, Valeria realised – 'Signor Vice Mayor, Signor Chief of Police, Signor Chief Prosecuting Magistrate, Vice President of the House of Commerce, magnificent Rectors, Parliamentary Deputies and Senators ...'

The Pugliese accent swelled from a powerful PA system. High up behind him, at the back of the stage, some metres above the heads of the important professors seated there, a huge screen lit up, showing the Rector in gigantic close-up, for the benefit of the students at the back of the big hall. Meantime Ottone went on greeting all those present one by one, group by group, drawing everyone in to this supremely institutional embrace:

'*Signori* representatives of the political, regional, territorial and military authorities, *signori* representatives of the students, distinguished *colleghe e colleghi, carissime studentesse e carissimi studenti, signori* of the administrative, technical and auxiliary staff, *signore e signori ...*'

At last Ottone paused, sighed, smiled, as if he had just completed the pleasurable duty of welcoming every aunt, uncle, niece and nephew round his table at Christmas dinner,

'Permit me if you will to read an email I received just a few moments ago from the Minister for Foreign Affairs.'

He cleared his throat:

'*Carissimo* Beppe ...

'It is with the greatest regret that I write to inform you that an urgent public duty has intervened, during the night, to prevent me from attending the Inauguration of your Academic Year as I had planned and ardently desired. It will be my very great pleasure and urgent concern to come and visit your university at the earliest opportunity to see the magnificent things my old friend is doing there, ever conscious as we all must be of the centrality of high-quality education to the prestige of a nation and its influence on the world stage.'

This, Valeria realised, was the merest self-regarding fluff, but quite suddenly the atmosphere changed. Ottone's voice grew emphatic and severe. No doubt, he said, the Minister was in good faith. After all, he was indeed an old friend. They went back a long way. Very likely he would do everything he could to promote higher education. But the truth was, *signori e signore*, that while everywhere in the world universities were cherished and respected institutions in the territories they both drew from and nourished in return, in Italy they were rejected and despised, like some poor, embarrassing relative forever demanding cash. And if the state universities, Ottone went on, were hard hit, the so-called private universities were devastated, treated as pariahs, as if they were not part of the collective endeavour to improve our society and render it competitive in the modern world. Here the Rector paused and looked up at the audience. His face, massively visible all over the huge hall, seemed at once severe and pained, as if let down by a loved one who really should have known better.

'We are hounded and browbeaten at every turn,' he said emphatically.

Now he began to list the measures the government had taken against universities in general and private universities in particular. He counterpointed each cut or offending regulation with some achievement this or that academic community had contributed to Italy's reputation. He began to introduce, in second counterpoint, mention of the government's and national bureaucracy's misdeeds. A corruption scandal. A sex scandal. The disgraceful nepotism of the Italian elite. The expenses, salaries and pensions that parliamentarians paid themselves. The extravagant misuse of electoral funds. As he spoke, this or that detail roused cheers or groans of assent. One or two people clapped. The more participation he got, the more slowly Ottone proceeded, relishing his success, piling up university virtues and government vices. Valeria could not help but admire his elegant Italian, his attentive balancing of pairs of nouns, adjectives and verbs, the feeling that a grand palace of rhetoric was being patiently constructed in the air above their heads, a cathedral of fine words that invited dignitaries and humble folk to come together in a shared enchantment of common values and purpose.

The Rector spoke earnestly now of the nobility of learning, the importance of its being available to all, rich and poor alike, the absolute need for well-educated young men and women to drag Italy out of its philistine torpor, its years of recession and institutional inadequacy. He had sworn a holy oath, this man from Puglia announced, never to sink into defeatism or resort to mere opportunism. 'Purity is a beautiful thing!' he announced. 'A precious thing!' He raised the volume. People laughed at purity in this country, Ottone said, with its *furbi* and *corrotti*, its barons and godfathers, but: 'Ladies and gentlemen, permit me if you will to appear naive, permit me if you will to embarrass you with my vision of a university that rejects every subterfuge,

188

every false rhetoric, every call to sit back on its laurels, a university that holds high for us all the example of the young man or woman who burns the midnight oil to improve the lot of his neighbour, whether in the next room, the next country or at the other end of the world, and who is able to do so because supported and protected by an alma mater proud of his or her endeavours and attentive to the inspiration of the founding fathers who gave us our wonderful constitution, making equal opportunity for all a central principle of our community.'

Listening to this extraordinary and quite unexpected speech, succumbing in the half-dark of the great hall to its powerful rhythms, thrilled by the Rector's evident fearlessness and vibrant passion for truth and learning, Valeria felt she was making up her mind about her future. She felt she could trust this mature, warm-hearted man, the man who had been head of the commission that had given her 110 *e lode*. She felt she could trust any institution he headed. She was glad he came from her part of the world, more or less. He would understand what it meant for a southern student to move north. She wanted to work under him, she thought, for him. And then, in a direct line between herself at the back of the hall and the Rector on the podium now declaring the academic year open, Valeria could distinctly see the sandy curls of Professor Furlan. He too was someone she would love to work with. Tomorrow she would ask him to be her tutor for her Magistrale Degree thesis on Francophile journalism in Africa. What a release it was then to clap out loud in the storm of applause as Ottone headed back to his seat.

GALANTUOMO

Over dinner that evening with the Lucana brigade, Valeria announced her decision to apply for a PhD after she had finished her Magistrale. She wanted to be an academic, if they would give her a scholarship, that is. Her folks could never afford it otherwise. She would apply soon and sit the exam in September.

'You won't be coming home then?' Paola said sadly.

'Never,' Valeria heard herself say. Her certainty surprised her. She would be one of those southerners who never go home. Not to live, that is. All at once her choice was made.

They were eating in a trattoria in Porta Romana. Superficially there was a festive air, as always when these old friends got together. Paolo had Paola up for the long weekend and the two seemed happy enough. Giancarlo, Valeria's old boyfriend, had left the melancholy girl from Trento and was here for the first time with a new woman, a nurse from Monza, petite, cheerful, amused by the southern company. The two joked and played constantly with each other's hands. If the girl, Bruna, was aware that Valeria had previously been Giancarlo's girlfriend, she showed no signs of it. Then Giancarlo rather pointedly asked after Michele.

'Will he come north, if you're going to stay here?'

'I don't know.'

Valeria was unsettled by the question. She hadn't thought about it. Michele wasn't part of her calculations.

A moment's silence fell on the group. The time of decision was upon them. The second graduation, not the first, was only months away. Giancarlo was already applying for jobs. He too planned to stay up north. There had been a Careers Day at his university and a number of engineering companies had come along to seek recruits. He had two interviews scheduled. He seemed bullish. But his friend Flavio was quieter. He was waiting for something to come up back home, he said. Or not too far away. Bari, maybe, Taranto, Potenza.

'Don't worry,' Giancarlo smiled across the table to Chiara. 'There are never any new jobs down there. And even if there were, they'd be sewn up by someone local before they were advertised.'

'Flavio *is* someone local,' Chiara observed drily. 'In his head he never left.'

It wasn't clear whether Chiara would follow Flavio if he moved back to Basilicata. She was so far behind with her studies. Nonna Rosa was more demanding than ever, sinking into dementia. Always slightly belligerent, the big girl seemed to be challenging the others to admit that she had been put in an impossible situation. She stabbed a fork in her food. How could she abandon her grandmother?

'Get the old witch to move back south too,' Paolo suggested. 'She's a Lucana herself in the end. It's normal to go back in old age.'

Giancarlo said his aunt, his great-aunt, wouldn't hear of going back. She would see it as a defeat. Everyone back home would crow. Her brothers and sisters and cousins. You had to go back as a winner. Or not at all.

Valeria felt a prick of anxiety. She too had begun to think of going home as a defeat. She had to make a success of it here in the north. Suddenly she was aware of a growing impatience with her friends, as if these reunions, with their easy nostalgia, posed a threat.

The trattoria was typical Milan. It had all the furnishings of a traditional *locale*, the old wooden tables and chairs, the simple red-and-white checked tablecloths, photos of the city a hundred years back, the first tram arriving in Porta Romana, horses pulling a barge along a canal. It had the traditional trattoria menu – *ossobuco, cotoletta alla milanese, risotto allo zafferano.* The wine list too was mostly local and all reassuringly predictable. Yet the waiters, and presumably the cooks too, were Chinese. Dutiful and efficient, if not exactly friendly, they moved rapidly between the tables, or surveyed their clients from door and cash desk. It was strange, these industrious people from China with their approximate Italian, preparing and serving Milanese food for students from Basilicata. And at significantly lower prices than you could find in the trattorias still run by Italians.

These people won't be going home, Valeria thought. She couldn't help feeling there was something sad about it, as in a dream where something or someone appears in the wrong place, in the wrong company, and you can't understand how this has happened.

The group was on the tiramisu now, or rather the boys were. Of the girls only Chiara indulged, her eyes a little glazed, her fleshy white fingers raising and lowering her spoon almost mechanically. She was obviously disorientated by Flavio's yearning for home. Her life was thwarted. Yet he was solicitous and thoughtful, pouring wine in her glass, picking up a napkin that had fallen, leaning to whisper in her ear, his lips warm and lively, constantly declaring them a couple, separate from the others. And he was definitely less childish than in the past, Valeria thought, less football obsessed. He cared for Chiara; it was just that he wanted to live his life in the world he had grown up in. He wanted to go home.

The waitress came and bowed and with a rare smile offered glasses of limoncello on the house. Again it was the boys who said yes, though this time Letizia joined them. Limoncello served the Neapolitan way in small frozen vase-shaped glasses with tiny handles at the base. And a plate of *cantuccini*, almond biscuits from Tuscany. It was amazing, Paola shook her head, how these Chinese knew all the Italian traditions.

'Except the rule that you don't compete on price,' Giancarlo laughed.

Draining the fierce liqueur in one, Paolo launched into a long story about a recent wedding back home in Basilicata and the bizarre behaviour of his older half-brother, Franco. It had been a cousin's second marriage. The bride, pushing forty like the groom, was seven months pregnant. He, Paolo, had had to go of course, though he hardly knew this cousin, who was his mother's elder sister's second son. Franco, on the other hand, his half-brother, knew the cousin much better, being the same age. But Franco had been offended when, instead of sending the official wedding invitation directly to him, it had been sent to his ex-wife and then hand-delivered to him by his daughter, Manuela, who lived with her mother. Worse, the invitation didn't specifically mention Franco's present partner, Marisa, who he'd been living with for more than a year now. 'He was absolutely livid!' Paolo laughed. 'He was kicking the wall.'

Chiara and Bruna, the northern girls, didn't understand. Who cared if an invitation came directly or through friends?

Letizia shook her head. 'If Franco's the cousin, why send the invitation through the ex-wife? It's asking for trouble. Why invite the ex-wife at all?'

'Because they were all friends from schooldays,' Paolo explained.

Like us, Valeria thought.

'Still, if the invitation comes with a wedding-present begging list, you'd have thought it could be sent directly,' Paola offered. 'Getting married is a business. If you want a present you treat your guests with respect.'

To complicate things – Paolo picked up his story – when Manuela, the daughter, brought the invitation to her father, Franco, she had told him that if he came with his new partner, he must warn her mother because in that case she wasn't going to let her, Manuela, go to the wedding, since she, the mother, had vetoed any meeting between her daughter and her ex-husband's new woman.

'*O dio santo,* how backward can you get?' Chiara picked up Flavio's limoncello and drained it in one. Rather than objecting, he kissed her.

That was crazy enough. But it was the way Franco *reacted* that was so fantastic, Paolo went on, showing an evident fascination for his half-brother, but also a sense of happy superiority, and distance.

'Not only did Franco swear he wouldn't go to the wedding, he also bought air tickets to Prague and booked a hotel for the weekend of the wedding with the money he'd previously set aside for the present for his cousin. That way he and his woman wouldn't have to tangle with the revellers. They'd be out of town. Because of course more or less everyone they knew was going.'

'You can't be around when everyone's going and you're not,' Letizia agreed.

'So why didn't he phone his cousin,' Bruna wondered, 'and just ask why he'd sent the invitation through the wife? Have it out.'

None of the Lucani saw fit to answer such a naive enquiry. An offended person does not phone an offender. Unless to curse him.

'How was the wedding?' Giancarlo enquired.

'Later,' Paolo promised. He was a tall, heavy boy with a shock of endearingly unmanageable hair. Looking around the table, he drew a deep breath and smiled. 'We still haven't got to the real madness.'

'*Avanti allora!*'

The fact is, Paolo said, there were two aunts of Franco's mother, hence of the groom's mother too, Zia Eleonora and Zia Matilda, both in their eighties now, one living in Ancona and the other in Frosinone. Of course they were both invited to the wedding, but there was the problem that they were too old to use the train or drive themselves ...

'He didn't!' Valeria said, understanding at once what had happened.

'*Sì, sì, proprio così!*' Paolo laughed. Franco had taken the day off work Friday, set off at the crack of dawn in his brand-new Bravo, for which he would be paying for the next five years, driven 500 km up the Adriatic to Ancona to pick up Zia Eleonora, then 250 km cross-country to Frosinone to pick up Zia Matilda, then another 500 km back home. After which he was just in time to pick up his own woman, Marisa, and drive her out to Bari for the evening flight to Prague.

'Respect!' Flavio breathed.

Giancarlo was surprised that this was even possible. 'Logistically,' he said. 'Amazing.'

'Then returning Sunday evening he takes Monday off as well to drive his aunties home. First Frosinone, then Ancona.'

'*Galantuomo!*'

'So the wedding cost him two days' work even if he didn't go!'

'Not to mention the weekend in Prague.'

'You're laughing at him,' Letizia objected. She seemed riled. She hadn't found the story funny at all. 'But what do you expect him to do? He couldn't go to the wedding after his cousin treated him like that. On the other hand, he could hardly let his aunts down either, could he, if they wanted to go. He did the right thing.'

Bruna was shaking her head in wonder. No one in Monza would ever dream of doing such a thing.

'To my mind you're missing something,' Chiara chipped in. 'To my mind there must have been something else going on, otherwise ...'

But Valeria realised her phone was ringing, or rather chiming. MAMMA, the glowing screen said. While the others speculated and joked she stood up and hurried towards the door where the signal was stronger.

'It's Carlo,' an anxious voice told her. 'You have to come at once.'

Some hours later, half asleep on the night train to Bari, Valeria was vaguely aware of the name Ancona – '*Stazione di Ancona Centrale, Stazione di Ancona Centrale!* Departing passengers are invited to check that they have not left any belongings on seats or luggage racks.' And suddenly she was thinking of Paolo's half-brother Franco; she had sometimes run into him as a child in Paolo's house when they all went there to do their homework, a separate, rather gloomy young man always arguing with his mother. Franco went to pick up those aunts for his mother, she thought, to show his mother what a good son he was, despite wanting to be a thousand miles from his family with his new woman. And I'm a good daughter, Valeria thought, and a good sister. But as the train pulled out of Ancona and accelerated to a steady rhythm, she realised that Dottor Furlan was sitting on the seat opposite. He was leaning towards her, eyes bright and sandy moustache bristling, talking about a conference in Marseilles. There was a call for papers, he said. This is a big opportunity, Valeria. No, I can't, she told him. I have to look after Zia Lella. Nonna in heaven will be upset. Dottoressa Lasala! Furlan was actually shaking her shoulder now. Dottoressa Lasala, are you out of your mind?

She woke with a start to find the conductor asking for her ticket. An elderly man with a Sicilian accent. Had he given her shoulder a little shake? To her left dawn was breaking over the Adriatic. The train was racing along an embankment above the empty beach. The sea was calm and grey, pricked here and there by lonely lights. Carlo had tried to kill himself, her mother had told her. He was in intensive care in the San Paolo hospital, Bari.

FONTAMARA

Where communities are tight-knit and pitted against each other, the figure of the spy is inevitable. There is always someone who appears to be on one side, but is actually on the other, or perhaps on neither, or both. In short, a traitor. Dante puts such folk at the very bottom of hell, in the ninth circle. If belonging is the greatest good, betrayal of those we belong among is the greatest crime.

But why would anyone do such a thing? For the past few months James has been looking into the translations, hence the writing, hence, inevitably in this case, the life, of Ignazio Silone. He cannot remember any story that has ever disturbed him more.

Silone is most famous for his short novel *Fontamara*, published in 1933. It's a powerful denunciation of the exploitation of southern peasants by wealthy landowning opportunists with the connivance of the Fascist authorities. It seemed right, James felt on first reading the book, that it should have been written by a man who came from an impoverished village, like the place Fontamara described in the novel, a man who had spent all his early adult life serving first the Socialist then the Communist Parties. Indeed, *Fontamara* was written and published in Switzerland, since its author, like all left-wing activists in the early thirties, was a wanted man in Italy. Only in 1996 did it emerge that Silone had been a Fascist spy.

Ignazio Silone wasn't born with that name. It was the pseudonym he assumed when he left the Communist Party, stopped spying and wrote *Fontamara*. Determined to end his double life, he invented a new name for himself. Prior to that he was called Secondino Tranquilli and he was born in 1900, third child of small landholders in the village of Pescina in the mountains of the Abruzzi, midway between Rome to the west and Pescara to the east. His infancy was a string of bereavements. Of seven children born to his parents, only he and a younger brother, Romolo, survived. In 1911 his father died. In 1915 an earthquake destroyed Pescina. Secondino dug out his mother's corpse five days later. Penniless and bereft, he and his brother were taken under the wing of Don Orione, a charitable priest, and sent to separate, live-in church schools in Rome. Secondino was bullied and Don Orione had to find him a new school, in San Remo far away to the north. When there were problems in that school too, the boy was moved to Calabria. No place, it seemed, was home for this poor orphan, but at least he had Don Orione to correspond with and the man quickly became both mentor and father substitute. Secondino wrote to him of his doubts about the Christian faith and his disgust with the corrupt environment in these church schools. Eventually, he abandoned his education and joined the Young Socialist Party; at which point Orione cut off all communication with the young man and washed his hands of him. Secondino was devastated. He hadn't been loved for himself, independently of his beliefs, but only for the service he could offer the Church.

Making the Socialist movement his new family, Secondino rose rapidly to positions of command. He was lucid, determined, and always ready to express the strongest views. In 1920 he was instrumental in leading the Young Socialists to join the Communist Party. However, in 1919, questioned by the police, he met Guido Bellone, an affable, well-respected, unmarried policeman in his late forties; as with Don Orione a special relationship formed. For all his achievements in the party, Secondino was insecure; he needed a father figure. In any event, Bellone was the man to whom he would now pass on information for more than a decade. Secondino wrote long reports for him about the make-up and goals of the Communist Party, its members and strategies. Far from betraying in return for money, Secondino sought to impress Bellone, to show him what a sharp observer he was. Elaborating on important party meetings in Moscow, Berlin, Paris and Spain, he developed and flaunted his writing skills, and through that process began to establish some critical distance from the increasingly demanding political movement he was involved in. He began, that is, to find in the Communist Party's totalitarian tendencies, some justification for his betrayal.

Thanks to Secondino's spying many of his comrades were arrested. Some died in prison. He himself was arrested on a number of occasions, a form of cover, but always released. Only when his brother Romolo was imprisoned in 1928, did he experience a crisis that led to his leaving the Communist Party and telling his Fascist minder he would spy no more. 'Life has thrown me down a slope from which I now want to save myself,' he wrote to Bellone in April 1930. He promised to withdraw from all political activity and dedicate his life to writing. One figure who would appear in many of his books was a young revolutionary saved from torture and induced to inform on his comrades by an understanding older policeman, then in a crisis of conscience declaring himself responsible for crimes he hadn't committed and dying a hero's death in prison. Romolo had died in prison in 1932. Secondino, having assumed the new identity of Ignazio Silone, lived until 1978, enjoying enormous respect as an independent left-wing intellectual with an impeccable war record.

James had just finished reading Dario Biocca's *The Double Life of an Italian*, which tells Silone's story, when he received an email informing him that the Rector was extending him the honour, as coordinator of the Higher Level Degree in Publishing and Media, of being present on the podium during the Inauguration ceremony for the new academic year. He should thus arrive to collect his gown and take his seat at least twenty minutes before the event was due to start.

Reading and rereading the email, James found that he did indeed feel honoured that he would be up on the podium, raised above all his colleagues. It was a new emotion. The Rector was inviting him to play a full and visible part in the life of the institution where he had worked for so many years. It felt good. And a few days after receiving this encouraging news, wonder of wonders, Ottone actually called to him across the foyer of the university and spoke warmly to him, in a manner that could only be described as fatherly, as if the age difference between the two were rather more than in reality it was. The Rector congratulated him on his academic achievements, expressed his pleasure that the university was now being properly mentioned in the credit line in his publications (how could the man know these things?) and told him (with a warm grin!) that he was counting on him to enhance the reputation of the university in the Anglo-Saxon world. Afterwards, James felt enormously cheered to be part of a positive collective endeavour in his adoptive country. Only now did he realise how hungry he was for this sort of recognition.

So on the big day he pulled out a proper suit for the occasion and even a tie. When was the last time James had worn a tie? Soberly besuited and be-gowned, he climbed the steps to the podium and took his seat at the back among the other coordinators and department heads, Federica included, for she coordinated the BA degree in Communications and Media Studies. It was good to feel he was up there with someone he trusted. It was good to look out into the audience and see colleagues who had not been thus honoured. Have I become politically astute? he wondered.

Fanfares sounded and one by one the speakers of the day took their places behind the table at the front of the podium: the Rector himself, splendid in his ermine; the Speaker of the Italian Senate, who was the main attraction and proof of the Rector's prestige; and finally Professoressa Modesto, now Head of Department, who would give the *prolusione*, the inaugural lecture, since every year these ceremonies included a kind of academic lesson on some topical subject, to show the important folks from outside the university – the local politicians and magistrates and heads of police and fire brigade – how useful it could be to turn the light of intellect and academic methodology on to contemporary issues. Professoressa Elisabetta Modesto would be talking, the programme said, about 'Italy and the Semiotics of Globalisation'.

Perhaps it was important that James heard the Rector's speech from behind, as it were. Unlike Valeria, or indeed most of the audience, he could not see the man's persuasive face and lips, nor could he look at the huge image on the screen immediately above and behind him. At once and to his surprise, as the Rector got into the meat of his talk, he found himself admiring what was being said. The picture of the universities' woes, the description of the fickleness and indifference of successive governments were spot on. He entirely endorsed the stirring call to work together for the young people of today – his own two children, for example. It seemed the older man's words carried real emotion, real belief.

Or did they? As the speech progressed, listening from behind, spared the Rector's smiles and grimaces, it did begin to seem a strangely disembodied voice, a voice in the air, as it were, saying too precisely what you had been hoping for. What would a speaker need to say after all, James suddenly asked himself, to win the approval of any group of Italians today? First of all he must condemn corruption in the most emphatic terms, because everyone knew corruption was endemic. This was what Ottone had done. He must eschew cynicism with passion and conviction, because everyone knew that cynicism was the ubiquitous response to corruption. And again Ottone had done this. Then he must signal to his dismayed and dispirited listeners that his was a flag they could rally round with confidence, that he had the strength of character to offer a way out of the miasma; he would lead them and protect them. This too Ottone was doing. The Rector is simply bound to say these things, James realised. He is performing to script.

As the Rector reached the persuasive climax of his speech, James found himself wondering what it must have been like to hear

Secondino Tranquilli address the Unione Giovanile Socialista in Rome, or the Communist International in Moscow, or any of the other groups of committed revolutionaries that the passionate young man had addressed through the 1920s, always speaking on behalf of the world's oppressed. You would have been persuaded, of course. Tranquilli was a wonderful speaker. You would have been ready to leave your home and follow this visionary young idealist. And then you would have been betrayed.

What had Ottone actually *done* in his nearly two years in power? James found himself thinking as another fanfare of music rang out and Professoressa Modesto walked towards the lectern for her *prolusione*. First of all, he had arranged for this unlikely protégée to replace him as Head of Department. Second, he had given research grants to two young men whose main task seemed to be to substitute for himself and Modesto in the lessons they didn't actually teach. Third, he had promoted all those close to him: the researcher on contract had become the researcher with tenure; the professor *associato* had become the professor *ordinario*, the professor *ordinario* had found him- or herself with some prestigious new role, perhaps invented ad hoc, Vice Rector with responsibility for teaching, Vice Rector with responsibility for research, and so on. Mightn't it be, James wondered, that Ottone's recent, more generous attitude to himself was an indication that the man somehow knew now that he had voted for him in the famous election?

Fourth, the new Rector had left his very few opponents to languish in limbo, or had systematically removed them. Professor Ventura had recently responded to a phone call from James in a state of indignation and distress. She had just received notification, she said, that the university was taking advantage of new employment legislation to oblige her to retire at the end of the present academic year; she had now passed the minimum age for retirement, hence no longer had an absolute right to continue. '*Mi stanno facendo fuori!*' They're kicking me out. Professor Scilli was also being forced to take his pension; to make way for the younger generations.

So that was that.

Fifth, last, and most momentously, Ottone had altered the university's legal statute, expanding its Board of Directors to admit three new members, all of whom already sat on other boards of which Ottone himself was a member in quite different areas of life. This expanded board also had expanded responsibilities, as, for example, electing the Rector and Heads of Department at the end of their four-year terms. So the professors and researchers would henceforth be spared the divisiveness of the so-called democratic process and the problem of attaching themselves to this or that bandwagon. The university would thus be given the kind of stable, long-term governance that attracts serious investment. Because it was understood that the board, as now constituted, would re-elect Ottone at the end of three years. And again at the end of six years, and nine and twelve. His was the only bandwagon there was.

All this had been achieved without so much as a whiff of protest; on the contrary, amid a general sense of relief that with this powerful man at the helm, the institution's future was assured. And perhaps the professors were right not to protest, James reflected. After all, wasn't he too being invited to take his place at the collective table, to tuck in his napkin and raise a glass to future collaboration? What did strong leadership matter if it was benevolent? Analogies with Silone were inappropriate. The writer's spying had been the pathological doubleness of a man with a deep flaw in his character, something that could be traced back to his orphaned childhood. James knew nothing about the Rector's background, but it was hard to imagine he suffered from a similar neediness. He might not be entirely honest when he painted himself as a campaigner for transparency and equal opportunity, but what did it matter if he got the university moving forward positively?

PROLUSIONE

'The signifier moves along a vector from the particular to the general, from the local to the global, from Treviso to Tokyo, Palermo to Peking,' Professor Modesto was observing between sips of water, 'while the signified remains a shifting and ambiguous target within a play of forces under-defined syntactically, but over-determined pragmatically, in an overlap of national and international arenas where stakeholders vie to put marketable flesh on ideas, theories and propositions that all too often reveal themselves as stereotypical formulations surviving from the pre-postmodern age of nation-state narcissism.'

What on earth was this about?

Immersed in conflicted reflections about the Rector, James had missed the woman's opening remarks. Apparently there was a Power-Point. Twisting his neck for a moment to the screen behind, he could just make out a tangle of arrows and coloured boxes, followed by a slide that was all text, the same text that Modesto was reading. Wearing a coal-grey dress with turquoise cashmere shawl, her hair freshly permed in a tight blonde helmet, she was reading her lecture with the earnest diligence of one determined to soldier on regardless of whether the audience was able to follow. Raising a glass to drink, her hand shook.

The talk went on. Polysemes and multifaceted intertextual connotations impacted on deconstructed iconic projections and paradigmatic feedback relations in a pile-up of pretension that left the listener despairing of some reality to which all this jargon might intelligibly refer. Half an hour. Forty minutes. Forty-five. Towards the back of the hall students had begun to whisper, or simply chatter. The famous 'authorities' in the front rows consulted their mobiles with restrained expressions of perplexity and embarrassment.

Modesto sipped some more water, shifted her weight from one high heel to the other, announced, 'and hence in conclusion' for the third time, then launched into another sentence as long as it was formless and meaningless. The words 'Lacanian mise-en-scène', then 'metonymy' and 'synecdoche' flashed by. James was lost, but also awed. He had sensed, along with everyone else, that Modesto had her limitations. He had guessed that the flaunted attention to footnotes, bibliographies and all the tedious machinery of academic endeavour was very likely pedantry. But he had not expected such an extraordinary misjudgement of this major public occasion. Had the audience been made up of independent agents they would have been laughing their collective head off. As it was, quite a number of students were now slipping away. The heavy black curtain over the rear exit twitched every few seconds as eager hands pushed it aside. But the professors were obliged to sit in solemn silence, as Modesto now announced her conclusion for the fourth time. And again didn't conclude.

James began to feel angry. He began to fidget. He turned to his left to look at Federica. She was impassive in her black gown, slim, knuckly hands resting quietly on her knees. He stared at her, eager to elicit some kind of response, until eventually she caught his gaze. Immediately, her eyes narrowed in warning. Don't show what you think. You're in full view.

James turned away and tried to settle his features, tried not to hear the amplified burbling of encoded this and deconstructed that. Then, abruptly, it was over, and with a brief shuffle of papers, a last sip of water, and a final Thank-you-for-your-attention, Modesto wrapped it up. At once the Rector led the enthusiastic applause. He got to his feet. And it was then, as the woman stepped back from the lectern and turned towards her place at the main table, that James was able to glimpse a smile of triumph flushing her face. She was delighted. She thought her talk had gone down a treat.

'A thousand thanks,' began the Speaker of the Senate a few moments later, 'to my old friend Beppe for inviting me along this morning, treating me to a few lashes of his sharp, anti-establishment tongue and giving me the chance to hear Professor Modesto's excellent analysis of Italy's image in the world today; I must say one rarely hears speeches of this calibre in the Senate.'

'It must be some kind of joke,' James found himself saying afterwards. He said it to Federica, first, then to Alessio and Antonio. He said it to Domenico Galli and Professor Scilli, to a researcher in economics and a professor *ordinario* in marketing. He said it to people he hardly knew, to secretaries and administrators. He even said it to two students from his class who greeted him on the stairs.

'How can Ottone speak passionately about learning, then applaud the nonsense we had to endure today?' he asked. 'How can a Speaker of the Senate pretend he was impressed?'

For the whole of that afternoon James just couldn't restrain himself. He even made jokes with the janitors. It was as if a spring screwed up tighter and tighter during the hours in that honoured position on the podium must now be released.

'What kind of honour is it to be subjected to gibberish?' he asked a young lecturer he had never met before. 'It's absurd to speak of meritocracy and give us Modesto! It's surreal.'

People smiled. They nodded and raised eyebrows.

'Weren't you asleep?' Alessio quipped.

'Surreal and absurd sounds more exciting than what I heard,' Federica remarked.

'You've no idea,' Domenico Galli sighed, 'what coded messages are being sent when politicians and magistrates get together. It's *meant* to go over our heads.'

But mostly James's colleagues just shrugged.

'What did you expect from a *prolusione*?' someone asked. Others said they thought the Head of Department's grasp of the complexities of globalisation was impressive.

This only wound James up further. In the bar for coffee, he ran into Cecilia Tamara, who had recently completed her PhD. 'How can the Rector speak of his commitment to talented youth and not even offer someone like you a research grant?' he exploded.

Cecilia was laconic. She had spoken to Professor Modesto, she said, who had promised she would speak to Ottone. The problem was funds.

'They have funds enough to bring in people to teach their lessons for them!'

Cecilia shrugged. She was a sophisticated Sicilian woman of good family in her late twenties, always elegantly dressed, always discreet, apparently savvy.

'Why not do this?' James suggested. 'Federica and I are planning a conference and a publication to conclude the research project on European journalism. That'll be in a couple of years' time. When we draw up the budget we could propose that they give you a grant to handle the organising and editing.'

Cecilia was listening carefully now. She took an iPad from her bag and started tapping notes onto the screen. Who was involved exactly? she asked. What reading should she be doing to prepare? Should she talk about it already to Modesto?

'Just don't encourage her to get involved!' James laughed. 'After what we heard this morning.'

Cecilia pulled a pack of cigarettes from the sleeve of her dress.

'It was quite a talk,' she observed.

The metro station close to James's home is at the end of the line where many of the travellers are Arabs, Chinese or African. In the past, the turnstiles here only had to be fed a ticket when you entered the metro;

they turned quite freely when you were coming out. But to reduce fare evasion the transport authority has recently introduced new turn-stiles that require you to insert your ticket to get out as well. A metro employee sits in a glass-walled cabin strategically placed in the middle of the long line of turnstiles. If a passenger tries to jump them, or slip through ticketless on the heels of the person in front, it is presumably this man's duty to intervene. But he never does. On the contrary, the wider turnstile, or rather swinging gate, for wheelchairs and the like, which is located right beside his glass cabin, is actually left open, so that those without a ticket can simply walk through. The employee doesn't challenge them. He doesn't raise his eyes. He's studying his phone.

What would a semiotics expert make of it? James wonders. First the notice – *Attenzione!* – that advises passengers exiting the station they will have to *riconvalidare il titolo di viaggio* – stamp their 'right to travel' again – then beside that notice the open gate with no one checking. The written text and the reality in flagrant contradiction; there must be some semiotic term for that kind of situation.

James smiles and shakes his head. Perhaps it is no surprise in a soci-ety like this that the dictator praises democracy, the crony denounces cronyism, and the dumb are asked to speak, *intelligently*. But he sud-denly stops. You're becoming obsessed, he warns himself. Chill. Just as he is climbing the stairs out into the open air, his phone rings. It's a number he doesn't know. All of a sudden he has Professor Modesto on the line.

A squealing tram makes it hard for him to grasp what is being said. He has never spoken to Modesto on the phone before and her voice is surprisingly low. Then he understands.

'I am seriously disappointed,' the Head of Department is saying. 'And I must say I had this information from someone whose word I trust absolutely.' It sounds as if she's genuinely hurt. 'I think you and I need to speak to each other face to face.'

CARLO

A sister finds herself fastened to a reef by a golden chain forged by a mermaid. From far away her brother arrives with a steel file to set her free. He has also brought along a rich king to marry her.

A young boy discovers he has three older sisters who left home before he was born and all married wild animals: a falcon, a stag, a dolphin. He travels the world, seeks them out and invites them and their spouses to visit his family home. During the long journey, they come across a princess locked up in a tower by a dragon. The falcon, stag and dolphin use their special animal skills to kill the dragon and free the princess, upon which they are magically released from a curse and revealed to be three handsome and very human brothers. The sisters' younger brother marries the princess and the whole troop of four couples return to their delighted parents to live happily together.

Brothers and sisters save each other. They find spouses for each other. So it's important to have children of both sexes. A woman who has had seven sons is fed up. The eighth time she's pregnant, it's agreed that if she gives birth to another boy, the seven brothers will all leave home for ever. If it is a girl, they will stay. The children's father isn't mentioned. A daughter is born, but the midwife sends the wrong signal and the boys head out into the world. Many years later, their grown-up sister sets off to find them and eventually frees them from the terrible ogre who has reduced them to slavery.

There is always a separation, a misunderstanding, a curse, a tyrant (ogre or dragon). Courage and youthful confidence turn the evil tide, upon which husbands and wives inevitably present themselves. So after great hardship the family is richer, more united and more knowing than before.

Needless to say, the worst thing brothers and sisters can do is fail to respond to the call for help when it comes. Then fate is implacable and the story can only end in weeping and gnashing of teeth.

Valeria responded. She travelled through the night, arrived in Bari in the early hours of the morning, took a taxi to the San Paolo hospital and sat beside Carlo for the following week. She talked to the doctors and nurses and tried to understand what had happened. But he lay under some kind of enchantment. Three months earlier he had begun a traineeship with the navy in the old port town. Something had happened; he wouldn't say what. At the same time his childhood sweetheart was working as an au pair in Marseilles. He was convinced she was seeing someone else. He wouldn't go back home to Mother, he said.

Valeria stayed in Bari. She found a tiny flat on the edge of the old town. Carlo started looking for work of any kind. Their mother came to visit. Home was a two-hour drive from here. She brought a *torta salata*, some *amarena* cakes she had made herself, and various items of clothing she had picked up for ridiculously low prices at the market. She thanked her daughter *di cuore* and said how wonderful it was to see the two of them, brother and sister, together again and so nearby. Carlo was sheepish.

Meantime, Valeria was missing her university classes and though she did what she could and emailed all class assignments to her various professors on a weekly basis, it was not the same. So soon enough she told Carlo she would have to go back. Her room in Milan was being paid for, after all. Likewise the lessons. If she didn't do well in her exams she would be throwing away a long-term family investment.

'Go,' he said.

It was April. Back in the city she threw herself into her studies, working all hours with great freshness and intensity. She had animated conversations with Doctor Furlan during his office hours. They talked about francophone journalism in Africa and on his suggestion she went to see the degree coordinator, her English professor, about the possibility of applying for a doctorate in Communications and Media. However, only three weeks after returning she received another late-night call from her mother. Again Carlo was in hospital; again she was the one who must go.

Carmela, Valeria's mother, runs a small catering business. It is impossible for her to get away for more than a day or so, and without the money she is earning who would pay for Valeria's studies and room in Milan, not to mention Carlo's flat now in Bari? Vanessa, the oldest of the three, is only a half-sister and anyway has a job to hold down. She has never got on with Carlo; he has always been spoiled, she thinks, because of being the youngest and a boy. Carmela always wanted a boy. Valeria's father, Marcello, is officially unemployed, but actually driving a van for Carmela, for although the two divorced twenty years ago, they have never entirely separated. Over the years the tug of war between them has driven the children mad. It doesn't occur to anyone that Marcello might be the person to help his son through a hard time.

Once again Valeria arrived in the night at the San Paolo hospital, a vast cement-and-glass sprawl. It seemed Carlo had made an unannounced trip to find his girlfriend in Marseilles, then returned almost at once and launched himself into the kind of binge that is hardly distinguishable from a suicide attempt. Eyes closed on his bed with a drip feeding into his arm, he smiled when his sister took his hand but shook his head to every question. Waiting for him to be well enough to leave, Valeria thought it curious that he had made the long trip back to Bari before going crazy, as if he wanted to be somewhere safe before doing something dangerous.

Carlo was tall and boyishly handsome. Hopeless at school, he had nevertheless been the darling of both teachers and friends. He was genuinely modest, and had a cheerful, lively temperament. But once school was over and unemployment began, the young man lost his way. About his weeks training for the navy he would say only that there were certain things he would never subject himself to. About the trip to Marseilles, he would say nothing at all. The girl who had been his close companion and only lover since he was fourteen must never again be mentioned. It was over. His endless refrain was that he wouldn't go home. Under any circumstances. His old friends would laugh at him. But nor would he come north with his sister to Milan. His home was in the south. 'La mia terra,' he said. Something would turn up, in Bari.

So began a long period of limbo for Valeria. Her university classes were not compulsory. Theoretically, she could stay in Bari as long as it took to get her brother on his feet and still take her exams. Dedication is what sisters do. And no, it was not the same, she thought, as nursing an incontinent grandmother. That was a form of masochism, or a cowardly way of hiding from the world. A brother was a brother.

They slept in the same room. He was sheepish, gloomy, sometimes angry, sometimes full of manic fun. He would buy outlandish clothes second-hand, hats particularly, and waste money on elaborate tattoos with infantile themes: swords, dragons and elves. Always friendly and engaging, he found jobs easily, only to abandon them in a matter of weeks. He had been taken for a ride, he complained. They were paying him little or nothing. It wasn't leading anywhere. Then he would stay in bed smoking dope for two or three days, hardly speaking. Valeria's heart sank.

She studied at home, or went to the university library. For comfort, she had her old friend Paola, who was just completing her Law degree in Bari. After which, Paola said, she had decided to go north and live with Paolo, since it was clear there was no future in the south for a man who had studied Economics. Of lawsuits, on the other hand, there was no end.

They walked through the old town together checking out shop windows, or along the promenade to the beach south of the port. Bari was full of colour and curiosity. In the clear air the sun felt good and the sparkle on the sea always lifted the heart. There were people here still living in the old world of dialect and family, traditional cooking and traditional jobs. That was what her brother wanted, Valeria thought. That security of tradition. But she knew it would not be her world, ever. On her laptop she changed her screensaver from a view of olive groves to a tram in murky twilight.

'Keep an eye on Carlo, while I go up for my exams,' she said to Paola. And she told her old friend about her meeting last month with the degree-course coordinator. He was a defeatist, she said. And a bit of a know-all. Perhaps, being British, he felt superior. He had advised her to go abroad. His view was that in Italy a PhD very likely led to unemployment, especially if undertaken at a small university like theirs. Then if she really wanted to do a PhD in this university, he said, she should have chosen someone powerful as her Magistrale thesis tutor, not Doctor Furlan. Professor Modesto, James had said, who was Head of Department, had to date tutored only two theses in this degree – most professors in the same time would have done twenty or more – but both those two students, and only those two, had won scholarships to do PhDs. The point was, Head of Department had the power, first to get you into the programme, then to find you a job at the end.

Valeria didn't tell Paola James's exact words, which had angered her and which would echo in her mind now for years to come. They had been in his small office, which he shared with another professor, a woman in her thirties, who had actually been present throughout the interview, tapping away on her computer by the window with a prickly cactus plant beside her. 'As soon as you finish your degree,' this man had said with his marked English accent, 'you can forget meritocracy. From then on, it's who you know.'

Valeria had felt the force of these words like a punch in the head. It was a scandal, she thought, that a university professor should tell her this so bluntly, so shamelessly, and that another university professor should sit calmly at the other side of the room without so much as raising an eyebrow.

'You have to prepare for that,' James had warned.

'The fact is,' Valeria had pleaded, 'this is the only thing I want to do in life.'

'Again, I'd advise you to apply abroad,' James said. 'You can count on me and no doubt Furlan for a reference.'

'But I like it *here*,' she told him. 'I'm really excited with the work I'm doing with Doctor Furlan. I want to go on with that.'

'In that case you had better ask for an appointment with the Head of Department, though I'd advise you not to mention Furlan to her. If Professor Modesto is encouraging, there's a passing chance you'll get in.'

So Valeria had contacted the Head of Department, who had given her an appointment the same week. She honestly couldn't understand James's evident antipathy to the woman who proved to be both gracious and understanding, albeit in a rather formal, old-fashioned way. She could sit the doctorate exam right after presenting her Magistrale thesis, she had explained. There was even a rather comical moment. As Valeria had got up to leave, Professor Modesto, sitting behind a large desk where tins of sweets and two packets of cigarettes were carefully lined up beside stacks of forms and blue-bound theses, had suddenly said, 'Signorina Lasala, wait a minute. That name. Lasala. Lasala. You're not by any chance a relative of Doctor Matteo Lasala, are you?'

She turned.

'In the Partito Democratico,' Professor Modesto clarified. 'Who runs the big charity, what's it called? In Rome.'

'Mattia,' she said. 'Not Matteo. He's my father's uncle.'

'Ah, how foolish of me!' Modesto seemed immoderately pleased. 'Do by all means give him my most respectful regards when you next see him, Signorina Lasala. And the Rector's regards, of course. A most remarkable man.'

'Which is hilarious,' Valeria told Paola, reporting the conversation. 'Because I never see him at all.'

'Perhaps you should,' Paola suggested.

FERRAGOSTO

Valeria took her Magistrale exams in May and got excellent marks, galvanised by the prospect of continuing and deepening her studies. Then there was the long summer in Bari, completing the Magistrale thesis for her degree commission in October and studying for the doctorate entrance exams immediately afterwards. Here there was a lot to do without knowing exactly what, since the directions for these three exams, two written and one oral, could not have been more vague: Communications Theory (a six-hour written paper), Project Description (another six-hour written paper), then an oral discussion including assessment in French and English. That was all she had to go on. What did they want her to write during those twelve long hours?

Meantime, her boyfriend Michele arrived in Bari to spend the summer with her. A staunch member of Comunione e Liberazione in occasional correspondence with Don Gabriele at their local church back home, he found a room in a seminary for next to nothing. Some days the two took a bus together to the beach; others they made love in her flat when Carlo was at work. He was serving in a pizzeria now. Valeria was fond of Michele and everything seemed natural and pleasant. They talked a great deal about the world and politics and religion and what they would do when their studies were over. He still had a year to go before finishing his Magistrale in Naples. She even went to Mass with him on Sundays and rather enjoyed it. It reminded her of old times. But they didn't talk about living together, or whether they intended to look for work in the north or the south. Why not? Valeria wondered how Paola and Paolo would get on now that they were about to make *il grande passo*, the giant step. Would they be happy in Milan? She wondered why she couldn't even imagine Michele coming north to live with her.

In August the whole *compagnia* went camping in the Gargano as they always had: Valeria, Paola and Paolo, Paolo's older brother Franco with his girlfriend Ilaria, Letizia and Maria Pia who never had boyfriends, Letizia's brother Mario who was still smoking more dope than was good for him, Flavio and Chiara, Giancarlo and Bruna. But Valeria's brother refused to go on holiday with his old friends. His girlfriend had always been part of the group, he said. Now he needed to forget it all. So he tagged along with Valeria and her friends and they did all the things one does on Adriatic campsites: hired a palm-frond sunshade and deck chairs on the beach, swam in the shallows between sand and breakwaters, lived in their bathing costumes, played beach volley and table tennis and boules and mini-golf. There was a karaoke evening, a raffle evening, a five-a-side football evening. Mid-morning the beach PA blared music into the still summer air. In the sultry afternoons there was silence and siesta. The camp disco throbbed through the warm evenings and the smoke from a score of barbecues drifted up through the dry branches of the umbrella pines.

It was fun. It was the same summer Valeria had always known, the only kind of summer holiday she had ever had, and it was good to see Carlo kicking a ball around with her friends and apparently not unhappy. But nor did he seem his old self. She sensed his need to have other people around all the time. He launched into games and jokes with too much energy, but no real enthusiasm. And her enthusiasm was flagging too. On Ferragosto, 15th August, when by tradition you swam nude at midnight and stayed up through the small hours to watch the sun rise from the sea, she began to feel like an impostor, an infiltrator. She didn't care about Ferragosto, she realised. She wasn't the least excited by the skinny-dipping. Shortly after dawn, Zia Lella, no doubt kneeling at her early-morning prayers in the convent, sent a WhatsApp with an image of the Virgin Mary drawn into the sky among angels. Because Ferragosto was also the Feast of the Assumption. But Valeria didn't care about that either. 'Our Lady prays for you,' Zia Lella had written. Not enough, Valeria thought.

Back in her tent, absurdly, she checked her email to see if Doctor Furlan had corrected the thesis work she had sent. But he was on holiday too, of course, with a woman, no doubt. The whole of Italy was on holiday, breathing sea air and tanning lotions, watching sunrises and sunsets. Only the degree coordinator, James, answered promptly to her mails, any time of day, any day of the year. He must be a sad workaholic. He sent her a reading list for the doctorate exam and two examples of thesis projects that had been successful. This unusual willingness to help only made his previous advice more ominous.

On the last night, around the barbecue, drinking beer and smoking dope in the mothy air under an awning strung between tree trunks with the friendly buzz of the campsite all around, she finally found herself telling her friends what this enigmatic professor had warned her: that once your education was over it was mainly a question of who you knew. At least in the university. 'I felt like saying, so why the hell did I bother to study so hard?'

There was an animated discussion.

'He's just jealous,' Paola thought, 'because he's never managed to fit into the system. Being a foreigner.'

'What do you mean, if he's a professor?'

'I think he was trying to help,' Chiara said.

'By making me feel like shit?'

'Because he's worried you might be starry-eyed.'

'Everyone knows the *concorsi* are fixed,' Giancarlo observed, passing a joint. 'On the other hand, if others can swing it, why shouldn't you?'

He blew out a smoke ring.

'You should hang around the Head of Department,' Paolo agreed. 'That's all the guy was telling you.'

Bruna said three professors in her hospital, a big university hospital, had recently been arrested for fixing *concorsi*. So maybe things were changing and by the time she'd finished her doctorate it would be different.

The others thought this was nonsense.

'It will never change,' Flavio said. 'Because they have no idea how to do things differently. It doesn't matter what the rules are.'

'A degree coordinator should be fighting corruption, not warning off his best students,' Michele said, but Valeria knew he was saying this to please her.

Their faces glowed in the light from the barbecue. They were all bare-armed, bare-legged, sitting on pine needles in the dark, sun-burned and dizzy with heat and smoke. After her turn with the joint, Maria Pia had to go to the bathroom because she felt sick. Photos were taken and messages sent. Replies came from similar groups of friends holidaying in similar locations and their photos were passed around. Emoticons arrived from anxious mothers who always said goodnight to their children. Perhaps a message from a grandmother, or aunt. Paola in particular always seemed to have a relative on the phone. Letizia's father called towards midnight. From Australia, she said.

By the food tent, Giancarlo had four or five bottles of different drinks he kept mixing in various proportions for everyone to try. There was ice in an icebox, though it was getting watery now. On the next pitch just beyond theirs someone was playing a guitar, people were singing, and from time to time Chiara and Bruna joined in, holding hands and swaying. The two northern girls had become good friends, in southern company. Everyone was laughing and joking. Yet even as she relaxed into it, Valeria was aware that they were no longer the same adolescents who had first camped here together seven or eight years ago. Was this the last time?

Talking of cheating, Paolo now said, had they seen the story about the student in Trento who had hacked into her university's software and managed to increase all her grades by a point or two to make sure she got 110 and *e lode* at the end?

They all marvelled at such ingenuity but agreed that cheating in written exams was almost too easy now. So long as the professors didn't actually frisk you for your phone at the door, you could look up anything, ask anyone anything. There was a secretary in his university, Flavio said, who could get you advanced photocopies of any multiple-choice exam for very small favours in return. It was incredible.

Not to mention Renzo Bossi, Chiara reminded them, son of Umberto Bossi, ex-leader of the Lega Nord Party, who had simply used the organisation's funds to buy himself a degree in Albania.

'Please remember he denies it!' Paola laughed.

Everybody chuckled.

Valeria hated all this. But she knew it was true. One of her most unsettling experiences recently had been when Dottor Furlan emailed her a copy of a previous Magistrale thesis that he thought particularly good, on feminist writing in Cameroon. It was the kind of structure she might adopt herself, the exciting professor had told her. Reading the thesis, Valeria had been struck by the marked changes of style from paragraph to paragraph. She had begun to paste a sentence or two into Google and sure enough whole sections of the thing had simply been lifted from other articles and books, while one entire chapter, as far as she could see, was simply a poor translation of an article that had appeared in *Jeune Afrique* two years before. She hadn't told Furlan because she didn't think he would be happy to realise he'd been taken for a ride.

Then Flavio and Chiara put an end to the conversation by announcing that they were going to get married. Next spring. Giancarlo raced off to see if he could still buy some *spumante* at the disco bar. It was pushing one o'clock. 'The first to betray the group!' Paolo accused

Flavio. 'His idea, not mine!' Chiara protested. 'I can't really see the point of pieces of paper.' But obviously she was delighted, Valeria thought. She had nailed her man. No doubt as soon as they were married, she would be willing to move south for him. They would live in Potenza or Matera. They would have children. It was the excuse Chiara needed to escape her incontinent grandmother.

Just as Giancarlo returned with a bottle, telling everyone to rinse out their glasses, Valeria realised that Carlo was no longer with them. His face had gone from its place in the shadows where he had sat quietly all evening. She stood and went over to the tent he was sharing with Paola's brother, but he wasn't there.

'Maybe the washrooms,' Letizia said.

Valeria waited a while. She raised a glass with the others. They shouted a toast. Then she went to look for him. She walked through the site under the pines, past tents and cars, down to the beach. There were rows upon rows of closed sunshades and stacked deck chairs, the disco still throbbing away to her right. Here and there groups and couples were smoking and drinking. The air was balmy and there was a silver sliver of moon over the sea. The sand was fine and dry and deep. A group of teenagers were splashing in the water, tossing a ball. Beyond them a couple of lights winked out at sea and she could just make out the lamps of men fishing out on the breakwaters. Valeria took off her sandals and began to walk fast where the sand was harder by the water.

She found her brother almost a kilometre away where the beach ended and the embankment carrying the railway line came right up close to the sea. He had opened a sunlounger and was lying on his back eyes closed.

'I'm not one of your group,' he muttered. 'I haven't been to university. I don't know the people you talk about. I don't know Milan. I don't know anything.'

'You're my brother,' she said. She sat on the sand by his feet.

'Your brother who should never have been born.'

This was a reference to something their mother often said: that she should never have had children and that above all she should never have had Carlo, knowing as she did her marriage was finished and 'your father a good-for-nothing'.

'But you're her favourite!'

He shook his head. 'I'm the favourite she never wanted.'

Valeria stood and took her brother's hand and pulled him to his feet. He folded his arms around her and sobbed.

SUFFICIENTE

Graduation in October was a replay of the scene two years before, but without the same levels of anxiety. Again the whole family came up from Basilicata to Milan and did all they could to prevent Valeria from studying. Again Zia Lella said her rosary, again Vanessa had to have the TV on low through the night, again Valeria hardly slept. But she was ready for the experience this time. When she sat face to face with the President of the Commission, Professor Modesto on this occasion, she knew the powerful woman was well disposed; Furlan was more than pleased with her work, James was sympathetic. All her classmates were there for moral support, as she would be for them when it was their turn. Michele had come, and Giancarlo and Paolo and Flavio. As friends must.

Switching on her PowerPoint she felt mature and confident. Later, when her name was called out to announce the final mark, it was no surprise to see the commission get to its feet for the 110 *e lode*. Her family were in awe. Her formal education was over.

The following week, she took the train up from Bari again and slept on the sofa in Paolo's flat the night before the theory exam for her PhD application. 'Compare the passage from manuscript literature to printed books with that from paper to screen-based text within a general theory of human communication.' It was the only question. The exam started at 9.30 a.m. and finished at 3.30 p.m. You were allowed to bring a sandwich. Valeria was astonished to see there were only three candidates in a classroom for eighty. And there were three scholarships available. Did that mean the exam was a formality and the result a foregone conclusion? Perhaps other potential candidates had gone to speak to Modesto and the professor had suggested there was no point in their applying. In which case she, Valeria, was already chosen and this ordeal a charade.

The thought upset her. But at once she feared a false sense of security. The six hours seemed interminable. She was unable to write anything but clichés. In the end, she handed in her paper ninety minutes early, discovering a week later, on the university website, that her work and that of one other candidate had been judged *sufficiente*, the lowest possible pass grade, while that of the third candidate was *insufficiente*. It was the worst mark Valeria had had in her life.

In any event, there were now only two students for the next six-hour marathon. Which meant the exam *wasn't* a foregone conclusion. Unless of course that third candidate had been unwanted from the first and warned that there was no point in applying but had applied anyway. There were people who did that, and then went to court demanding that judges assess whether their exam really was *insufficiente*. These reflections were distracting. But this second exam was easier, since it was simply a question of writing at length about the project she was proposing for her doctorate. The work would be assessed overnight with the doctorate oral exam taking place the following afternoon.

This final test of character was to be held in the Rector's suite on the fourth floor with the Rector himself presiding. CCTV guarded a polished oak door. You activated the intercom, you explained who you were and why you were there and a young male secretary came to open up. Valeria was shown into a bright, windowless, air-conditioned boardroom dominated by a long table with a gleaming glass centre and wood surround. Beneath the glass, computer monitors were tilted so that people round the table would be able to follow a PowerPoint without cluttering the conversation space between them. A dozen swivel arm-chairs were upholstered in pale blue leather while the walls were lined with complete collections of Italy's most famous encyclopedias. The carpet was a deep cream pile and the air drenched with the fragrance of expensive cleaning products. Sitting on the edge of her chair, Valeria felt intimidated. There would be no friends to support her here.

A young man was shown in, a boy wearing a red jewel in his ear, a ponytail, a dark jacket and pink tie. The other surviving candidate. It seemed they were to be examined together. A woman with thick wavy hair appeared, bringing with her a cloud of sweet perfume. 'I'm a new arrival,' she said cheerfully. 'Professor Valente, Television and Media Studies.' Fleshy and pleased about it, she smiled, smoothed the lap of a fluffy trouser suit and began to rummage in a deep blue bag, eventually pulling out a tube of mints. 'Anyone want a suck? Cover the smell of fear.' She laughed. Large hoops of earrings tinkled. Both candidates declined. The woman popped a white sweet between her lips, moving her mouth with evident pleasure. 'Let's hope it's brief and painless,' she laughed again.

Modesto arrived and Valeria understood at once that the two women disliked each other, and in particular that Modesto resented the other woman's flamboyance. Her own face seemed to be made up with grey pencil, mouth pinched, cheeks chiselled. There was some desultory talk about a new bill in Parliament that threatened to change university career structures. The other candidate said his name was Alessandro and he was from Genoa. Valeria explained she was from Basilicata. '*Caspitina!*' Professor Valente whistled. My goodness. As if she had said 'outer space'.

Ten minutes passed. Modesto couldn't settle. She got up, went out of the room and came back in again some time later, announcing rather gravely that the Rector had received an urgent call from the Minister for Education and would come as soon as he could. Valente stood up, pushed glossy hair off her forehead and said in that case, if there were no objections, she would sneak out on the fire escape and smoke herself the day's first cigarette. She was just approaching the door when the Rector burst in. 'We're late!' he announced. A head taller than the others, striding swiftly across the room, he imposed a masculine urgency, as if the women were responsible for a delay that was already unforgivable.

Ottone had changed, Valeria thought. He was peremptory and almost grim, but with sudden menacing smiles. 'Do come and sit down, ladies,' he said with heavy sarcasm to the two professors, opening his arms to lay them along the backs of the pale blue chairs each side of him.

'Beppe!' Valente said and greeted him with a touch of the cheek.

Modesto sat on the edge of her seat, straight-backed, silver pen gripped in her slim fingers, and began to pass the Rector various papers.

'Ah, yes. Dottoressa Lasala.' He opened the folder in front of him which, Valeria saw, contained her written exams and university records. The others were silent while he leafed through them, breathing slowly and deeply. He looked up. 'But I've seen you before, of course ... The southern damsel who took on the European film institutions. Excellent.'

Valeria was astonished that this powerful man should remember her first-degree thesis of two and a half years before, and acutely embarrassed to be called a 'damsel'. Removing his spectacles, pulling a large blue velvet cloth from his jacket pocket to wipe them, Ottone turned first to his right, then to his left to scrutinise his two colleagues through the heavy lenses held some inches from his eyes. 'We could do with a bit more of that kind of courage in this university,' he said pointedly, looking at Valente. 'That kind of freshness,' he said, turning to Modesto. Valente laughed with determined good cheer. Modesto's smile was more pained. 'Bettina, go and order some coffee, will you, please?' he said, as if disappointed that he should have to remind her to do this. 'For you too?' He turned to Valente who nodded. '*Decaf-feinato*,' she said. Modesto got to her feet with evident reluctance. Ottone frowned and opened the other file. 'Alessandro Cimaglia. Your project, please. Explain.'

The boy launched into a spiel: the use of metaphor in political discourse. He seemed too young, Valeria thought, but was obviously smart, speaking as though he had memorised whole volumes of linguistics and past political speeches. Modesto returned to her seat and a few moments later the male secretary brought three espressos on a silver tray with tiny sweet biscuits.

'Don't mind us,' the Rector gestured to Alessandro. 'Go on.'

Since no one was asking any questions, the boy, now quoting Montesquieu, had begun to speak faster. He seemed afraid of boring them. No one had told the candidates how much time they had or how long the exam was supposed to last.

Trying to decide how she should play her own cards, Valeria realised that the two women professors were waiting to see how Ottone would respond. They needed a cue. He was the only person who mattered. When Alessandro suddenly stopped talking, Valente passed a book across the table and asked him to start reading and translating from the top of the page.

'Just the first paragraph.'

'*La liberté que nous assure ce désengagement critique (à tous le sens de ce mot) est donc sollicitude e ouverture sur la totalité.*'

Valeria recognised Derrida. Her heart sank. But Alessandro read confidently, as if familiar with the text. Could he have known what was coming? Ottone leaned slightly towards Valente, muttering something very close to her ear, then turned to look at a message that vibrated on his phone. All at once he thrust the phone aside.

'The "s" is not pronounced, young man! *Per l'amor del cielo.* All these years studying French and you don't know when the "s" is not pronounced.'

Alessandro hesitated. He wasn't aware which word he had got wrong.

Ottone shook his head, reached for his phone, pushed his chair back and walked swiftly out of the room. In the uneasy silence that followed they could hear him giving an order to the secretary. 'Sounds like it must have been a difficult call with the Minister,' Valente observed, rummaging for her mints again. Modesto kept her head down, making notes with an air of dogged scrupulosity.

'Forgive me, *colleghi, signorina, signorino*.' Ottone was back, smiling more generously now. '*Avanti la prossima!*'

In fifteen minutes it was over. Professor Valente quizzed Valeria on her understanding of the concept of *différance*. Modesto agreed that the candidate did not seem to have grasped the subtlety of Derrida's decision to spell the word with an 'a'. 'Nonsense,' Ottone cried. 'The *lucanina* has understood perfectly! It's just that she's unimpressed!' For five minutes he launched into an anecdote about a conversation he had had with Derrida at a conference on the Island of Capri in the early 1970s, during which the French intellectual had thanked him for finally explaining the exact meaning of the Italian words *dietrologia* and *insabbiare*. 'But that's enough. I'm happy with what I've heard.' He pushed his chair back, reached over the table to shake hands with both candidates, and left the room.

On the esplanade outside the main entrance, Alessandro was in tears. He had been taken apart, shat on, he said. Yet aside from one tiny reading error, he had got everything right!

'For sure calling us *signorini* was a bit rich,' Valeria observed.

She offered her companion a cigarette. The early November air was cool and damp. 'I was wondering, though,' she said, inhaling deeply, 'if the whole thing didn't have more to do with them than with us. I mean, they didn't really try to find out how much we knew, did they?'

A week later both candidates learned that they had been accepted for the twelfth cycle of the university's Doctorate in Communications and Media. It meant three years of scholarship at 1,100 euros a month. Net of taxes and national insurance. A decent salary. In retrospect, it had all been far, far easier than you would have thought.

GENERAZIONE ANTICAMERA

Federica's husband, Ernesto, is reading a new poem he has written. It's about Joseph, not quite the father of Jesus. The last lines read:

> *We've no end of stories about the deaths*
> *of his wife and Son, and even that other Father;*
> *there are fancy tombs dedicated to them,*
> *and paintings showing them up above*
> *on sofas of cloud with angels in attendance,*
> *but who knows a damn thing of what became of poor Joe?*

It's a story of exclusion. Joseph was drawn in to avoid scandal, exploited, then cold-shouldered, *bocciato, non-amesso*. His family could do without him. Christianity could do without him.

James is listening to the poetry reading in a small venue in the centre of Milan, run by a wealthy cultural foundation. Four poets read their work, moderated by a tubby fellow with curly hair and catarrh who spends more time expounding his own ideas than allowing the poets to read. Federica, sitting next to James, whispers that alas, this man, a failed poet, now in his late sixties, is the *barone* of poetry readings in Milan. You can't read anywhere decent unless you're on good terms with him. He tells you which publishers to go to and who to hang out with if you want to make it as a poet.

James has heard similar stories from local musicians. Someone or some clique more or less dictates which bands can play where. Everyone has to suck up. But he is surprised that such power could have accumulated in a field that brings no one any money, or even much prestige these days. There are fewer than twenty people present and after the reading it turns out that everyone knows each other and many are themselves poets who read on other occasions when no doubt those who read today will be in the audience. Everybody is eager to say a word or two to the overweight impresario who wears a mauve cravat of the kind popular in London, James recalls, in the 1970s. There is much discussion as to which poets are the most *gettonati* of the moment, a *gettone* being a token, for use in a machine, and, by extension, or various extensions, the money paid to a performer for their performance, so that 'the most *gettonato*' comes to mean the person best paid, or most frequently in the public eye. In short, the flavour of the month. A few names are mentioned, for the most part with contempt. 'Too bad there is never actually a *gettone*,' Federica observes.

Federica and Ernesto are among James's best friends these days. Tall, bespectacled and stooped, Federica teaches German literature, has a lively mind, a dry wit and no illusions about the world she moves in. Her husband, who lectures at another university, is, if anything, even more resigned than his wife. He has just written a new poem called *Generazione anticamera* – Waiting Room Generation. James hears him reading it in a seedy fourth-floor flat out in the suburbs where a would-be rival impresario, a high-school teacher in overactive middle age, holds court with his breathy second wife, bringing together a circle of downbeat acquaintances, eager for culture and discussion.

Travelling in James's car, they find the venue with some difficulty, since there seem to be no street names in this area of town and all the buildings, at least ten of them, being part of the same development, amazingly bear the same street number. No doubt it is safely assumed that no one would ever come out here who did not already know the place. Ernesto has to call three times on his mobile before first the building then the correct wing of the building are finally identified. Even as they climb the stairs, they understand it was a mistake to accept this invitation. There is a smell. Federica pulls a face. They would like to flee. It's the smell of yesterday's cooking, damp masonry and stale cigarette smoke in old carpets.

A narrow corridor with laundry draped on a drying rack leads into a cluttered sitting room. Chairs have been crammed to focus on a table, behind which the school-teacher and poet will be sitting. The audience are the kind who do not remove their raincoats and occasionally fish old toffees or half-used handkerchiefs from the pockets. To one side, a whole wall is taken up with a poster of the Golden Gate Bridge at sunset. Improbable glamour, discoloured by age. White wine is served, warm, in plastic glasses. Bending with the tray, the wife shows the tops of her red stockings under an unexpectedly short black skirt; she seems to be the youngest person present; rather, the only young person present. Meantime her bearded husband, in tweed jacket and corduroy, fusses over setting up a webcam so that the event can later be launched on the community's Facebook page. It takes a while as he goes back and forth, pointing and activating the camera, which is perched on a pile of paperbacks. Ernesto has to shift his seat six inches to the right. Remember not to slump! he is told. A spotlight is belatedly turned on. The wine, James notices, settling into a thread-bare armchair, is on the tart side.

The host launches into an introduction, rubbing his hands together and speaking more to the webcam than the guests. He keeps his chin tilted up. He recalls the history of their little reading community and its ups and downs over a dozen years, their determination to forge an exciting avant-garde in an increasingly conservative world, their consequent decision not to seek sponsorship, since that would inevitably have led to a loss of control. There are nods among the various members. One is leaning forward with his beard on his walking stick. An elderly lady keeps her eyes closed. After perhaps twenty minutes the host mentions Ernesto. He talks about the poet's trenchant

231

independence, his exploitation of both dialect and conventional literary traditions, cites influences, teases his guest with reminiscences of shared political affiliations in student days, and so on. Towards ten, Ernesto, who has now given up trying not to wince, is allowed to read. Without any preamble of his own, he begins:

> *The room is packed and the air, with open windows, unbreathable.*
> *At least the winter heat is free.*

Life is imagined as a waiting room, but ...

> *No, this isn't a Kafkaesque affair,*
> *that door doesn't conceal the Law, the State, the gods,*
> *though the rare figures who appear on the threshold, glowing*
> *with arrogance, might prefer you to think so.*

It is simply the way people in Italy wait for some possible job, some possible promotion, ever promised, never delivered, remaining meanwhile in a constant state of fearful obedience. Above all, it is the world of the university:

> *Round me I see only young people, or that's what I've been taught*
>   *to call them*
> *though they rarely raise their voices, many have grey hair*
> *and every day the morticians lay someone in his box.*

On the other side of the door, where power lies, people are made of stronger stuff.

> *It's strange that I, who've been here now for forty minutes,*
> *six hours three days two months and thirty years,*
> *have never seen anyone taken from the other side.*

On the contrary, the noise beyond the door is all tinkling glasses
    and music,
eternal partying.

This is indeed the constant impression: that the powerful, be they TV celebrities, politicians, industrialists, university barons, or the *sui generis* octogenarian Berlusconi, stay right where they are deep into decrepit gerontocracy. Ogres. It is not a country, as they say, for young men.

So when sirens shrill in the street, a shiver of hope runs round the room,
'Emergency', 'change', 'morgue', people whisper with the same pleasure
you might say caviar, vacation, supercool.

But it's a false alarm, and the poem winds up:

On TV an eminent man has promised that from now on
something must be done to stop this show of desperation.
Something must be done for the youngsters waiting at the door.
Lock up the windows as well.

Ernesto finishes and there is silence. His audience knows *exactly* what he is talking about. They shift uneasily in their seats. They all understood that observation that although those in the waiting room are forever to be described as young, still they never raise their voices as young people might be expected to, they never protest, all cowed by the thought that one complaint could set them back years.

'Ippolito Nievo,' observes a man sitting at the back in a corner. 'In *Confessions of an Italian*. Remember?' Everybody turns to look at him. 'Called the Italians "a sheep-like flock of men without faith, strength or illusions who reach the threshold of life already half dead".'

'What a wonderful memory, Ranieri.' The host claps his hands.

'Ranieri has a quote for everything,' a woman in the front row declares admiringly.

'The group's historic conscience,' the host's wife observes.

All attention shifts to this lean man with his straight back and proud shock of white hair. Severely complacent, Ranieri leans forward from his chair. 'A "gesticulating, chatterbox, superficial, carnivalesque people", Mussolini called us, while Garibaldi –'

'Excellent,' the host declares. 'Next poem, please.'

Ernesto sighs, turns a page, begins:

The everlasting emperor, that swanky blowhard
has exiled me to the black sea
of my bile
        for no reason, with no trial,
nor had I realised I was upsetting his plans ...

James doesn't know it, but these words will prove prophetic, not for the husband who wrote them, but for his wife who is listening. For we are moving now into the last phase of our long fable, the events that will bring James and Federica and Valeria and Antonio Furlan together, as companions in eventual exile, banished by the everlasting emperor, or ogre, Ottone.

GUFO

It all began with the decision, decades before, to measure and compare the value of research done in different universities, and, as part of this drive, to privilege collective over individual research. The idea, in the eighties, was that many academics were taking it far too easy and not really producing anything. It's hard to imagine anyone wanting to argue with this assessment. And that even when they did produce a little research or reflection it was done piecemeal, haphazardly, and didn't amount to anything you could get a major corporation to sponsor or invest in. This was also broadly true, though it was nevertheless the case that left to their own devices some academics were producing research that was both extremely interesting and potentially valuable. There are always exceptions, always people who insist on working well, even when underfunded and ignored. Excellence dies hard. However, the perception was that such quality, where it existed, was accidental rather than schematic; the whole system, qua system, wasn't *serious* enough, hence it had to be made so, or made to *appear* so, as soon as possible. It had to be on a par with France and Germany and Britain. It had to be able to compete for the generous research funds now being offered by the European Union.

The government's solution was to oblige all universities to set up research departments and all academics to subscribe to them. These departments would then excogitate collective research projects that members would be forced to participate in. So no sooner did James become a fully fledged *concorso*-winning professor than he found himself obliged to choose between various grandiose department projects that held little interest for him: Funding for the Arts in Lombardy from the Risorgimento to the Present Day; a CD Rom Encyclopedia of Oriental Influences in Mediterranean Poetry; a History of Subtitling in Italian Silent Cinema. And so on.

Perhaps collective research makes sense in the sciences where an awful lot of interrelated laboratory work might need to be done to explore a single hypothesis. But James's feeling was that in the arts the collective obsession simply impeded what interesting work was being done individually. Projects were kept as vague and inclusive as possible to allow all department members to find a niche within them, which rather defeated the original intention. Niche found, no one bothered to read anyone else's work, concentrating entirely on getting their own task out of the way in the shortest possible order, so as to return to doing what they really wanted to do. Or perhaps to doing nothing at all.

In any event, there was little cohesion. Where a project was lucky enough to secure funds from outside backers, or the government, or, wonder of wonders, the EU, the money was used to hire young people who would then spend most of their time teaching lessons for those powerful older professors more interested in politics than pedagogy. Or it was spent on expensive trips to foreign capitals, ostensibly to toil in antique archives, but more likely to take a mistress shopping. Or to invite some old friend, or friends – a professor from Paris or Berlin or Barcelona – to come and lecture at your own university so that the two of you could get together for dinner, after which your guests would hopefully return the compliment, inviting you to wherever they were based with their own research funds. This generous spirit of reciprocation was particularly true with regard to the ambitious conferences that were held to mark the end of any project and whose seriousness was judged by the number of people attending from foreign countries. 'Internationalisation' and collective research were understood to go hand in hand and there was a widely shared assumption that if foreign academics were willing to sign up to your project that was conclusive and undeniable proof of its value. As if foreigners were always serious; as if it wasn't well known that professors from northern climes – Britain particularly – are always happy to come to sunny Italy for a few days, pick up a modest *gettone* for repeating a paper they've given a dozen times elsewhere and then disappear to the *pinacoteca*, or the *paninoteca*, or even the *discoteca*.

After the end-of-project conference came the project publication, a kind of tombstone laid on the whole endeavour to permit its decorous decay beneath a glossy engraving of supposed achievement. Made up largely of papers given at the conference, plus a few articles from junior colleagues for whom space had not been found on the podium, this was essentially a form of collective vanity publishing that allowed reputable but cash-starved publishers to take a slice of the university research budget to print works that could never command an audience, but whose existence brought 'points' to the university (useful when the government assessed its funding) and to individual academics (useful when being considered for promotion). So after all this effort to make research serious, the genuine originality or simply interest value of the publication was very likely the last thing on anyone's mind. All too often the Rector or Head of Department would muscle in to ensure that his or her protégés got their names in print hence establishing a claim for the *concorso* they were being groomed for. Only on rare occasions did a project coordinator feel sufficient levels of *vergogna* to turn down a Rector's protégé when his or her paper was unacceptably poor. Often the most remarkable aspect of such books is the ingenuity of the coordinator's introduction in giving the impression that there is indeed some connection between the hotchpotch of contributions that make up the whole.

But if you can't beat them – and James knew you really couldn't – then join them. Try to make it fun. Try to make it *work*. It shouldn't be impossible. After all, there were projects, now and then, that allowed interesting research to be financed and led to publications in which at least one of the articles was worth reading. Sometimes more than one. Have a go, James thought. With the arrival of Ottone as Rector, and his apparently limitless ability to attract funds to the university, it was probably worth at least proposing a project. Then if your idea passed muster and money became available, you could use it to help some young person get his foot on the academic ladder, someone you had tutored for their thesis perhaps. That was a worthy thing to do.

So it was that Federica and James dreamed up *European Journalism in a Globalised World*, a project that would assess the flow of articles by European journalists inside and outside the continent; that is, who was writing what for whom, and how much did each European country know about what was being said in other European countries. It seemed the kind of catch-all topic that might allow all the university's academics in languages and communications to find something they could say. It was fashionable enough to guarantee the presence of a couple of heavyweight international names at the final conference. Maybe even attract some press coverage. And hopefully, they could give some work and income to a young PhD or two. Cecilia Tamara, James suggested, to start with. Only three years later was he to realise that this young person, for whom he and Federica did eventually pro-cure a research grant, was the spy who had so promptly informed Modesto what James thought of her *prolusione* at the Inauguration of the Academic Year.

The most striking consequence – to go back a little way – of that first phone call James had received from Professor Modesto, inviting him to explain himself – was the extraordinary level of anxiety it caused him. At first James assumed this must be guilt: he really shouldn't have spoken so ill of a superior working in the same institu-tion, and to so many people, showing such evident contempt. It was morally wrong of him. Chastened, he went to the university library and looked up Professor Modesto's publications. She had scheduled their meeting in a week's time. He would go, he decided, equipped to show a broad awareness of the woman's achievements and intimate his respect and appreciation. He was ready to change his mind.

At first, bringing up the list of her titles on screen, it seemed there were too many books for him to look at all of them; he must choose, and this was as it should be, of course, for a professor *ordinario*. Such people were at the pinnacle of academic endeavour. On closer attention, however, it appeared that most of the books cited were collections of essays for which Modesto was a non-contributing editor, and all published, James discovered, by publishers or institutions in which Ottone was present on the Board of Directors, or himself an editor, or in one case simply the owner. This was also true, it turned out, of the four books Modesto had actually written herself. None of these was more than a hundred and twenty pages long, while two were less than a hundred. So there wouldn't be too much to read after all. And none was published after Modesto had become a professor *ordinario* at the remarkably young age of thirty-six. Goal achieved, she had shut up shop.

James went to the desk and ordered the books, causing the old librarian to raise a wry eyebrow. But this was not the moment to start exchanging remarks. James slipped the slim volumes into his bag, took them to his office and began to read. After just fifteen minutes with the first, he found he couldn't go on. It was impossible. He closed the book and opened the second. This time he lasted only ten minutes. It was the same wayward, tautological, jargon-driven rhetoric he had heard at the Inauguration of the Academic Year. 'The following monograph,' the third book (ninety-two pages long) began, 'undertakes to posit as indisputably essential in the analysis of any act of textual communication those metaphors whose energy is constitutive of any eventual interpretative analysis.' The more James looked at this sentence the less sense it made. And the less guilty he began to feel. His amazement at the mindlessness of Modesto's drivel had been perfectly legitimate.

239

Why then the extraordinary anxiety he felt on confronting the woman? Because you feel vulnerable, James realised. Because Professor Modesto is Head of Department, your direct superior. Or no, because Modesto is so close to Ottone that Ottone has made her Head of Department, despite being perfectly aware (he must be!) that she is academically a basket case. And if he has done this it is because he is safe in the knowledge that no one would ever dare to criticise, even indirectly, through his protégé, a man of his power and prestige.

No one but a dumb outsider like James.

But how had all this come about? Promotion far above one's ability normally meant only one thing; yet it seemed unthinkable that Ottone and Modesto should be lovers. Not that either was outside the age range, or even unattractive. But there was something so falsely proper and rigidly self-protective about Modesto that surely no man however desperate would even want to break her defences down. It was known, of course, that the two regularly travelled back to Puglia together on weekend flights. But what did that mean? No doubt they spent their Saturdays and Sundays in their respective homes, Ottone with his wife, Modesto, apparently, with her widowed father. They had also published a book together. But again, many people in mentor–protégé relationships published books together. Except that in most cases the protégé was intelligent, or at least a help of some kind. Whereas Modesto surely was the merest ballast. James shook his head. The other woman Ottone had brought in recently, he thought, the colourful Suzi Valente, from Cagliari, was a far more likely candidate for the role of mistress. Certainly Modesto seemed unhappy with her arrival. It was strange.

So were there other relationships, James now wondered, of a peculiarly Italian nature perhaps, that might explain this determination on Ottone's part to conjure up an academic career for someone so spectacularly unsuitable? Some family connection? Ottone and Modesto's father perhaps? Or now deceased mother? An old relationship there? Or some concession Ottone wanted from Modesto's family? A property he wished to acquire?

'Freemasonry,' Domenico Galli pronounced over his Pink Lady. 'Whenever something seems inexplicable, it's Freemasonry, or Mafia.'

James hadn't realised there were women Freemasons.

'Giuseppe Garibaldi, as first Grand Master of Italy, allowed women into Freemasonry in acknowledgement of their contribution to the Risorgimento. It's hard to keep women out of anything these days.'

'A nightmare,' Federica laughed.

'More likely,' Alessio thought, 'Ottone wants his butt covered by someone who owes him everything but who couldn't survive ten minutes in a university without him. Any other professore *ordinario* with even a shred of vocation, would be tempted to go their own way at some point, to develop their own career. But that can't happen with Modesto. She's dead meat without Comrade Otto. So he has someone who will do everything he says and can't even blackmail him by screaming to the world that she's been his lover. Because she hasn't. He has a *portaborse* and *sicario* – a lackey and an assassin – all in one. To do his dirty work. And the fabulous thing is that being a woman people just don't suspect how dangerous she can be.'

'What about Otto's wife?' Federica wondered, stirring a Spritz. 'Older, isn't she? Protective. Controlling. So they say. She must know that powerful men are constantly being preyed on by sexy young opportunists – Valente, for example – so she encourages a close relationship with a woman who admires him and is totally indebted to him, but is sensationally unsexy. More a bodyguard than an assassin.'

'Fantastic. So the real relationship is between Modesto and Otto's wife!'

'Perhaps.'

They were all round a table by the canal in spring sunshine, supposedly to discuss their research project on European journalism. They had decided that any funding they managed to attract would be used exclusively for only four purposes: to give a research income to a young PhD; to pay for all necessary books and research material; to bring some really smart people to an eventual conference; and to pay for a properly edited, published and promoted collection of papers. There would be no travel allowances at all and no dubious purchases of personal computers or expensive software.

'Far too noble,' Domenico shook his head. 'Who will want to get involved?'

When the others laughed, he added, 'You are allowing your identity to be determined by other people's sleaze. You want to be virtuous, so as not to be like them. But in the end all this moralism is just an excuse for conforming to their obsession for collective research, which is a complete waste of time. I refuse to be involved, morally or immorally. I won't join a research project.'

'Bravo!' James said.

The waiter arrived and there was a break in the conversation while people ordered drinks and Alessio rolled a cigarette and Antonio Furlan lit it for him and offered his own Marlboros to everyone and Galli took one and fitted it into his gold cigarette holder. One should never, he observed, breathe poison without a filter. 'And Ottone is poison of the most venomous variety. You'll regret this project. You'll regret not voting for Tedeschi.'

'*Gufo*,' Federica said to him. Which is to say, owl, grump.

ITALIANIZZAZIONE

The blond-bearded Antonio Furlan, who was enjoying his first *aperitivo* with the group, proposed that they bring Valeria Lasala into the project to consider European journalism in and from Africa. It would fit with her PhD.

'She could work alongside Cecilia, organising a web page and making sure everyone knows what the others are doing,' Federica suggested. They had decided that this project would be genuinely coordinated so that each person's work could be enriched by the group effort. With bi-monthly updates on everyone's progress.

Again Domenico shook his head. 'No one wants to know what the others are doing.'

'We'll see.'

'About your problem with Modesto, though.' Antonio turned to James. 'You know I have to sit in her courses as assistant and sometimes teach part of her lesson?'

'So?'

'It's embarrassing,' the young man grinned, twisting his moustache.

'In what way?' James asked.

'If anyone knew the nonsense she spouts, it would be a national scandal.'

'Par for the course,' Alessio observed.

'Could you record her?'

'Sometimes I can barely resist an urge to tell the students she's got it all wrong.'

'But you do resist,' Domenico pointed out.

'I'm afraid it shows on my face.'

'Then you'd better watch it,' Federica said gravely. 'Because while His Majesty's subject here already has tenure, you don't. Not yet.'

'Lick arse a little longer,' Domenico advised, drawing on the Marlboro that Antonio had given him. 'After all, this particular example seems fairly clean and dry.'

'Depends how long your tongue is,' Alessio thought.

'In general,' Domenico insisted, shaking his gold cufflinks, 'you folks like to think of yourselves as good, but you all eat at the same filthy trough, which is why Ottone is sitting pretty. He knows you need him.'

'So how should we all behave, Sir Pink Lady?' Alessio enquired.

'I'm not a "should" merchant,' Galli said. 'But wisdom suggests you might relax and enjoy your good luck. Think of all the people who would kill for your jobs. Or, if you really feel so squeamish, then get the hell out.'

It was good advice, James agreed. But he put it to Domenico that the world is never static. Circumstances change and a person needed to understand the point at which a bar might tip and a change of strategy be required. He himself had been fine with his job until Ottone had arrived and made Modesto Head of Department. Now it was more difficult.

'Some guidance, please,' he asked his friends, 'as to how I might handle my forthcoming meeting with the dear lady.'

'You voted for Ottone,' Galli again reminded him. 'I did suggest that Tedeschi was the better choice.'

'You were right,' James conceded. 'But life can't end because one made a mistake. What do I say to Bettina? How do I explain why I've been slagging her off as dumb and stupid?'

'Think of it this way,' Alessio proposed. 'Modesto is the ultimate test of your *italianizzazione*. If you can deal with this, you are ready for honorary citizenship.'

'That's an interesting idea,' Galli acknowledged. 'You thought you had become Italian, you naively imagined you had got used to Italian ways, but now you have to prove it.'

'I'm up for it,' James smiled. 'But how?'

Unexpectedly, it was Federica who said very quietly, 'I'll tell you how ...'

Having insisted on this confrontation, Modesto had made James wait a full week. She was away 'on a mission', she explained. 'To enhance the university's internationalisation.' She didn't say where and he didn't ask. He had thus been given plenty of time to suffer extremes of anxiety and unhealthy tension, playing the eventual encounter over and over in his head, wondering about the consequences and generally wishing he had kept his big mouth shut. At home, his son was sympathetic, but had difficulty seeing the problem. 'You're unfireable, Papà. Who gives a shit? Everyone under thirty-five is unemployed these days. That's a serious problem. Anyway,' he added, 'your friends have told you how to play it. It will be fun.'

'I'm not sure I can do it.' James put his head in his hands. 'I feel sick thinking about it.'

'The problem,' his son said, 'is you, not your Professor Modesty Blaise.'

Majoring in fine art, his son was an avid reader of old comics.

The four Heads of Department had their offices on the fourth floor near the Rector's office. James knocked on the polished door exactly at the appointed hour. Modesto, freshly permed and soberly dressed, sat behind a polished expanse of desk, signing her way through a pile of exam registers. She continued to sign, keeping him waiting at the door, then looked up, smiled cordially, invited him to sit and reached across the desk to offer a box of chocolates. Taking one, and immediately regretting it, James became aware of a photograph of Margaret Thatcher on the wall to the left.

'Margaret!' he exclaimed.

Modesto nodded. 'Your most illustrious compatriot of the last fifty years, I would say.'

James thought it wise not to disagree.

'Rolled back the boundaries of the State. Would that we had seen her like in Italy.'

The idea of Margaret Thatcher in Italy was so surreal James was silenced. There was a whole side to Modesto he knew nothing of.

'Now ...' the professor *ordinario* frowned. 'About the things I was told ...' She hesitated, evidently finding it painful even to think of criticism.

James leaned forward on his seat and swallowed his chocolate. The time had come.

'Complete and utter fabrication, Bettina,' he announced emphatically. 'Not only would I never have said such things – as you know the British are great respecters of collective responsibility and institutional solidarity – not only would I *never, never* have criticised a colleague so crassly, but more to the point I simply do not see how anyone at this university, above all anyone present at your remarkable Inauguration speech, could possibly question your academic excellence, or imagine that in doing so other colleagues would give him the time of day. Most of all, I do not see how you, Bettina, the author of four extraordinary, highly praised and widely cited monographs on Communications Theory, could suppose, or even begin to suppose, that I of all people would be so stupid as to do such a thing. I'm astonished and disappointed that you could underestimate me like this.'

As he spoke, he was aware of a slow smile of relief spreading over Modesto's prim face and realised his colleagues had been right. Her only aspiration was to live in blissful denial.

'The more over the top the better,' Federica had advised.

PART FOUR

Scandalo

UNA BELLA RAMANZINA

Respect is everything. A real *capofamiglia*, a king, a Mafia leader, a university *barone*, or simply a father who really is a father, must be able to command respect and must react when it isn't shown. For honour's sake. Not that a single slight or affront means the end for the perpetrator. A *capofamiglia* loves his family and cultivates all its members and wins respect from everyone when he manages to bring a rebel back to the obedient fold.

So second chances abound. The cold shoulder, your initial punishment, is not permanent. It's a goad to better behaviour. The door is open, or at least ajar. Bow the knee and you'll soon be basking in the warmth of paternal approval once again. You will even be cause for rejoicing; there is more joy in heaven over the one sinner who repents than the ninety-nine ... etc. The disrespectful person is a challenge. His courage is recognised, his pride appreciated. Or hers. Perhaps especially hers. When, for example, as Giambattista Basile recounts, the King of Bello Paiese courted the Princess Cinziella, daughter of the King of Surco Luongo (Long Furrow) and she spurned him, he didn't give up on her. First he disguised himself as a peasant and tricked her into a situation where she could be ravished in her sleep. She grew to enjoy the experience. Pregnant, she was obliged to marry him. Married, he took her back to his palace in Bello Paiese and confined her to a stable in the grounds, outside his house and family circle, where the only food she got were the hunks of bread he speared on crossbow bolts and fired at her from his distant window. Only when she was delivered of two baby boys, two handsome new family members, did the king at last relent, and then 'this moment of consolation seemed far sweeter to her than all her past suffering'. Though she realised that in the future she must 'keep her sails lowered'. The drama had been for the good.

Similar stories are told for any number of sons who show disrespect to their fathers. Actually, the Italian expression is *mancare di rispetto* – fail to show respect, not deliberately show disrespect. Respectfulness must be active and ongoing and even simply omitting to show it now and then will be more than enough to provoke displeasure. In fact, forgetfulness of your duties is more offensive than a deliberate slight; it implies that the *capofamiglia* is insignificant. He can be forgotten. But even in this scenario you do get your second and, as fables suggest, even third chances. The same will be true for the daughter too proud to accept an appropriate suitor and for young people in general who do not express proper gratitude to the uncles, aunts, barons, fairies and even ogres who have furthered their careers. In general, the person who must show respect is perceived as younger, greener, ingenuous. This is important. '*Round me I see only young people,*' said Ernesto's poem, '*or that's what I've been taught to call them.*' It's this being perceived as young, or younger, hence not yet entirely responsible for your actions, that provides the *capofamiglia* or *padrone* with an alibi for offering you a second chance. Otherwise, if you deliberately insulted him, as a knowing adult, he would have to get rid of you, *e basta*.

So one morning Antonio Furlan received an email offering an olive branch and possible redemption. Despite the snub to Professor Modesto entailed in his signing up to the research project promoted by James and Federica, but not to the project proposed by the Head of Department (*Global Feedback: The West through an Eastern Mirror*), Antonio was contacted by the Rector's secretary and invited, at fairly short notice, to present a paper at a conference convened by the Society of

Italian Linguists, of which Ottone had once been president and was now a sort of honorary and benevolent *éminence grise*: 'Lingua franca past and present – Latin, French, English', the conference was called. 'What future for Italian?'

It was hardly his field, Antonio thought. He consulted his diary and then Google Maps too, for the venue was new to him. There was also the problem that he would have to get out of a previous commitment undertaken many months before. On the other hand, it might be dangerous, he realised, to turn this invitation down. A door open today might not be open tomorrow. Antonio's contract as a *ricercatore* had been renewed two years ago for the last legal time. A year hence, either they offered him a professorship, or he was out of a job. Then he remembered something.

'*Cara Valeria,*' he began an email. '*Do you know anything about a town called Madonna del Buon Cammino? Isn't it in your part of the world? The Rector has invited me to speak at a conference down there. Perhaps I could propose that you present your own research at the closing roundtable discussions.*'

When this email arrived Valeria was cooking *pettole* for the eve of Santa Caterina. Her brother had been working for some months now in a busy trattoria in the old port of Bari. For the first time he seemed to be enjoying his job. He had discovered cooking and had applied for a place at the Top Chef Academy, which, despite its British name, was only fifteen minutes' walk from where they lived. Perhaps he had found his vocation. Yet the boy still seemed fragile, leaving Valeria marooned in the spell of his vulnerability.

At the same time her PhD was proving a disappointment. Initially it had seemed there would be a cycle of high-powered methodological lessons for all doctorate students, to give them a start with their research; but this had been repeatedly postponed, then hastily organised towards the end of the second semester in a muddle of near-meaningless encounters – forty hours of them all told. Rumour quickly had it that the main reason for these lessons was to allow the professors to complete the annual number of classroom hours that they were obliged by law to teach.

In the last days of October she had travelled north, taking a night train without a couchette to get the cheapest possible price; all the PhD students were required to be present at a *collegio di dottorato*, a sort of grand committee, for their first assessment. The meeting began at 2 p.m., or shortly thereafter, in a classroom on the third floor, but the doctoral students were required to wait outside the door until they were called in. The Rector wished to address the professors in private first. At three they still hadn't been called in. They couldn't go down to the café in case the door opened and the call came. They couldn't smoke. Younger students hurried back and forth along the corridor to their lessons. There were no seats to sit on, no windows to look out of. The young would-be academics leaned on the cement wall and gossiped. What else? This professor was gay, someone said. This one was in a relationship with a student, not even good-looking. One spoke about the research he was doing in Paris, another the archives she was examining in Spain. Three of their number, Valeria realised, had fathers or mothers who were *professori ordinari* at other universities. They feigned anxiety and were quietly confident. They could see in their parents' lives the careers that naturally awaited them.

Valeria went down the corridor beyond the central stairwell to get a coffee from the machine. She waited her turn, since it was always busy, eventually slipped in her coins, selected an espresso, and in that very moment, heard a distant voice shouting, 'Valeria!'

They had been called in. 'You take it,' she told the boy behind her.

It was an ordinary classroom where the Rector sat up front behind a large desk speaking into a microphone; Modesto was beside him taking down the minutes with her usual diligence.

A young researcher ushered them towards the front row, and crossing the room Valeria's heart sank. There was something intensely unwelcoming about the atmosphere. Twenty-five men and women were arranged in knots of two or three, often with coats strewn on the seats beside them as if to prevent others from getting too close. The desire for apartness was palpable. No one had taken a place in the first three rows. Antonio Furlan was towards the back, studying his mobile. Ippolito Preti, the old Philosophy professor, ever on the cultural pages of Sunday papers, never in class, had a large book open on the desk in front of him. Federica was way off to one side under the window, a good six seats from anyone else. The only thing that seemed to unite them all was an expression of glazed and disheartened submission. James alone, on seeing Valeria, raised half an eyebrow of recognition, as if to welcome a fellow sufferer to the banquet of humble pie.

'Things,' the Rector began even before they were properly seated, 'have been lamentably lax here, and I have decided to impose a little order.'

His voice was soft, but menacingly amplified through the room's PA and he smiled with the air of one who has just carried out a severe punishment to his entire satisfaction. 'That, *dottori* and *dottoresse*, is why you have had to wait a while outside. I apologise for the delay, but I assure you it was done for your own sakes. The truth is that some of your illustrious guides on the path to wisdom have been taking it rather easy, and I have given them a *bella ramanzina* – a good scolding.' He paused as if to relish this homey colloquialism. '*Un predicozzo. Una pappina. Un rimbrotto.*' He reflected: 'I could go on. As I recalled, the Crusca dictionary has some twenty synonyms for this concept. A sad confirmation I suppose that such things are so frequently necessary.'

Again he paused, looking around the room, as if inviting someone to be so bold as to join in the discussion. No one was. Or perhaps the pauses were a further demonstration of his power to dispose of their time.

'There has been too much cosiness in this doctoral school. Yes, I'm going to call it that, however few of you there are. This is a school, an academy, a seminary, and as such it requires a curriculum, a pro-gramme, a project, an ethos of dedication, and above all a clear hierarchy between those teaching and those taught. Instead all I see are charming one-on-one relationships, tutor–student couples, love-birds almost, excellent no doubt for promoting mutual self-regard, but hardly propitious when it comes to training serious academics, hence enhancing the reputation of this athenaeum.'

Again the pause of power. No response was required or even possible.

'Attendance at your cycle of lessons, *signore e signori*' – he consulted a piece of paper on the desk in front of him, lifting it to his eyes, turning it over two or three times – 'was, how shall we put it, less than wholehearted? Is that the right expression? Sporadic, perhaps.' He put the paper down and looked directly at Alessandro, the boy with the earring from Genoa. 'Is that what you would say, Dottor Cassola?'

The boy didn't respond. Ottone smiled as a parent does when he has caught out an erring child. Indulgent and severe.

'Someone in our little community obviously felt it was more useful to be in London, rather than Milan, forgetting where his bread was buttered. *Non è vero*, Alessandro? Please do correct me if I'm wrong, my friends.'

This time the silence was even longer, until Suzi Valente, with a sort of grave cheerfulness, said, 'Perhaps the timetable was set up with too little notice, Beppe.'

Rather than easing the tension, this intervention and above all the marked use of the Rector's first name, merely confirmed for all present that Valente must be in a special relationship with Ottone. She felt invulnerable, but they did not.

'Suzi!' The Rector shook his head. 'You are too indulgent, *cara mia*. Or would you like Professor Modesto to include that justification in our minutes? That we arranged these lessons at rather short notice.'

Modesto frowned. Suzi Valente hazarded a deprecating wave of the hand.

'Don't these young ladies and gentlemen study here, work here? Don't they have a responsibility towards this institution? Couldn't I expect them to be here *tomorrow*, if I have some duty for them? Well? Suzi?'

She laughed as if they were joking. 'Of course you could,' she said.

'Good. I'm glad to hear it. Well, *dottori* and *dottoresse*, I have decided that there will be an exam on the content of these lessons. At the beginning of the autumn term. Your continued enjoyment of this university's patronage, your income, ladies and gentlemen, to be perfectly explicit, will depend on the results of those exams. Let no one imagine they can play the *furbo* here, collecting their cash while gallivanting around the world doing … doing what?' His face darkened and this tall, elegant, white-haired man spat out, 'Doing whatever the fuck they want!'

He sat back and smiled, removed his glasses, pulled a blue cloth from his pocket, began to polish them with care.

'Excuse me, ladies and gentlemen, but I am obliged to be vulgar. There are some smart-arses in this room who think they can do just what the hell they like. They can live where they like, see whom they like, publish whatever clever crap they like, in whatever rag they like, without proper reference to this academy, without seeking the permission, or even the opinion, of the president of this committee.'

Ottone replaced his glasses, leaned forward across the desk and adjusted the distance between mouth and microphone.

'Well, *signorine* and *signorini*, you had better think again.'

COLMARE QUESTO VUOTO

The Rector's performance went on for some thirty minutes. It was hard to believe it was the same man who had spoken so eloquently against corruption and cynicism at the Inauguration ceremony. Or perhaps not. Valeria saw the connection; there he had been attacking lazy, opportunist politicians. Now the target was lazy, opportunist doctoral students. Yet at no point was it clear to her, hunting back and forth through her own behaviour that year, whether Ottone was referring to specific misdemeanours, specific students and professors, or generally to a whole pattern of behaviour. Was her living in Bari a problem, for example? Certainly it had caused her to miss a few quite useless classes. Had she done the right thing to publish two articles with minor French academic reviews? Was there some rule that required her to seek permission from Ottone before publishing? If so, why not say so openly?

Finally, the great man sat back and invited various professors to read out reports of the work of the doctorate students they had been tutoring. As they spoke, he unwrapped small sweets and sucked on them, finger scrolling idly over the tablet on the desk in front of him. 'Dottoressa Silvini!' he suddenly interrupted to address the oldest student of the group. 'This is not a kindergarten or a travel agency. Is that clear?' His speech was slurred by the sweet in his mouth. 'I'm a tolerant man, but before the next meeting of this committee you will produce two completed and satisfactory chapters of your thesis, or suspension will be automatic.'

Did he have that power? Valeria wondered. Had they been given their scholarships mainly so that they could be threatened with losing them?

Professor Modesto rather nervously read out a report on Alessandro Cassola's project – 'Community and Communication – the modern heritage of the *commedia dell'arte*'. Again Ottone cut in, this time with unexpected indulgence. 'Leaving aside some rascally behaviour and disgraceful liberty-taking on the student's part, this is an extraordinary piece of research and something the university has reason to be proud of. You are really being over-cautious, Bettina, in presenting these ideas as promising. The student already shows a quite exceptional mastery of his sources and has found a most intriguing and original approach for interpreting their relevance today. Credit where credit is due, Bettina.'

Modesto smiled like a flustered girl.

Valente began to speak. She started buoyantly, presenting her student with the kind of smiling warmth that assumes approval, but again Ottone intervened. 'It's not enough, Suzi *mia cara*, to be enthusiastic about an *idea*. Is it? Some serious spadework is required.' He turned to the student in question. 'Facts, not froth, *per favore*.'

Valente, who, unlike the others had stepped to the front to present her report, never once stopped smiling or agreeing, as if, despite all, the occasion was going swimmingly.

'The student,' she said, 'has been diligently establishing a bibliography and carefully circumscribing the exact area of his interest prior to a period of study at the University of Austin, Texas, where there are archives that should yield original results.'

'We will see about that,' Ottone observed. 'We must never forget that all travel for research is paid from restricted and quite precious funds.'

Valeria was the last to be assessed. Furlan began to talk from three or four rows behind her, in a brisk, reassuring tone. He outlined her area of study, the articles she had written, spoke of her focus on Congo, the largest French-speaking country in Africa, where she intended –

'Who else is following our little Lucanina?' Ottone interrupted.

'I am.' James raised his hand.

'Ah.' The Rector met his eyes and frowned. 'Our British friend is hardly an expert on francophone Africa, I wouldn't have thought.'

'I am helping Dottoressa Lasala establish a proper methodology,' James explained.

Ottone hesitated, raised his eyes theatrically to the ceiling, then lowered them to examine his nails. 'It's all too cosy,' he pronounced. 'Too intimate, too complacent. There will be no further trips abroad without my express approval.'

'Actually, Rector, Lasala is the only student who has not yet been abroad ...'

'From now on, ladies and gentlemen, each candidate will be followed by a mini-college of six supervisors who will assign work, all of them, read work, all of them, and all produce a joint report that they will all, repeat all, without exception, sign off on. Then and only then can a student move on to the next year of the doctorate and receive the next year of their scholarship. *Dottori* and *dottoresse*, you will be given notice of your respective supervisors in the coming days, after which you will go *immediately* to see all of them to discuss your research and writing. Colleagues, this university needs to get serious.'

The Rector stood up and swept out of the classroom, quickly followed by Modesto. At once the atmosphere changed. As if a sudden infantile vitality had rushed into the company, silence gave way to chatter and even giggles. Valeria's friends too were grinning and chuckling beside her. But she felt emotionally exhausted and utterly confused as regards her duties and aims. Why am I even doing this? she wondered.

Ten days later she came back to Milan and tried to see the six professors who had been named as her supervisors. One, however, the youngest, who taught Television Journalism, did not reply to her emails. Modesto responded politely to explain that she was unavailable but asked to be remembered to Valeria's great-uncle in Rome and promised she would read with interest any work she might send. It was not necessary, however, for them to meet in person.

Professor Preti, who was apparently in charge of the six, saw Valeria for a few minutes in an office decorated with posters of conferences at which he had spoken.

'I know nothing of Francophile journalism in Africa,' he told her frankly. 'It is madness making me your main supervisor. No doubt you understood that. One of the Rector's whims. Naturally you will be working with Furlan as before. He seems to have an excellent head on his shoulders.'

'And the report?'

'Report?'

'I believe there has to be a report on my work which all six supervisors have to sign before I can pass the year and get my grant.'

'Yes, right. Well, you must write that report yourself, of course,' he said. 'I wouldn't know what to say. Email it to us for eventual rectification, then come by during office hours for our signatures.'

When Valeria returned to Milan some weeks later for the signatures, she had to stay two days longer than she expected to track down Marcello Masini, the TV Journalism man. Caught without a place to stay, she phoned her old room-mate Costanza who let her sleep on the sofa in the flat she was now sharing with the middle-aged owner of a gym called Energy. 'Don't mention Massimo,' she whispered as Valeria got out of the lift. Her boyfriend in Piacenza.

Woken by a flushing toilet in the middle of the night, Valeria felt disheartened. Why was it taking everyone so long to grow up? Why didn't Costanza leave her boyfriend in Piacenza or go and live with him? Why wasn't she herself living with Michele? Or even talking about living with him? Why did she have to keep phoning back to Bari to check that Carlo was all right, then home to tell Mother that he was all right, then answer a call from Zia Lella to tell her that *she* was all right. When I'm not all right, Valeria thought. I'm not all right at all. And how could she ever say anything original about francophone Africa if she was not to be allowed to go there herself and experience the place?

The following day she persuaded the department secretary to give her Masini's phone number and left a message on his answer service. When he did not reply, she phoned again, and again, and at the third attempt got a response. He was busy, Masini said, but if she could drop by his house, could she? he would gladly sign the report.

The place was in a rather noble building in the Brera area. Old families, serious money. Valeria had been anxious about visiting the man alone in his home, but as it turned out he was looking after his two-year-old child. His wife was curating an exhibition in Venice, he explained, and signed the report cheerfully, without so much as glancing at its content, the little boy grabbing at his arm as he did so.

Some days later, intrigued by a TV programme entitled *The Right to Study*, Valeria saw Masini talking earnestly about the lack of democracy in educational institutions, and the need to *colmare questo vuoto* – fill this void – at all costs. 'Fill this void,' she repeated to herself. She found herself mouthing the words for days. 'Fill this void.'

PRESENZIARE

Years later it would occur to Valeria that the shape of her life had been determined by two academic conferences: the first, though frustrating, had had wonderfully positive consequences; the second, though stimulating, catastrophic repercussions. But that was eight months down the road.

Meantime, nobody knew why the linguists' annual conference was to be held in the remote location of Madonna del Buon Cammino in the dusty landscape of the Alta Murgia national park. It wasn't the easiest place in the world to get to. Valeria, who had now been officially invited to speak at the concluding round table, met Furlan and Cecilia Tamara, the Sicilian researcher, off the day's first flight from Milan in the arrivals lounge at Bari airport, where, at the express request of the Rector, it seemed, they were to be met by a driver to take them the forty kilometres inland to Madonna del Buon Cammino.

The young man presented himself in jacket and jeans – it was February – took them outside to a rather dilapidated Skoda and proceeded to drive hard through the heavily trafficked roads around the southern town. Cecilia sat up front and Valeria and Antonio in the back, all listening to the driver's constant patter, which was of the I'm-a-survivor variety, I can get by any how, any way, no matter how hard times are. He pointed out businesses along the circular road that had closed down in recent years, including a petrol station he had worked in. One of three or four petrol stations he had worked in. Not to mention a warehouse sharing depot. Laughing, he invited Cecilia to open the glove compartment and pull out a scatter of business cards. Fabrizio Fanelli, Authorised Taxi Service; Fabrizio Fanelli, Authorised Night Nurse; Fabrizio Fanelli, Registered Plumber; Fabrizio Fanelli, House-hold Clearing Services, With Discretion. References. Fabrizio Fanelli, Funeral Assistance, With Discretion. References. It seemed there was no service the young man with jet-black hair and a gold chain round his neck was not authorised to carry out, with discretion, and the assurances of satisfied clients.

'Do you really do all those things?' Cecilia enquired.

'And more! If you could register yourself for burglary, I'd do it!'

'That's called politics where I come from,' Cecilia joked.

Valeria was surprised how flirtatious the young woman was being, compared to the rather dry, correct figure she cut at the university.

'Last night I was sitting up with some old guy with Alzheimer's and a broken hip,' Fabrizio continued.

'But you slept, I hope?' Cecilia asked.

'Here and there.' Fabrizio Fanelli let the wheel go a split second so that the car took a small swerve.

'*Cristo!*' Turning to the back, Cecilia said, 'We should be ashamed of ourselves, having such cushy jobs.'

'For as long as we do,' Antonio observed.

'You'll be OK,' she told him. 'Now he's inviting you to conferences.'

Valeria noted that Cecilia didn't seem at all concerned about her own position, though she too only had a temporary contract. And neither of the others seemed concerned about her.

But perhaps she was wrong. Turning to her left, she caught Antonio looking at her. He didn't turn away but lowered his voice to ask, 'What would you do, Valeria, if you had to leave the university?'

She shook her head. 'No idea.'

Cecilia laughed. 'Marry a millionaire. Or a *mafioso.*'

'Same thing, isn't it?' the driver quipped.

Valeria felt a welling of emotion. 'I'd rather serve *ossobuco* in the cheapest trattoria in Milan,' she announced.

'*Bravissima!*' Fabrizio Fanelli cried, turning from the driving wheel for a fraction longer than seemed safe. His girlfriend was a waitress, he said. '*Affanculo i miliardari e i mafiosi. Anche i politici.*'

'*E i baroni,*' Antonio added.

'Why, what have the *baroni* done to you?' Cecilia asked, apparently with real curiosity. 'I think it's too easy to criticise these people. They had to get where they are.'

'What haven't they done?' Fabrizio demanded, imagining the question was meant for him. 'Made the world the *schifo* that it is.'

Valeria turned to Antonio and found he was still looking at her. As their eyes met he raised an eyebrow as if to ask something, silently.

The venue wasn't in Madonna del Buon Cammino itself, but in a brand-new conference centre perhaps a kilometre beyond and with a four-star hotel attached. 'We opened last week,' the man in reception explained to Antonio and Cecilia as they took their respective keys. 'You'll be the first ever guests in your rooms.'

Waiting for them in the lounge, since she would be sleeping at her mother's home, Valeria understood that the conference was being held here as a favour to whoever had opened the centre. To get it off the mark. No doubt at a discount. Ottone was a big man in Puglia. Very likely he knew the investors. Then she thought how ugly it was always to be thinking in this way, always seeking to understand the secret things behind every public arrangement, and pictured instead Antonio's blond moustache and that wryly raised eyebrow. He was a good twelve years older than her. What question could he be asking?

The conference hall had the atmosphere of some modern chapel or airport prayer room. The podium was polished wood, the chairs upholstered in a soft lime green, there was a general smell of fresh masonry. But the mood could not have been more different than that miserable *collegio di dottorato* Valeria had attended some months before. Giving the opening address, Ottone was in high spirits, complimenting everyone on their distinguished careers, their wonderful publications, their brilliant minds, setting a tone of collective, almost euphoric, self-congratulation. And the talks were interesting for the most part. Valeria allowed herself to relax and enjoy. She took notes, even asked a question or two, saw all kinds of interesting connections with the ideas she had been pursuing. It had been a while since she had felt the excitement of so much intellectual input. Over coffee she discussed the politics of European language use in Africa with a man who was still teaching at the University of Tripoli despite all the troubles there.

Meantime, Ottone and various other older professors interrupted the speakers at liberty with playful remarks. There were anecdotes, reminiscences. The theme of Italy's marginal status in the global world did not seem to trouble anyone. One elderly lady spoke at length on the worldwide perception that, however unimportant, Italian was the most beautiful of all languages, and received loud applause. The timetable began to seem notional.

Lunch, more than an hour late, was a time for networking with thirty or so other academics from all over the country. At a pleasant buffet. Away from their home university, everyone seemed relaxed and expansive. Valeria felt she was getting on with Cecilia, for example, in a completely new way, though she had talked to her any number of times in Milan and constantly liaised with her over the web page of their research project. It was a serious mistake, the Sicilian woman observed at one point, for Antonio not to have signed up to Modesto's research project. *She* had. It was always going to be seen as a slight.

'But if it didn't interest him? Or he didn't have the time to do both?'

Cecilia shook her glossy head. 'You know that's not the point. Nothing would have been asked. It was a question of signing up. And he should have brought you in too. You could have read a book or two for Bettina.'

It seemed Professor Modesto got her assistants to read books for her and make easily digestible summaries.

'Can't she read herself?' Valeria laughed.

'She's busy running the department. She still does a couple of jobs for Beppe back in Foggia too.'

Valeria wasn't used to hearing the Rector and Head of Department referred to as Beppe and Bettina.

'When are you speaking?' she asked the Sicilian. Her own round table was the following afternoon.

'I'm not,' Cecilia said.

'No?'

'I came just to be here. *Presenziare*. I'm paying my own expenses.'

'Oh.' Valeria turned and saw Antonio in earnest conversation with two women in tightly permed middle age. He was definitely the best-looking man in the room. Could Cecilia have come for him?

A voice called. 'Lucanina!' To her immense surprise she and Cecilia were being invited by the Rector and Professor Modesto for a coffee in the hotel bar. 'Talk of the devil,' Cecilia chuckled. The Rector waved to Suzi Valente who had given a very clever paper on the excellent health of the Italian subjunctive. And to Antonio who was still with his female admirers. 'Come along, come along. Colleagues should stick together,' Ottone cried. Crossing the road, he actually took Valeria's arm, in a fatherly way. 'It's good to see one of our young people here,' he said. 'I'm sure you'll do us proud tomorrow. Are you going to take the opportunity to visit your family?'

Valeria said she was. She didn't say she was presently living in Bari.

'You must give them my warmest regards,' the great man said. 'Especially your Uncle Mattia.'

'My father's uncle,' she said.

They stood by the black marble counter drinking espressos, laughing and joking, as if the best of friends. Ottone wore a dark tweed suit and waistcoat, a red handkerchief in his top pocket and a gold pin on his blue tie. Smelling warmly of cigarettes and aftershave he traded anecdotes about the other elder members of the association. Suzi Valente laughed and poked fun. She told him his glasses needed cleaning and brushed some ash off his sleeve. Only Modesto seemed prim and distracted, twice not hearing questions addressed to her.

'Let's step outside for a smoke, if you don't mind,' Ottone proposed. 'Bill on 376,' he told the barman. In the mild air by the porch, he offered a packet of Dunhill Top Leaf and everyone took one but Modesto. The Rector shook his head:

'I fear Bettina's worried about her paper.'

Trying to be affable, Modesto admitted that departmental duties had prevented her from adding the kind of finishing touches that made the difference in a good talk.

'You'll blow 'em away,' Valente joked.

Valeria glanced at Antonio and he winked.

AL PREVALERE DELLA LINGUA ITALIANA

The novelty at dinner that evening, in the hotel dining room, was the presence of Ottone's wife, a heavy and heavily bejewelled lady, intensely feminine in an elderly way. She sat in the centre of one of two long tables with her husband on one side and Modesto on the other, the younger woman in her inevitable grey *tailleur* looking almost masculine in comparison, as if the southern lady had found herself a beau. To the other side of the Rector was Suzi Valente in a low-cut blouse, drinking a great deal and clearly enjoying life.

The arrangement was so intriguing that in moments phone messages were flying from remotest Puglia to Milan and back. *'The grande dame a sort of maîtresse?'* James responded to Antonio. *'With whip?'* wondered Federica. *'Could this explain Modesto's castigated look?'* Antonio suggested, tucking into a plate of lamb. *'Chastising as she has been chastised?'* suggested James, who was watching football with his son. *'Our submission and impotence make us childish,'* Alessio joined in rather gloomily. A few moments later he upped the stakes with, *'Us tittering while they triumph.'* *'Whining while they win,'* Federica proposed. *'Sighing while they succeed,'* James chipped in.

The lighting around the newly furbished room was so white and bright that the food on the table seemed oddly artificial. The decor of the hotel with its blandly international patina, extravagant chandeliers and expensive-seeming laminates would have been disquieting had anyone allowed themselves a moment's awareness of the abandoned countryside outside the window, the sagging fences and tumbledown housing. But no one did. The meal's main course now over, Ottone patted his lips with a napkin and stood to announce a toast.

'Ladies and gentleman, in the fifteenth century, pilgrims crossing our country built the sanctuary of the Madonna del Buon Cammino. Our Lady of Safe Passage, you might say. A place of refuge from wind, weather and bandits. Six hundred years on, we enjoy a quite different place of refuge on a different but not unrelated pilgrimage. Our association of linguists protects those who devoutly serve the Italian language, one of the great wonders of the world. So without more ado, *signore e signori*' – the great man lifted his glass – '*al prevalere della lingua italiana*' – to the ascendancy of the Italian language – '*sul Global Stage!*' Ottone finished to loud cheers of applause.

'Was that an Anglicism or a Frenchism?' Antonio whispered archly to Cecilia, for the Rector had pronounced '*stage*' *à la française*. The young woman, however, was on her feet clapping with fervour and showing off a long salmon evening dress on a willowy physique. From the other end of the table, Valeria watched and wondered. Perhaps Furlan was just another Don Juan, she thought. He and Cecilia in adjacent rooms very likely. Beds never slept in before, the receptionist had said. In a while her mother would be arriving to pick her up. She would make her evening call to Michele during the drive home. He had had an important exam today.

A half-hour later she got to her feet and made her excuses, very few because no one seemed interested. Nor had anyone made her an object of their networking. Still, no sooner had she crossed the lobby and passed through the sliding glass doors out into the cool evening than Antonio slipped out behind her, pulling on his coat. To smoke, he said. 'It's too ridiculous, isn't it, that Ottone uses an anglicism to toast the Italian language. The global stage, for heaven's sake.'

Valeria accepted a cigarette and confessed she had wondered if he had meant it as a joke. Then breathing out the first puff of smoke, she said, 'Sometimes, I think I should just give up now, while I still have time to find another career.'

Her phone rang as she was speaking. Her mother had got lost, it seemed. She would be another ten minutes or so. 'My mother's the only person who gets lost more often now she has a satnav,' Valeria laughed. In truth she felt like crying. There was such a mismatch between the life she aspired to and the reality of her circumstances.

'You mustn't give up,' Antonio said quietly. 'I've almost given up a dozen times, but it's worth holding on if you have a passion for what you do.'

He suggested she come back into the hotel if her mother was going to be a while. It wasn't warm out here. But she said she'd rather wait outside. The company had tired her. She'd been talking to a woman who clearly thought it was a waste of time studying the use of French in Africa. Or Africa in general. And who seemed to think of the Italian south as part of Africa. 'She kept saying, "But in the south you do this, don't you. In the south you think that." As if we were foreigners.'

Antonio said he would wait with her. They could walk to the village maybe.

'Won't they notice you're gone?'

He looked at her and raised an eyebrow as he had in the car.

They began to walk along the road in the cool evening. The country could hardly have been more nondescript: cement walls around flat fields of ageing olive trees, the occasional low house with a cluttered vegetable garden and makeshift scarecrow, scaring no one. No kerbs, no pavements. Cracking asphalt. A chastened, subdued, gritty world.

'Is the sanctuary worth seeing?'

There was a sign pointing left.

'Huge car park and small schlocky chapel,' she said.

They walked in silence for a while in the breezy winter dark until Antonio asked her why she was living in Bari these days; surely it

269

would make more sense to be in Milan. Valeria explained about her brother. He still needed company, she said. And she could find all the books she needed at the university library in Bari.

Valeria's mother phoned again to say she was already at the hotel, and they turned to hurry back.

'*Dottor Furlan, mia madre*, Carmela.' Valeria did the honours.

Her mother was at her worst in these situations, nervously smoothing out her skirt, afraid of showing her ignorance. 'Ah, I've heard so much about you,' she began, shaking his hand with both of hers. Her voice was warm and hoarse. 'What an honour, Professore. I'm so grateful for all you're doing for Valeria, really. It's so –'

'I'm not a *professore*,' Antonio said rather abruptly. 'Not yet.'

The older woman began to invite the academic to come and visit their home, since he was so near. Really it was only half an hour in the car. Tomorrow perhaps. They could prepare something special. *Pasta con le vongole*. Or –

'Mamma, he has a flight.'

'We're so much in your debt, Professore.'

Offering a smile, Antonio was apologetic. He really couldn't make it. 'But why don't we have breakfast together tomorrow, *signora*, when you bring Valeria? There's bound to be a café in the village piazza. At eight thirty. I like to take a walk in the morning.' He bowed and hurried into the hotel.

Valeria was astonished. So much so that she forgot to phone Michele on the ride home, with the result that he called her just as she was climbing into bed.

He had got thirty, he said, but he had been hoping for a *lode*. Then he wanted to talk to her about politics and corruption, but she told him she was tired.

LINGUA FRANCA

The following morning Antonio was in the small piazza before them, sitting outside the only café. Four rickety tables with plastic chairs. They were fifteen minutes late, as was to be expected.

They ordered coffees and *cornetti* and Antonio insisted on orange juice for everyone. Carmela was dressed and made up this morning. Her earnest voice, quick smiles and intense determination to please, leaning across the table, touching the young academic's wrist, were so embarrassing that Valeria withdrew into silence, watching the blond Furlan as he nodded and smiled at her mother's inevitable spiel about the joys and woes of Basilicata. Finally, he said, 'Signora Lasala, there is something I wanted to talk to you about.'

Again the women were taken aback. Antonio pushed his plate away and sat back. He had kept his raincoat on over a suit and tie, for he would be speaking first. Everyone knew it was important to look smart for the Rector.

'Signora Lasala, your daughter needs to move back to Milan at once, urgently, if she is to make anything of this doctorate programme. I felt I should warn you of this personally. She needs to be seen around. She needs to be available to assist professors when they have to miss a lesson. Otherwise, this period of study is going to be all time wasted.'

As he spoke, Valeria's mother did everything a body can do to show respect and assent. Is that so? Ah, I see. No, you're right. It's so good of you to tell us this. She leaned across the table nodding and murmuring, her perfume settling over the breakfast like a mist.

'So perhaps some other arrangement needs to be found for her brother,' the academic concluded.

Signora Lasala sighed. 'If only he would come home,' she said.

Back at the conference, Valeria could barely concentrate. Antonio spoke about the determination of the French to keep control of the way their language was spoken and written at global level, so different from the English tendency to surrender their tongue to whatever mouth chose to chew on it. As he stood at the lectern, Valeria watched his mouth, which was pale behind his golden moustache, authoritative, without being emphatic. When he finished his presentation right on time even Ottone joined the applause.

Professor Modesto, the other contributor on the panel, chose to speak sitting down behind the big table on the podium. She coughed and made some preliminary remarks, fussing with a PowerPoint that wouldn't load up. Her lips were pursed and brow wrinkled. With the PowerPoint loaded, she skipped a couple of slides saying she did not wish to go over her time. There was always too much to say. She brought a Word file up on the screen and took a while to find two quotations in what looked like a rather long article. Then the text, all in italics, was too small for the audience to follow and had to be expanded. Being a Mac person, Professor Modesto explained, she wasn't used to Microsoft. Again she apologised for these *inconvenienti* of modern life. Now the text wouldn't fit on the screen. Speeding up, and slightly lowering her voice, she read a very long sentence, perhaps fifteen lines, mentioned a Russian name twice, then switched back to the PowerPoint, skipping a few slides that were not, she said, 'altogether essential'. Only when she showed one with a comic example of Chinglish – a photo of a food product and the caption 'Explodes the large intestine' – did Valeria realise it was the same PowerPoint she had used at the Inauguration two years ago. 'The lingua franca thus – but how am I doing for time?' the professor interrupted herself. 'I fear I am already over my limit. Am I?' She raised her eyes to look to the chair whose kind smile indicated that she was indeed a good ten minutes over. 'Ah. Slaves of time! But I will conclude here then. The lingua franca thus constructs a competitive international community whose discreet internal feedback modality guarantees a complex hierarchical displacement of autochthonous linguistic strategies.'

In the front row Ottone got to his feet to applaud and the listeners behind him took his cue. But in the ensuing panel Q&A all the questions from the floor were directed at Furlan who spoke eagerly and fluently. After the fourth or even fifth question specifically for Furlan it would have become embarrassing had not Cecilia Tamara raised her hand. She had very much appreciated Professor Modesto's learned talk, she said, particularly her fascinating consideration of terminological categorisation in different varieties of pidgin English. However, her question was, if this supposed lingua franca, English, was really spoken so differently in the many different countries that used it, could it really be called a lingua franca at all?

Modesto puckered her brow and pursed her lips. Her hair, as ever, was pinned tight to her face. She was glad, she said, such an intelligent question had been asked. The implications of course were enormous. The Italians with their many dialects knew better than other nations how much a language could divide as well as unite. 'I'm from Foggia myself,' she confided, 'and find much of what I hear spoken in Palermo or Brescia incomprehensible, *n'est-ce-pas*? Though that is hardly the worst of it.' She smiled. 'Is that, then, one has to ask, the case with speakers of Chinglish, Spanglish and Franglais? There is clearly an important opportunity for research here and an urgent need to establish a working bibliography.'

Surely, Valeria thought, I can't do worse than that when my turn comes.

In the event, she didn't have a chance to find out, since her turn never came. There were eight of them at the round table, the last session of that Friday afternoon, all junior colleagues from universities. Each had just ten minutes to speak. Scheduled for three thirty, they started at four. Many of those attending the conference had already left. A coach was due at five thirty to take people to the airport. Sixth on the programme, Valeria wasn't aware of a problem until the second speaker took twenty minutes and the third half an hour. The chair, an elderly Sardinian woman, suggested they might speed up, but now the Rector intervened with a long reflection that he had forgotten, he said, to make in his own talk. It had to do with the importance of ensuring government sensibility to the need for sustained funding for linguistic research in view of the aggressive competition from German and French language policies on the European scene. He had met the Minister of Culture himself recently and had made his point forcibly, but it could only help if others present were also made to lobby the appropriate authorities. And it would be terribly useful if someone would volunteer to coordinate such lobbying so that everyone could know who had said what to whom.

Two or three other professors raised their hands and spoke of the influential contacts they had either spoken to or planned to speak to and still other names were mentioned as targets of further lobbying in the event that anyone had access to them. Over-prepared, her brief and hopefully interesting talk on the tip of her tongue, Valeria wanted to scream. But she knew that a young person earns her place in the community by showing patience and respect. She sat and smiled while one by one members of the audience got to their feet and hurried off to collect their bags and check out of their rooms. So in the end there were barely a dozen people scattered around the hundred seats of the brand-new conference centre when, halfway through the fifth talk – Lingua Franca and Gender Equality – it was announced that the coach had arrived, so that the chair was sadly obliged, she apologised, to bring the meeting to a close.

The important thing was to be there, Antonio told her at the airport. *'Presenziare.'*

Cecilia and various others had already left on the flight to Milan. Antonio was waiting for a flight to Venice, whence he had a train to Padua.

'Come and wait with me and let's talk,' he said, 'if you have time.'

Valeria sighed. She was in no hurry to get back to the small flat and Carlo.

'We still haven't discussed a strategy for getting Ottone to agree to your going to Africa for a semester.'

They drank a glass of wine at the airport bar and spoke of the exams she would have to do in the summer. They would be a formality, he thought, and she laughed and told him she felt it had been unwise of him to make Modesto look so second-rate at the panel. 'If you really want them to let me go to Africa, you'll have to do a bit more to get Modesto to like you.'

Antonio looked hard at her, then smiled. 'Right,' he said, 'I didn't think. But you too. You'll have to get yourself back to Milan if you want to make progress. You can't throw your whole career away to hold your brother's hand, just because your mother dreams of keeping the family together down south.'

Valeria felt such a powerful cocktail of emotions rising that she couldn't respond. I'll take the bus to the beach, she thought, and give my famous conference talk to the fish. Then Antonio's gate came up on the departure board. 'Time to go,' he said, but as they got to their feet and gathered their bags, she checking that her phone was in her pocket and wondering if there was any shopping she should do, he bent down towards her and turned an ordinary goodbye brush of cheeks into a kiss on the mouth. Startled, she was returning the kiss before she knew it. Neither had their arms free, but they stood perhaps thirty seconds, glued by the lips only. Then he broke off and put his bags down and his arms around her and they kissed deeply until she was struggling to be free; she pulled away and said she was sorry but she couldn't, she really couldn't. She had a boyfriend, she said. She wasn't a cheat. 'This isn't me.'

UN SANTO IN PARADISO

What should be public tends to be kept secret, while what should be private is broadcast from the rooftops. So it goes. Back from his summer holidays James heads up to the fourth floor to deal with a matter of some urgency. Modesto is not in her office. She will be present on Wednesdays, Thursdays and Friday mornings, the secretary says. The rest of the week she spends at her other job, in Foggia.

Why, James demands of the secretary, has Franca De Sanctis been allowed to move her course on journalistic sources to the second semester, after Christmas? It should be obvious that this is a crucial component of the first semester.

Modesto's secretary, Gaetano, is a fleshy young man with glassy hyperthyroid eyes and an anxiously diligent manner.

'I'm sorry, Prof,' he says. 'Hardly for me to say.'

James knows this. He knows his question was a form of impotent complaint. He is standing at the open door of the department's admin offices where Gaetano sits opposite a petite creature from Calabria – Tania, who is Ottone's personal secretary. As always, he is aware of a certain uneasiness in the room. The secretaries of the two powerful allies do not trust each other.

James hesitates. He feels he needs to sort out this problem quickly, before lessons start. He feels that if he can't ensure a certain logic in the organisation of the courses it is pointless his being course coordinator.

Tania's phone rings. Her mobile, not her desk phone. She glances at the little screen, jumps to her feet and hurries out of the office, a soft *'pronto'* on her lips. Immediately Gaetano's manner changes. *'Entri, entri,'* he beckons, getting to his feet and lurching across the room to close the door. The young man has a club foot.

'Prof,' he says now with an earnest expression, 'please, don't even *try* talking to *il capo* about it.' Gaetano always calls Professor Modesto *'il capo'*. 'It's not worth it. She won't change her mind.'

James sits down on a swivel chair opposite Gaetano and at once feels sorry for the young man, an ex-student of his who should have gone on to better things.

'Tell me,' he asks.

Gaetano hesitates, grimaces, doesn't speak.

'De Sanctis,' James insists, 'hasn't written the article she was supposed to write for our research project. She never makes any effort to integrate her course with the other courses in the degree. She doesn't tutor any student theses. If you could tell me what's going on, I could decide whether it's worth making the effort to speak to Professor Modesto.'

'Prof,' Gaetano says, 'what if we run into each other for coffee after lunch?'

James stands, moves to the door and opens it wide so the boy can see that no one is there, then closes it again.

'Prof!' Gaetano is appreciative. 'Whenever De Sanctis wants something, or more usually when she doesn't want to do something that she's been asked to do, the Rector gets a phone call from a certain person. Right? He passes that call on to Modesto, saying that she, as Head of Department, is responsible for De Sanctis's duties; and *il capo* passes the call on to me saying that I must have made some kind of mistake distributing the various department duties. So then I have to listen to a tirade from this certain person for about fifteen minutes before promising to arrange things as De Sanctis wants.'

'Un santo in paradiso,' James says.

'Right.' The excitement of betraying his trust brings a little colour to Gaetano's cheeks.

'So can we know,' he asks, 'who the holy man is and what other miracles he has performed? I just need to understand whether there's any point in tackling Modesto.'

Gaetano shakes his head. 'I'm sure Professor Galli knows.'

'Oh, come on!'

'*Il capo* would –'

'*Il capo* won't know.'

The secretary hesitates. 'A Rector.'

The two look at each other across Gaetano's desk.

'In a prestigious university.'

The young man twists his mouth in a see–what–I–mean face.

'OK,' James reflects, 'so some other Rector – correct me if I'm wrong – has organised a *concorso* in his university for someone whom our Rector is protecting, hence he, the other Rector, is in a position to dictate how we treat his lover who very likely has her job here thanks to this ... exchange. Hence my students have to follow their courses in the wrong order.'

Gaetano's features shift into a that's–about–it look.

'So there's nothing to be done.' James sighs and shakes his head. Then his attention is caught by a package on the boy's desk, in silver wrapping paper with a red ribbon.

'Do I have to say Happy Birthday?'

'It's not for me.'

'It's on your desk.'

Gaetano gets to his feet, picks up the package and unlocks a wall cupboard where, among stacks of paper and envelopes and bottles of photocopy toner and suchlike, three or four other bright packages wink on an upper shelf.

'Beginning of a new term,' the young man says. 'Always time for presents.'

★

He had been so happy, James reflects, riding the lift down to the less rarefied atmosphere of the first floor, during the summer break. Back in his office he considers resigning his position as coordinator. He is not paid for it. What has the job brought him if not an awareness of all the reasons why things don't work at the university? Before accepting an administrative responsibility, he knew nothing about what went on behind the scenes. He was happy. Now with each new issue, he discovers hidden obstacles, vested interests and veiled vetoes. He tries to bring them out into the open at department meetings, but his objections are ignored. 'You must be careful what you say,' Modesto warns from her place on the podium, speaking into a microphone. 'You cannot know the deliberations that occur at the level of the Board of Directors.' 'Perhaps you could tell us,' James suggests. Without a microphone his voice sounds weak. 'These matters are reserved,' Modesto says, 'this is a private company.' 'But it is also a university,' James insists. 'It requires government authorisation and is obliged to conform to university regulations.' 'You must be careful what you say,' Modesto repeats.

Is this a threat? If James forces a vote, he finds he is the only person voting against Modesto. Being initiated into a position of power, or supposed power, has merely shown James that power cannot easily be exercised, or not in the way it is supposed to be exercised. There are Italian Prime Ministers who have made that observation.

Wouldn't it be better to resign altogether then?

James can't decide. Perhaps he still entertains half an illusion that one day, maybe, they will let him do a few of the things he feels ought to be done to make this degree course work. But why should he care about that if others don't?

Thwarted, in the administrative side of his work, he has been dedicating more and more energy to the research project on European journalism worldwide, reading mountains of material, posting reflections on the project's web page, discussing matters with Federica and Alessio and Antonio and Cecilia and even the PhD student Valeria

Lasala, who has turned out to be eager, efficient and sharp. Papers have been called in. Some have arrived and a few are halfway good. An ambitious conference has been organised. The head of the German Press Association has agreed to come. The editor of *Le Monde* likewise. The European Commissioner for Culture. The president of the World Association of Newspapers and News Publishers. The head of the UK's Society of Editors Press Awards. Plus a half-dozen opinion-makers and professors from the LSE, Heidelberg and Barcelona. Even the editor of *Corriere della Sera*.

James and Federica can hardly believe they have managed to put together such an impressive group of speakers. At the beginning it seemed a pipe dream. But bit by bit, telling this important figure that the other even more important figure had already agreed to come, offering two nights in a hotel in Milan and the possibility of networking with other important folk, it has been done. James is excited. Perhaps he is reluctant to resign his position as coordinator because he feels the conference may change his profile at the university. Ottone will be pleased to see such big names coming together at the institution he governs. James will become a more important figure in the academic community he has served for so long. Is it wrong to want that?

CECILIA

Three people are waiting to see him on the first floor, where he is now late for office hours: Cecilia, Valeria and a heavily bearded student. He gives the two young women appointments for later and sees the student first. He's a troubled boy who is seriously *fuori corso*. He has come to ask if he can resume a thesis he started three years ago and gave up. He has had big personal problems, he says, but hopes he has now put them behind him.

James knows at once that the boy has not put these problems behind him. He's unsettled, crossing and re-crossing his knees, squinting right and left. On the other hand, someone who manages to confess his difficulties may at least be confronting them. Choosing his words carefully, James asks the student if he feels he is receiving proper support and the boy says, yes, he is seeing an analyst.

'Good. Let's go back to your thesis, then.'

James opens his computer and calls up their correspondence of two years before. But the student hasn't finished talking about his personal problems. The analyst, he says, has been explaining to him that having moved house and region frequently as a child he never developed that core group of friends, *la storica compagnia*, essential for structuring adolescent identity; as a result he had difficulty fitting in at the university and began to feel vulnerable and paranoid. What makes him confident

281

that he is getting over things now is that in the last year he has formed two steady friendships.

'I'm pleased,' James says, wondering if an English analyst would ever have come to such a conclusion. For his thesis the boy had chosen to contrast disaster reporting in Italy and America; how terrorist attacks are described, photographed and headlined. Not a bad idea. Apparently, the Italians always report a higher body count. James sends the student away with some simple instructions. 'Let's get this finished soon now,' he says.

With Cecilia he has to talk over some organisational issues, vis-à-vis the conference, and, delicately, to ask about her own paper for the event, which she still hasn't sent in. It's late in the day.

Cecilia is her usual efficient, contained self. She has a blue skirt and jacket, a helmet of glossy hair, the merest touch of make-up on a dark complexion. Pulling out papers from a folder, she explains the arrangement they have come to with the hotel for visiting speakers. She has phoned four restaurants about the closing dinner and is awaiting quotations. She has called in programme bios and abstracts from all the speakers and shown the programme layout as proposed by Federica to the printer. Delivery will be seventy-two hours after receipt of the finalised text.

'Brilliant. And your paper?'

'It's done,' Cecilia says.

'Did you send it? I don't remember seeing it yet.'

The young woman says coolly. 'I'll give it on the day.'

'But you know we're taking a look at all of them, Cecilia, to check the English and so on.'

What James means is that he and Federica, as project leaders, want to avoid one of those situations where a home speaker gives a paper so ridiculous as to bring the university into disrepute. Fortunately, Modesto has said she is too busy to offer a talk of her own, while Ottone will be away at a conference elsewhere.

Cecilia frowns. 'I don't want to show my paper before the day.'

James is taken aback.

'I am concerned other members of the committee will appropriate my ideas.'

James opens his mouth to speak, then closes it.

'It's happened to me twice before,' Cecilia insists. 'I send out a paper to a journal. It gets rejected, then I see my ideas appear in the same journal, under someone else's name.'

James has never had the impression that Cecilia's is an especially original or cutting-edge mind.

'If you are quite sure, you should have reported it. I believe ANVUR has a complaints department.' The Agenzia Nazionale di Valutazione del Sistema Universitario e della Ricerca is the body that watches over academic activities.

'If I file a complaint, no one will ever publish me again.'

James can't hide his exasperation. 'You're making me terribly curious about what you're actually going to say, Cecilia. Couldn't you let me have a peek?'

'I'm sorry but it's really too easy for journal editors to steal ideas from young people with no reputation and pass them on to their powerful friends.'

James does not believe that this happens in any regular way. On the other hand, it is the kind of thing a certain sort of person might suspect.

'Perhaps,' he can't resist tossing in, 'that's why Professor Modesto only publishes with journals where Ottone is on the editorial board. Do you think?'

'Very likely,' Cecilia replies. 'It's getting to the point where most people won't send to a journal if they don't know someone on the editorial board.'

'But you do know us, don't you?' James laughs. 'And actually, you owe your present research grant to our launching this project.'

Comes a soft knock at the door and Valeria pokes her head in.

'Think it over,' he tells Cecilia as she stands up to leave.

Valeria slips a red backpack from her shoulders, takes out a slim computer and pulls a chair to the desk.

'Someone seems pleased with themselves,' James observes. The young woman is all smiles and willowy ease.

'I've moved to Milan, permanently.'

'Ah.' He watches her as she fires up her computer. She wears no rings or bracelets. Tapping on the keys, her quick fingers are full of life.

'I wish the city had the same effect on me.'

'It's just that I don't have to travel any more. I'm getting a lot more work done, which makes me feel good.' She can't stop smiling. 'And I love Milan. Always have.'

Love was the important word in that sentence, James thought.

'Well, you'll be travelling again, pretty soon, I'm afraid,' he told her. 'I was speaking to Professor Preti and he now has an official invitation for you from the University of Dakar. At which point it gets hard for Ottone to keep saying no.'

Valeria was thrilled. Dakar was reputedly the best francophone university in Africa. 'Thank you so much.'

'Don't thank me. Preti has a contact there. I think the idea is that you go in the New Year, after we've got all the conference papers ready for publication.'

For half an hour they worked on the conference programme, deciding the order of the sessions and the speakers, discussing who should be asked to chair what. By now it was well past one.

'Want to eat?' James asked. 'In the canteen?'

But then checking his mail before leaving the office, there was a message from Federica addressed to all those involved in the organisation of the conference. So professor and PhD student read it together, half on their feet, standing over the screen. Essentially it was a reminder that both the programmes and the conference poster would have to be approved by the Rector's office before publication, meaning, as soon as possible. *'If nobody has any objection I'll submit it this afternoon,'* Federica wrote. However, she had added a PS.

'*Saw this today in a book called* Codes of the Underworld *by Diego Gambetta. He says, "Where promotions are based less on merit than loyalty, displaying incompetence credibly signals one's reliability."*'

Under the quotation was a winking emoticon.

'Fantastic,' James chuckled.

Valeria smiled too, but with a faint cloud in her eyes.

INNAMORATA

In the canteen, James chose chicken and rice. They queued at the till and found seats at a long table full of laughter and clatter. Chairs scraped and friends called to each other. There was a good warmth in the air.

'What part of Milan are you in?' he asked.

'Isola,' she said.

'Alone?' he risked. He was suddenly interested in the girl. She seemed transformed.

'Boyfriend,' she said at once.

'To be frank,' he told her, 'you've got *innamorata* written all over your face.'

'Have I?' The young woman flushed.

'Don't worry. It's charming.'

'Well, I am,' she confessed. Again the colour came to her cheeks.

'And what does the lucky man do? If I may ask?'

She hesitated.

'Sorry, I shouldn't ask.'

'He works at the university.'

'Better and better!'

'Oh, not *this* university.' She began to eat rapidly.

James pretended not to notice. After a moment, he said, 'Let's hope it's some fantastically powerful figure who can get you a great job.'

Mouth full, Valeria shook her head vigorously.

'No, no, that's not what I want at all!'

'Just joking.'

'To tell the truth, he's on contract himself.'

She stopped, so evidently worried she had said too much that James began to wish he hadn't enquired.

'But what about you?' she asked.

'Me what?'

'Where are you in Milan, Prof? With your family, I suppose.'

James explained that he lived with his son to the south of the city. 'I thought everyone knew I was divorced.' The boy was studying Fine Art at Brera. 'From what he tells me, it's chaos. But he loves it. And he has any number of girlfriends.'

Valeria frowned. 'I've always thought one was enough.'

'Right.'

James concentrated on his food. The conversation had unsettled him. Eventually, he wiped his mouth and offered, 'Funnily enough I was with a woman from Basilicata until recently. Same accent as yours exactly. But she was obsessed with going home and in the end she managed to get herself transferred to Melfi. Some administrative job.'

Valeria sighed. 'True. It's no reason for you ending your relationship, though. You could see each other some weekends and holidays. Basilicata's a great place to visit.'

'I don't believe in part-time love,' James observed. 'I'm an all-or-nothing guy.'

The girl caught the shadow in his eyes.

'Unfortunately, these days it seems to be more nothing than all.'

Suddenly she decided to confide.

'About that mail from Professor Motta. Her funny PS.'

'Yes?' James was happy to change the subject.

Valeria wiped her mouth, lined up knife and fork on her plate. 'I'm not sure it's a good idea sending mails like that to … to everyone.'

James frowned. Valeria made a face.

'Could be,' he said.

'What do you think?' he asked his son later.

'Someone in the mailing group is a spy. You're always saying there must be someone blabbing on you.'

'I thought it was Ricci.'

In his late fifties, Ricci taught a basic writing course in James's degree. The third time the students complained of his being tipsy at lessons James had tried to get something done about it, without success. Ricci was another with 'a saint in paradise'.

'But he wasn't on that mailing list?'

'No.'

The boy was packing a bag to go away for the weekend with his mother. Once a month the two would book a hotel in a distant town – Ravenna, Pisa, Arezzo – and spend a few days visiting the museums there. It seemed strange to James that a young man in his twenties who always had half a dozen girls in tow should take these regular holidays with his mother. But perhaps one had more than one girl in order to have none at all.

Valeria and Antonio also discussed her conversation with James.

'I almost let it out.'

'He's a friend. He wouldn't tell.'

'We mustn't. We'll be vulnerable.'

It was a conundrum. They were in love. Valeria had fired Michele just one week after the kiss, the now mythical airport kiss. She had told her boyfriend it made no sense. It was over. And she had left Bari to return to Milan. You can look after yourself now, she told her brother. You don't need a nurse. I'm not a babysitter, she told her mother. I love Carlo but I'm not going to ruin my life just in case he falls into depression.

Back in the northern town, she rented a single room in a miserable block of flats in Bovisa. It hardly mattered, because it wasn't more than a week before she found herself in Antonio's bed, and in his heart too, and he in hers. But he was one of her six doctorate supervisors.

'One year of secrecy,' she said.

'Six months of which you'll be in Dakar.'

They raised glasses of Prosecco.

'To Dakar!'

'I'll miss you.'

'You'll come and visit,' she told him.

James spent that Saturday and Sunday writing mails to the conference speakers, editing various papers again, thinking through the talk he planned to give for the hundredth time, making lists of journalists to contact, other academics to invite along, examining the details of the budget to see if there was anything left that could sensibly be spent. Even when he went running, to the south of the city, through fields of harvested maize on mud paths between black ditches and silver poplars, his mind was going over the conference timetable, the venues, looking for glitches, trying to decide whether a coffee break should be fifteen minutes or half an hour.

Come Sunday evening he was quite exhausted, turned in to bed towards midnight and immediately fell into a vivid dream. He was swimming through a sea of slime, in the dark. He could barely free his arms from the heavy liquid mud to make the strokes that would allow him to lift his head and breathe. The mud was getting thicker and thicker but somehow louder and louder too, and now his right arm really would not shift. He was sinking in sludge.

Suddenly his elbow jerked upward. His hand came out of a muddy tangle of sheets and reached for the ringing phone on the bedside table.

'*Pronto?*'

'You're not going to believe this, but the Rector just called me.' Federica's voice was quavering. James struggled to sit up.

'What? What time is it?'

'The conference is off,' Federica said. 'We have to cancel.'

PERFIDA ALBIONE

Sometime before these events, jokingly, over dinner, Federica's poet husband, Ernesto, had suggested that his wife's life was like a Cesare Pavese novel repeated over and over. There are eight such novels written between 1940 and 1950 and the pattern is always the same. The hero is an outsider. He, or sometimes she, is attracted to people living together in a tight-knit community and intensely engaged in some exciting project. It could be a couple planning a family or farm labourers at harvest time; a group of women setting up a fashion shop or a band of partisans planning a raid. Enthusiastic, the hero tries to join them, become part of their *compagnia*, or to start a relationship with one of its members. But no sooner is he, or she, involved than some terrible truth about the others is revealed. What appeared to be positive energy conceals a rape, a murder, an incest. People *together* are people with something to hide. Disgusted, fingers burned, the hero retreats to the sterile loneliness of his solitary world, where at least there is purity, at least there is integrity. 'The only difference with Federica,' Ernesto joked, 'is that she keeps going back and back.'

Years later, James would remember that conversation and start to think of the famous phone call from Ottone as the moment when, fingertips scalded, Federica began her long withdrawal from university life, renouncing any desire to climb the academic ladder or make a professorial career for herself. So, gradually the whole sad affair was to take on a clear trajectory and become understandable, to the point that one day they would laugh together by the canal over the inevitable *aperitivi*, remarking that at least she had not committed suicide, as Pavese eventually did. For the moment, though, in the immediate aftermath of that late-night phone call, James could do nothing but go over and over what she had told him.

The timing had been extraordinary. Eleven, Sunday evening. The forty-five-year-old professor of German had been cleaning her teeth, she said, when her husband knocked on the bathroom door holding her trilling phone, which had the words *numero privato* on the screen.

Who could it be? Given the late hour, Federica might perfectly well have chosen not to answer. Curiosity got the better of her. She rinsed her mouth and pressed the green button.

'Professoressa Motta!' Ottone began in a loud warm voice. 'Do excuse this intrusion, please. The fact is I have just been looking over the conference programme you sent me. It's remarkable.'

Federica couldn't remember how she replied. His voice and presence had obliterated hers.

'I hear such wonderful things about you, Motta,' Ottone went on. 'Excellent publications. Excellent student-satisfaction ratings. Just last week Professor Valente was telling me about a paper you gave in Florence, on translations from German during the Fascist period. Fascinating subject. Suzi was most enthusiastic.'

'I thought,' Federica told James, 'he meant to compliment us for the programme.'

'People speak very highly of you,' Ottone repeated. Then left a pause. Perhaps Federica said *grazie*.

'And I believed them.'

The tone had changed.

'I believed them,' Ottone repeated.

Now the pause was ominous. Shivering in her underwear, Federica took the phone into the sitting room so as not to disturb her husband who was climbing into bed.

'But I was wrong, wasn't I, Motta?'

Again the powerful man waited.

'I was completely wrong.'

Federica realised she was pressing her knees together, like someone afraid of peeing in their pants.

Ottone sighed theatrically. 'What did your masters teach you, Motta? Professor Ventura? Professor Scilli? They were serious people. I can't believe they didn't give you a decent education.'

Pause.

'Was it that they didn't teach you, or that you are incapable of learning? It must be one or the other, Motta.'

When James asked his friend how she reacted to this, Federica told him she had no idea. She was lost for words, standing half-nude in a corner so as not to be seen through the window. It was like being mugged in your own home.

'Respect, Motta. Didn't they teach you to show respect?'

'I should have told him to call back at a reasonable time,' Federica told James.

'Or is it our miserable *inglese*,' Ottone insisted, 'who has been giving you ideas of greatness? Eh, Motta? Our would-be Wellington?'

'I think,' Federica remembered, 'I finally got out something pathetic like, What have I done exactly?' However, her only reason for believing this was that she remembered so clearly his next words.

'What have I done? The miserable Motta has the effrontery to ask what she has done! *Exactly!* Are you trying to take me for a ride?'

Again she was speechless.

'It's not enough to make a complete fool of me, to invent a conference as a showcase for yourselves, to invite every swanky name you can think of, every *fottuta presidente* of every *fottuta associazione*, except of course your own Rector, except of course your own Head of Department, as if you owned the university that puts bread in your mouth, as if you could use it as an advertisement for yourselves; not enough to hand the opening address in front of all these bigwigs to a supercilious British turd, a presumptuous, puffed-up, insolent piece of foreign shit, who spits in the *minestra* he eats from, not enough to act as if your Rector *didn't exist*, as if your Head of Department *didn't exist*, no, you then have the effrontery to ask me *what you have done!* *Exactly.* You have the presumption to take me for a fool. An utter fucking fool.'

So this was the rub. The conference programme – *European Journalism in a Globalised World* – or rather the provisional draft of a possible programme, sent to the Rector's office precisely for the great man's approval, did not mention his name. Or the name of Professoressa Elisabetta Modesto, Head of Department. Federica had tried to object, she told James, or at least she seemed to remember having tried to object, that Modesto *had* been invited to speak at the conference but had declined, that the Rector himself had been informed of the dates of the conference some months ago and had said he would not be able to attend. But her excuses had been ignored. Or perhaps Ottone had talked her down, spoken over her.

'This is not how the world works, Motta. I did not get where I am now organising extravaganzas behind my superiors' backs. This is the worst kind of deviousness, vainglory, cockiness.'

He spat the words out.

'Condescension. Pomposity. Superciliousness.'

Pause.

'Dressed up as seriousness, what's worse. Dressed up holier than thou, more serious than thou.'

Pause.

'You northerners think you're so fucking superior. Don't you, Motta? So fucking correct. So fucking serious. So fucking focused on your so-called fucking studies.'

Pause.

'Fuck your seriousness, Motta. Fuck your fucking self-righteous talks on German translations under Fascism.'

Pause.

294

'*Chi se ne frega*, Motta!' Who gives a shit!

Pause.

'Remember who puts bread in your mouth, Professoressa. Remember where your easy fucking life getting paid to sit in nicely heated libraries comes from!'

It went on. Ottone was shouting, he was kicking an opponent who was down. There was no referee. Ernesto had come into the sitting room to see what was going on but did no more than raise an eyebrow in wonder. Federica was crouched in the corner, on the bare tiles.

'This conference is not going to be, Motta. Understand? It is not going to happen. Tomorrow you write to all your famous fucking friends and tell them it is off. Tell them you've had to cancel. Any air fares your international heroes have already paid for you will pay yourself. Is that clear? Or yourselves. You and your British accomplice. Any train tickets or hotel charges, you'll pay yourselves. You and the *perfida Albione*. You won't have a penny from the university. Is that clear? Then when you're ready, when *I'm* ready, you can come to my office and fucking apologise. On your knees.'

Ottone closed the call.

VERGOGNA

All night, James lay awake. Were they really going to call off the conference? He tried to imagine the emails, the phone calls. Were they going to tell the European Commissioner for Culture that at the last minute his trip to Milan was cancelled? And the editor of *Le Monde*. And the president of the World Association of Newspapers and News Publishers? Important people who had perhaps prepared a talk already, arranged to meet friends, booked a ticket at La Scala? Not to mention the flights they had paid for and expected to be reimbursed. Would he and Federica have to foot the bill from their own savings? Thousands of euros. What would life be like in the university henceforth?

Through the early hours James tried to understand how this had come about. Aside from comments to friends, he had never thought of himself as actively showing disrespect to the Rector, to the Head of Department. Not in the way he worked. At a push, he could no doubt recover the email proving that Modesto had been invited to get involved in the project and to speak at the conference. At a push, he could track down the exchange with the Rector's office about the dates for the conference, find the mail in which the Rector's secretary had said that the great man regretted that he would not be able to attend. But by nature James was suspicious of self-righteousness, most of all when he found it in himself. And gradually, going over the events that had led them, he and Federica, first to propose the project, then to try to run it in a rather different way from the way most research projects were run, then to organise a conference that was more ambitious than most end-of-project conferences – gradually it dawned on him that Ottone might have a point. The truth is, he acknowledged, we did not want Ottone and Modesto to be involved. We were only too glad when they showed no interest. We did not specifically warn them that we had invited major names to come to the university and that their absence would look odd.

Was this arrogance? A typically British arrogance? Or was it *vergogna*? On his part and Federica's. We are *ashamed* of working for Modesto, he realised. We didn't want intelligent folk from outside the university to see that we served Modesto. That we served Ottone. We are ashamed of the community we depend on. We hid our heads in the sand and hoped no one would notice. We were dreaming of a genuine, intellectual community, free from university politics. It had been a mistake. And maybe it was arrogance. But not something I could change in myself, James decided. Because I do feel superior, to people like Ottone and Modesto.

Was it time to leave then? To abandon Italy. To go home?

In the early hours, with no hope of sleep, James felt shaken to the core. Why am I here? he said out loud, in the dark. A person whom the Rector refers to as *perfida Albione*, your accomplice, the British turd.

But the university is not Ottone and Modesto, he quickly corrected himself. If anything they have hijacked the university. If anything you owe it to the university to oppose them, to *depose* them.

These were heady reflections. James tried to think seriously of going back to the UK, packing his bag, selling his flat. It didn't seem real.

Britain is no longer your home, he reflected. Britain has changed. Twenty and more years have passed. You have changed. There is no home to go back to.

And who was to say that such miserable goings-on might not equally well happen in the UK? Or if not the same things, things that were equally unpleasant and disheartening. You're in your fifties, he reminded himself. It's too late.

Towards five the first tram squealed by, rattling the windowpanes. James got up and walked around the apartment, looking into the mess of his son's room, staring at a photo or two, a painting he had of a landscaped English garden with a Gormenghast-style mansion in the background, beautiful and ominous. He went out onto the balcony and looked over the street corner where the traffic light flashed yellow through the night; to the left was a small park where respectable folk brought their dogs to shit, and youngsters traded drugs, or on hot evenings Arab women sat chattering with their children waiting for the air to cool. Then, as he leaned on the parapet, watching, telling himself once again that there was no way back now to that English garden and that Gormenghast institute, a van stopped and a man hauled up the steel shutters over the window of the corner café. They would be serving cappuccinos quite soon. With fresh croissants. As soon as they're open, I'll treat myself, James thought.

And he thought that the destiny of expats was to be constantly comparing the society they had left with the society they now lived in, growing less and less sure what the old world had been precisely as they grew more and more disillusioned with the society they had arrived in. Because life itself, perhaps, was a process of disillusionment.

From his balcony James watched the barman unloading trays of pastries from his van. His own favourite was *la brioche alla crema*. And a cappuccino with thick foam and cacao, warm but not hot.

James's mouth began to water and he smiled. The fact is you belong here now, he told himself. In Milan. You belong in this country, this street where you live with your son, this university where many fine people work and teach, and where you have some excellent friends, like Federica, who is going to need all the support she can get.

His mind went back to the problem in hand. Fight back, he decided. Contact the editor of *Corriere*. Ask him if the newspaper could host the conference. They must have a conference room in their building. Give them an interview explaining how absurdly the university was run. Do it.

For an hour and more, first showering, then sitting in the café, James grew bellicose. He began to feel strong and determined. But when he spoke to Federica later in the morning, she said no. 'If we do that we're really dead.' For the moment it was just disrespect, she said. 'But that would be war. And Ottone doesn't lose wars.'

'What can he actually do to us? He can't even fire us. We're protected by the law.'

'I don't want to find out what he can do.'

James was chastened. She had thought it over, Federica was saying, through the night. Perhaps there still was some room for manoeuvre, if only because when Ottone really thought about it he wouldn't want to risk the fallout in terms of the university's image, cancelling on all those important people.

'And so?' James asked. 'You think we should go and talk to him?'

'First to Modesto, use her as a go-between. Then to him.'

'OK. When?'

Federica sighed. 'It's better if I go alone.'

'But why?' James was exasperated.

'You're from a different world.'

So Federica knelt. And if the late-night phone call wasn't quite the end, bowing the knee was. Actually kneeling, deciding to kneel, before this odious man. It was the end. Afterwards she hurried to the bathroom and vomited. She sat in a cubicle for fifteen minutes before going down into the plaza to call James. Once again, he had to hear the dramatic events at second hand.

On the Monday Federica had apologised to Modesto who had spoken to Ottone who on the Wednesday afternoon conceded an audience. Federica had apologised, profusely. She had begged the Rector to spare the conference, to rearrange his schedule and give the introductory address himself; she had beseeched him to persuade

Modesto to give the first paper of the first session. She had agreed that she and James had behaved foolishly, arrogantly, too concentrated on their studies and their own careers to understand the politics of the thing and show proper respect for the university authorities.

Having gone over and over this in her head for the previous forty-eight hours, Federica had begun quickly and nervously. Ottone showed neither interest nor emotion. He took phone calls while she spoke. He made phone calls. He went out of the room and came back in. He leafed through the papers on his desk. He looked at his watch, flicking the cuffs of an expensive jacket, showing bright cufflinks. Every time she started speaking again he would half listen for a few seconds, then make another call, or press a button and speak to his secretary on the intercom, uttering a sharp remark, ordering up coffee. One coffee.

'Till finally I realised what he was waiting for and just did it,' Federica admitted. She had slid to the floor. Her knees pressed on the parquet. '*Perdono*,' she had whispered.

'You what!'

James was beside himself. When the call was over he hurried out into the street and walked aimlessly through the town, this wonderful town in his beautiful adopted country with its magnificent art, its food to die for. It was a sun-blessed autumn day, Milan was sublime in its gritty bustle and old-world elegance, and James was furious with regret. He should have been there! He would never have gone on his knees! His friend would not have gone on her knees if he had been there. He wouldn't have allowed it.

But of course that was why he hadn't been invited.

And maybe he was wrong. Maybe he had underestimated the power of these situations. Maybe he would have gone to his knees. And that would have been the final act in this seemingly endless process of changing skin.

James shook his head. At least the conference has been spared, he thought. There was that.

BUON GIORNO E BUON LAVORO

The conference was to go ahead, but ...

'I'm afraid I can't send out these emails,' the Language Department secretary said.

'I'm afraid we can't put anything on the homepage or in Facebook,' the girl in the web office told James.

'I'm afraid we can't print any posters for you,' the publications office warned Federica.

'No, we can't bring meals, or even coffee and biscuits,' the bar manager sighed.

Meeting James in the corridor, Professor Modesto's secretary, Gaetano, was explicit: 'All the secretarial and administrative staff have received orders that they must not help with your conference in any way. Pain of losing our jobs. Nor will any expense claim of any kind be accepted from you, beyond the flights and the hotels already paid.'

Later that week, Cecilia Tamara announced she had to return to Sicily for 'urgent family issues'. She would not be seen at the university again until the morning she gave her paper *Mapping Local, National and International Sources for Italian Newspaper Reporting*.

'At least you know who your spy was,' James's son observed.

So this was when Valeria Lasala became close friends with Federica and James. The research-project leaders had been entirely isolated. They shared the story of their humiliation with the young doctorate student. And with Antonio Furlan, of course. Meantime, without publicity, catering or logistical help of any kind it was perfectly possible that no one but the speakers themselves would actually come to the conference. The event had been permitted in order that it flop.

For three weeks the four friends worked day in day out, identifying possible attendees, finding addresses, sending out hundreds of invitations, studying the logistics of bringing the speakers from the hotel to the university without too much expense, negotiating a deal with a restaurant for a gala dinner that Federica and James now understood they would have to pay for themselves. But they would rather pay it, they decided, than let their guests down. They would pick up the speakers at their hotels, walk them to the metro and provide all the tickets themselves. They would seat them in the university café at coffee time and serve them and pay for them themselves. Likewise at lunch. They calculated the whole thing would set them back a thousand euros each. It seemed worth it, not to grant Ottone the satisfaction of their humiliation.

A new community formed. Valeria was invaluable. Antonio was invaluable. They worked the social media, built up mailing lists, dealt with their visitors' glitches, found students willing to accompany them here or there. They were encouraged by the positive side of the event and electrified by their loathing for Ottone and Modesto. Valeria in particular found the challenge exciting. The day before the conference she spent meeting speakers at the airport and driving them to their hotels in James's Fiat Punto. It felt good to be talking to the editor of *Le Monde* and the head of the German Press Association. At home with Antonio, the conference was the only topic of conversation. 'Do the others know about us yet?' Antonio wondered. 'Don't be tempted to tell them,' Valeria warned.

'After Dakar,' they agreed.

When the great day came, they were not allowed to put up signs in the university foyer directing attendees to the seminar room where the

conference was to be held. Valeria stood outside the main doors holding a piece of A3 paper with the conference title written in block
letters and directing anyone looking lost to the fourth floor. In the
event, after sending out almost a thousand invitations, there were just
enough people present to avoid embarrassment; fifty, or fifty-five in a
room for a hundred.

The Rector's condition for allowing the conference to go ahead was
that Professor Modesto must speak first. At least it would be over soon,
James thought. Glancing around the room, he realised that aside from
those engaged to speak, not a single member of the university staff had
come along to hear the European Commissioner for Culture.

Modesto fussed with papers and flash drive in her usual way, evok-
ing yet again the mystery of 'feedback loops in global identity
stereotyping'. No sooner had she finished than the Rector pushed
open the door and strode into the room. Could the two have synchro-
nised watches? The tall man came directly to the front and asked
James to move aside. Flicking out the sleeves of his jacket, he sat down
in the chair's seat and smiled to right and left with angry satisfaction.
'I know,' he began, having waited just long enough for everyone to be
apprehensive, 'that the conference language is English, but as Rector
of an Italian university speaking in Italy I will nevertheless address you
in Italian. Perhaps you will interpret for me, Bettina.'

'Of course.'

The Head of Department seemed nervous; the Rector spoke in
rapid bursts, then sat back as Modesto translated:

'I am afraid that an urgent commitment I have undertaken with our
Minister of the Public Instruction is not going to allow me a proper
participation in this interesting event.'

James smiled quietly.

The Rector frowned. He was speaking in Italian, he said, because
as an Italian linguist he wished to defend the language from what was
now an all-out assault from English. 'With all respect for our colleague, Her Majesty's subject,' he observed (and Modesto translated),

303

'the globalisation is a threat to the very same idea of a culture which is always based on the shared values and shared language of a peculiar people.'

Having made this emphatic statement, the Rector got to his feet, said, '*Buon giorno e buon lavoro,*' and left the room. The odd thing, James thought, was that had the man paid the slightest attention to his or Federica's research, he would have realised that on the question of globalisation and national culture they were in total agreement.

So began two and a half days of talks and discussions, a whirl of ideas and organisational hiccups, coffees and croissants, assertions and rebuttals, statistics and ideology. The European Commissioner for Culture painted a rosy picture of a world that was ever more an international space and ever more at ease with foreigners and foreign cultures. The professor from the LSE argued fervently that on the contrary each European country was locked into an internal debate and largely closed to voices from outside. The editors of *Le Monde* and *Corriere della Sera* protested, but good-naturedly. Alessio had everyone in stitches with comments from famous philosophers on the shortcomings of neighbouring nations. Federica spoke lucidly of the discrepancy between Germany's economic power and cultural insignificance. Cecilia appeared, mapped sources for Italian journalism, did some networking, and disappeared.

Friday morning the research students presented their work. Valeria was efficient, despite nerves. Likewise a young man from Toulouse who argued that European journalism had been more cosmopolitan under Napoleon than at the present time. Overall, James reflected, a lot of execrable English had been spoken, but in good heart. And he was impressed by how faithfully the speakers came to each other's events and how at ease they seemed with the modest cafés and bars he and Federica were obliged to choose for their refreshments. No doubt spring helped. The northern Europeans were happy to get a flavour of Milan. Most were staying on over the weekend at their own expense.

And quite suddenly it was over; all they had worked towards for months was done and finished and behind them. Late Friday afternoon, the four organisers – the Gang of Four, as they now called themselves – took a table together by the Naviglio, ordered a bottle of Prosecco and sat down to debrief and unwind. They basked in the sunshine and raised their glasses. 'I am so happy with you,' Antonio told Valeria in her arms that night and she said, 'Me too, Toni.' None of them had paid attention to an email earlier in the day announcing an addition to the agenda of the following Monday's *consiglio di dipartimento*.

SCAMBIO DOCENTI

This was late April. Very few colleagues were present at the *consiglio* because the following day, the 25th, was Liberation Day, a public holiday marking the end of the Fascist regime and the German occupation in 1945. Hence it was understandable that many were taking the Monday off. Had they not been distracted by the conference, James later reflected, they might have realised how odd it was to hold a *consiglio* on that day.

Still, James was there, Federica was there, Cecilia was there, and Preti, the old Philosophy professor, and Suzi Valente and four or five junior colleagues, close allies of Modesto's. This wouldn't have been enough for a quorum were it not for the rule that anyone who justified their absence prior to a *consiglio* was counted as present: Antonio Furlan, for example, who had sent an email a few days earlier pleading a doctor's appointment when in fact he was taking advantage of the post-conference weekend and public holiday to show Valeria around Padua and introduce her to his parents. This, as it turned out, was a mistake.

As ever the first item on the agenda was news and announcements. Modesto liked to read out lists of events that were to be considered university success stories. An internship for three students had been inaugurated at the European Parliament. An agreement had been reached with the catering company to extend canteen opening hours and increase the range of food on offer. A new Erasmus exchange with a Spanish university was almost agreed on. The previous week's conference, involving the European Commissioner for Culture, was not mentioned.

An inordinate amount of time was now spent communicating quantities of information that could easily have been distributed by email. All teaching allocations for the coming year were to be agreed and authorised and so all were read out, one by one, scores of them, despite the fact that with only two exceptions they were all identical to those of the previous year. This took more than an hour.

'We should have realised,' Federica remarked later, 'how ominous this was.'

They had begun at nine thirty. Towards noon, everyone was checking phones and watches while Professor Preti openly turned the pages of *Corriere della Sera*. Moving directly from item seven to item eight, in a monotone so low as to be barely audible, Professor Modesto announced, '*Scambio docenti* – professorial exchange. I'm sure you will be aware that for many years our colleague, Professor Busacca, Mario, that is' – here she smiled at an elderly man who only rarely made appearances at department meetings – 'has been eager to return to his home town of Genoa, for both personal and health reasons. Professor Busacca is, as you know, in Sector L–Lin/01, where in fact we have more teaching staff than we actually need.'

Modesto paused. L–Lin/01 meant linguistics, where, since Ottone had become Rector and brought in various old linguist friends, the university did indeed now have more supply than demand. Looking around the room, the Head of Department seemed satisfied that no one was paying serious attention.

'Professor Busacca has now identified a professor at the University of Genoa who is eager to return to Milan and the two have made a formal request for an exchange. Francesco Contini is a professor of French Literature with a distinguished career in structuralist approaches to early nineteenth-century French narrative.'

Never raising her eyes from the papers before her, Modesto proceeded to read out Professor Contini's CV and publications. Her voice droned on. No detail was spared. But Federica had understood at once.

'Bettina,' she interrupted. 'If you'll forgive me. Surely we already have all the French teachers we need. All the courses for next year are covered, as we've just heard.'

Modesto's face was a picture of nerves and defiance. James was struggling to appreciate the problem. Federica spelled it out.

'Since our colleague Dottor Furlan is due for renewal this September, isn't there a danger that, in taking a tenured professor in his field, we could compromise his future? There will be no teaching for him.'

Modesto shook her head vigorously. 'No, no, that is a quite separate matter. We are merely called on today to approve this exchange or not. Let me pass around Professor Contini's CV so that you can see for yourselves. There are only four pages.'

Cecilia Tamara sprang to her feet, went to take the CV from Modesto and handed it to Preti, who looked it up and down before passing it on to the young researcher beside him. The idea was that they were now free to read this professor's credentials, while the discussion was going on.

'I think you will have to agree,' Professor Modesto was saying, 'that Professor Contini would be a great asset to our university.'

James asked, 'Can we feel confident that this will not have a detrimental effect on Furlan's career?'

'For heaven's sake, Furlan is an entirely separate question,' Modesto insisted.

'Professor Preti.' Federica turned to the elderly man on her right, the only other professor *ordinario* present, the only person with sufficient prestige to turn this into a real debate. 'Professor Preti, what's your position? Can we really vote for this exchange without considering Furlan's renewal?'

'Me?'

Professor Preti looked up from his newspaper. He hesitated, wriggled. 'Well, if I am not wrong, there has been some talk, has there not – Professor Modesto will tell us, I'm sure – of a new course of International Studies in the Economics Faculty which I believe will require a French teacher. So there may well be more French teaching, er ...' his voice tailed off.

'Indeed,' Modesto latched on to this diversion. 'But it's getting late and I would very much like a unanimous decision on this exchange so that Professor Contini can feel quite sure he is welcome here.'

DON ABBONDIO

All Italians know a Don Abbondio. Very likely more than one. At the beginning of Manzoni's great novel *The Betrothed*, the object of interminable study by every Italian schoolchild, the parish priest Don Abbondio has the simple task of uniting the book's hero and heroine, Renzo and Lucia, in holy matrimony. But local tyrant Don Rodrigo has his lascivious eye on Lucia and wants her for himself. Returning home the day before the wedding, the ageing cleric finds his path blocked by two thugs who warn him the ceremony must not take place, on pain of death.

Chronically phobic himself, so afraid of the streets he would never leave his house if not accompanied by another man, Manzoni sketches in Don Abbondio's character with a mix of comprehension, contempt and comedy. The priest only took the cloth, we hear, so as to have an easy income for life. Complacently spineless, he 'maintains an unarmed neutrality' in all the quarrels that break out around him, bowing 'with the most profound respect' to everyone he meets. Nothing irritates him more than a fellow priest who defends the poor against the rich. For isn't the victim always partly responsible for his woes? Hasn't the dead man always done something to provoke his murder? Happily, Don Abbondio occasionally finds those even weaker than himself on whom he can vent the pent-up frustration of his bad conscience.

James first wondered about Professor Preti, who had come to their university somewhat inexplicably after ten prestigious years at Yale, when he poked his head into a room where the older man was conducting oral exams and saw him reducing a young examinee to tears. Otherwise, he was always the most affable colleague, showing James unusual deference and respect. He seemed a man you could trust.

In *The Betrothed* Don Abbondio caves in to the bullies and finds all kinds of bizarre excuses for not performing the wedding. His abject failure to respect a young couple's legal rights opens the way to years of eventful misery before the great wrong is overturned in a picture-book happy ending. In our case, however, the Don Abbondio figure appears not at the beginning of the story, to provoke an unhappiness eventually overcome, but at the end, when he fails to defend a happiness that seemed all but achieved.

In May of every year the Rector would announce a *collegio di dottorato* and, as we've seen, the PhD students would appear before the professorial staff and explain what they had been up to, after which the student's supervisor (and future protector) would read out his or her report (fulsomely positive) and the *collegio* would announce their promotion to the next year of the doctorate. But given Ottone's punitive rhetoric at the previous year's *collegio* and the fact that Valeria had clearly collaborated with a conference the Rector had tried to block, there was every reason to fear that this year things could be different. Certainly Antonio felt this was the case. Two other students he was partly supervising were safely under the wing of Professor Galli and the seven others under review were all attached either to *professori ordinari* or to *professori associati* close to the Rector. They would breeze through. But precisely because they were untouchable, Valeria would be even more vulnerable. In particular, she was the only student asking for permission to spend some months abroad and the Rector seemed obsessed with the idea that doctoral candidates went away chiefly to waste the university's money and have a good time.

To complicate matters there was the novelty of the six supervisors, not to mention Antonio's feelings of guilt that not only had he taken on a student he was unable to protect, but that he had now become her lover. Had he become Valeria's tutor *because* he was interested in her? It hadn't felt like that. She had asked for him, not vice versa. But it was what people would suspect.

After discussing the matter with Valeria, Antonio phoned James, ostensibly to ask whether the supervisors were to write separate reports, or whether there was to be an agreed group report. James hated bureaucratic considerations and said that being the most senior of the team, Professor Preti was the person to ask about this. For his part he had read Valeria's work and it looked OK. He would have no trouble recommending her promotion and the fieldwork in Dakar.

'Should I talk to Preti, then?'

'About the question of the report, yes.' But Preti wouldn't be a problem, James said, since it was he who had set up Valeria's place in Dakar. He wouldn't have done that if he meant to make trouble at the *collegio*.

Antonio wrote to Preti and Preti replied that each supervisor would just give a separate opinion at the *collegio*.

'Since you are the only one who really understands her project,' the older professor went on, 'I think you should have a quick talk with the others, reminding them that they will need to prepare a few words.'

Reassured, Antonio phoned Marcello Masini, the lecturer in TV Journalism, who admitted he hadn't yet read the work Valeria had sent him, but was quite happy to go along with the opinions of the others.

Antonio then phoned another tutor, Vanessa Catrone, a professor of Comparative Literature. She was impressed, she said, by the girl's commitment and energy, but perplexed by a naive methodology that sought to combine a linguistic approach and a more traditional textual analysis approach. 'How did she react to your observations?' Antonio asked. Professor Catrone said she hadn't yet had time to communicate her concern to the student.

It did not seem an insuperable problem. Antonio told Valeria to be in touch with Catrone at once. Otherwise, everything was falling into place. In early May professors and doctoral students received an email, inviting them to the important meeting on the 28th.

Aside from this forthcoming hurdle, Valeria and Antonio were on tenterhooks following the announcement of the exchange between old Professor Busacca and Francesco Contini, the new French professor. Contini would be arriving at the beginning of the following academic year, on 1st October, exactly when Antonio's present contract expired. The young man asked for an appointment with Professor Modesto which she eventually granted, though it was hardly up to her, the Head of Department said at once, to offer reassurance on a matter which was the prerogative of the university's Board of Directors. Naturally, she added, the board, which included herself, would need to establish whether there was space at the university for Antonio, whether there were courses for him to teach.

'My present courses will go to Contini?' he asked. He had been teaching them for six years.

'Since Contini is your senior, if he asks to teach your courses, they will inevitably be given to him.'

'And he will have to teach something, since he is coming here.'

'Of course.'

'You are telling me to look for a position elsewhere.'

'I'm not telling you anything of the kind.' Modesto hated to be pinned down. Both of them knew that to look for work elsewhere in the present climate was a counsel of despair. Arms folded, back erect, the woman stood stiffly at the window, looking out over the plaza and the other buildings of this institution where she had become so important. She turned:

'Antonio, I know you and others feel I am behaving heartlessly, but this is really not the case. The arrival of Contini was a separate matter that had to be considered on its own terms. An exchange was proposed and I had to refer it to the department who I must say voted unanimously for it to go ahead. Obviously it's a matter of concern to me to have to lose an excellent young researcher like yourself. In the coming months I will be exploring ways of avoiding that, you can be sure. These responsibilities weigh heavily on me, something none of you appears to appreciate. However, the decision will not come until late August or September and it will not be mine. To reassure you now would be irresponsible.'

'In short,' Antonio told Valeria, 'I'm to be roasted on a low flame over the summer.'

L'INFAME

Another complication in the life of these new lovers was the unexpected arrival of Valeria's old friend Paola who was now sleeping on their sitting-room sofa. Having taken her degree in Law in Bari she had come to Milan to be with her 'historic' boyfriend Paolo who had found an excellent job in the multinational Price Waterhouse. After six years of weekends travelling back and forth from one end of Italy to the other, it was adult cohabitation at last, the bliss they had always looked forward to. But after six months the two were falling apart. Paolo was unhappy, he announced: Paola was always on the phone to her mother, her grandmother, her sisters, her aunts, her cousins. 'You haven't left home,' he accused her. 'You're not really *here*.' She accused him of hiding something. Or more likely someone. He denied it. He was overwhelmed by her gloom, he said, her yearning for home. She admitted she was frustrated, but this was because not having the necessary contacts in Milan she had had to settle for an internship that barely covered her expenses. She hated the weather. She hated the smog and the cold and the grey streets. The two went days without speaking to each other. Paolo announced that they needed a 'period of reflection'. 'Reflection!' she shouted. 'We've been seeing each other since we were ten!'

They had never shouted at each other before. Deeply offended, Paola moved out to force his hand. 'Can I stay with you?' she phoned

Valeria to ask. 'For a few days?' Paolo wouldn't last more than a few days without her, she said. But she had been with them for a month now, sinking deeper and deeper into depression. Meantime, the old group of friends, the various Milanese Lucani, could hardly get together without Paolo and Paola. Everyone phoned Paolo to encourage him to patch it up. Letizia was indignant. Their relationship was written in the stars, she told him. They had *always* been together. Since they were little children. Wasn't that worth something? Their parents were practically in-laws already. 'Are you mad?' she demanded. When Paolo was evasive Letizia told him she would never forgive him for hurting her friend like this. 'How do you think people will react when you go home? They'll spit at you in the street.'

Valeria's old boyfriend Giancarlo also called Paolo and told him to stop fooling around. 'I hope you're not making all this trouble over a bit on the side,' he said. Flavio and Chiara went to visit the villain and sang Paola's praises. All those years on night buses up and down the Adriatic? It was something to treasure.

Paolo told his friends he was thinking it over. He was playing a lot of football and tennis. He had found a new gym. Sometimes it felt like Paola was his sister, he said, not his girlfriend. Paolo's mother phoned Paola to say she was ashamed of her son and was doing her best to resolve the problem. Paolo's older half-brother – he who had driven a thousand kilometres to bring his aunts to a cousin's wedding – phoned Valeria and demanded she intervene. 'You're a childhood friend,' he said. 'You sat next to Paolo at primary school, go and tell him how to behave. He's a disgrace to the family.'

All too soon, Valeria noticed, the word *infame* was being used – traitor, rat. *Io, l'infame* is the title of Patrizio Peci's autobiography describing how, following his arrest, he decided to betray his companions in the Red Brigades. In revenge, they killed his brother. If Paolo had another woman, his friends agreed, then he was truly *infame*. They would cut him out of their *compagnia*.

Valeria went to see Paolo with a heavy heart, and without telling Paola. They met in a bar in Isola. The young man was defensive.

'*You* left Giancarlo,' he observed. 'And now you've left Michele.'

'Because I fell in love with someone else. And you?'

Paolo shook his head. 'I need a little time.'

'Paola's going crazy.'

The young man stirred his Spritz.

'I went through this with my brother,' she said, 'when his girlfriend ran off to Marseilles. They'd been together since they were twelve. He tried to kill himself twice.'

Paolo opened his mouth and closed it again.

'I do understand, though,' she said eventually. 'I mean, the feeling that something is old and a kind of prison.'

She watched him. Paolo was looking away. Lifting his glass, his hand shook.

'I know you don't want to go home,' she said. 'I feel the same.'

'I would die.'

He began to cry. He was such a big hunk of a boy, she would never have imagined.

She sighed. 'You have someone else.'

He nodded.

'Is it serious?'

Paolo was rocking back and forth.

'Very.'

'Tell Paola, get it over with.'

He shook his head. 'I thought it would be easier to let time pass. I don't want to hurt her.'

'She's bound to be hurt.'

The boy looked confused.

'Do you want me to tell her?'

'No!'

'But you're happy with this other woman?'

'Yes.'

'Then just tell her. She won't believe it's over until she knows there's someone else.'

They sat looking at their empty glasses. The waitress saw something was up and hung back.

'They'll hate me,' he said. 'No one will talk to me for years.'

'*I'll* talk to you,' Valeria said. 'Just do it.'

But in the coming days it didn't seem Paolo had told Paola, and she continued to wait for a change of heart on his part, sitting mutely with Antonio and Valeria at meal after meal, saying nothing, until her mother phoned, or her aunt, or her grandmother, and then slipping off to the bathroom to talk to them about her woes.

'She was never like this before,' Valeria apologised.

'So long as she doesn't do anything desperate,' Antonio said.

PLAGE DE LA VOILE D'OR

Two days before it was due, the *collegio di dottorato* was postponed. It would be rescheduled shortly, the brief email said. Meantime a Professor Cottin had written from Dakar to say that if Valeria was planning to come in September it would be wise to pay a preliminary visit as soon as possible to choose suitable accommodation, since housing could be scarce at the beginning of a new academic year. This would allow her to meet the professors she would be working with and see the university facilities. They would be expecting her to teach Italian Literature, they said, and it would be good if she could indicate what books she would be using.

Valeria hadn't been aware she was supposed to teach. But all the better. She waited until the new date of the *collegio* was announced – 11th June – then booked flights for herself and Antonio for the following week. They would take a little holiday together. Nobody in Dakar would know that Dottor Furlan was one of her supervisors in Milan. They could go to the beach and get some sun. However, on 6th June another email announced that the *collegio* would once again have to be postponed due to the Rector's heavy schedule. It would now take place on 18th June. As they were flying.

This was serious bad luck, and the urgent question was, should they cancel these flights, and lose their eight hundred euros (almost a month's income), so as to attend the *collegio*? It was well known that

Ottone insisted on doctoral students being present. On the other hand her head supervisor was Preti and it was he who had contacted Cottin and Cottin who had invited her to make this preliminary trip. She asked for an appointment with Preti, but he was busy. She wrote to ask him how she should behave and he didn't respond. Not wanting to seem too close to Antonio, she phoned James and explained the situation, minus the fact that she would be travelling with Antonio. James said he would talk to Preti.

The older professor was watering the plants in his third-floor office when James knocked and let himself in. He loved plants, Preti enthused, because they were reliable and predictable. They brought colour into your life, but not the capriciousness and, frankly, treachery that inevitably came when you kept animals, not to mention people. 'Wives, children, mistresses!' He laughed, passing a small green watering can along a line of a dozen pots.

James explained Valeria's dilemma and said she was concerned that Ottone might take it amiss if she wasn't present at the *collegio*.

The professor sat down, spread his arms wide and smiled. This university was ridiculous, he said. It offered absolutely nothing to its PhD students. And the students themselves were only taken on so that the university could boast it had a doctorate programme and apply for funds accordingly. What nonsense it all was. 'You can't imagine the picture they painted when they persuaded me to come here,' he complained, 'compared with the wretchedness I found on arrival.'

'What do you think Dottoressa Lasala should do?' James asked. 'If she's not present, can we guarantee the *collegio* will be OK and she will pass the year?'

Preti seemed perplexed. 'There are six of us supervisors, aren't there? I can't see the problem.'

'The problem is Ottone. Plus the fact that it seemed Furlan already had a conference set up in Paris for the 18th. So we won't have him with us. Though he'll give us a full report, of course.'

Preti pulled a face. 'I can't imagine what Beppe could have against the girl. She will have to do her fieldwork at some point. As for absences, the meeting has been postponed twice, so the Rector can hardly complain if someone can't be there at the third time of asking.'

'I'll tell her she can fly,' James said.

The *collegio* was on the Monday. Early Sunday morning James received a phone call from his brother in Bristol to say their father was in intensive care after a stroke. At once James took the train to Malpensa and the first flight to Gatwick, spending the night with his mother in the waiting rooms of Bristol General hospital. Nevertheless in the morning he remembered to write a group email to Preti and the other supervisors summarising the things he had intended to say at the *collegio* with regard to Dottoressa Lasala and asking the others to read out his assessment. Reassuringly, Preti responded at once, telling him not to worry and to give all his attention to his family at this difficult time. Towards evening of the same day, James's father died without recovering consciousness. His mother insisted on sitting up another night beside the body in the morgue and James and his brother again kept her company. Hence it wasn't until the following morning, Tuesday, exhausted and dismayed, that he saw Federica's email.

Carissimo,

How are things? How is your father?

Unfortunately, the collegio went badly yesterday. Not only did the Rector refuse Valeria permission to go to Dakar, but he also refused to promote her to the third year. Instead, she has to produce half of her final thesis before the October term, otherwise she is to be thrown out of the programme altogether.

I really can't tell you in a mail how the meeting went, in particular the extraordinary hostility of some of our colleagues towards Valeria (that is, towards us, I suspect). It was horrible from beginning to end.

I tried to get involved and defend Valeria, but I'm not one of the super-
visors and they just didn't want to listen, especially when all I could really
say was how useful she had been preparing the conference. I had the
impression the decision was taken before the collegio began and was simply
made the easier by the fact that you and Antonio and Valeria herself
couldn't be there. The Rector was ferocious with all the students, but only
Valeria was disciplined.

Reply on this private mail, please.

James was upset, what with trying to come to terms with his father's
death, which seemed quite unreal, and now this new development,
which was grotesque. A young woman had been punished, he realised
at once, because of her involvement with himself, and Antonio, and
Federica.

'But Preti?' he wrote. 'Didn't Preti say anything? And Catrone?
Masini?'

Federica replied towards evening.

The whole parade of hypocrisy, mediocrity, venom was beyond absurd.
There was a general relief that you and Antonio weren't there to protect
Valeria, and that she herself wasn't there to see who was speaking against
her. I think a lot of people must have been upset that we arranged that
conference with such prestigious speakers. Preti began positively, but as
soon as he saw which way the wind was blowing, he started mumbling
and backed down. He didn't even say it was him who had made the
arrangement with Dakar. He didn't say he had encouraged Valeria to go
ahead with this preliminary visit. He let it seem as if it was presumption
on her part arranging a period abroad before permission was granted, and
even going out there to arrange accommodation right when there was a
collegio. *Then Catrone started talking about naive methodology, even*
though that problem was supposed to have been settled. Masini com-
plained she had never come to his office hours; he would have advised her
but couldn't help if she never showed. By the way, there's worse, I forgot

322

to tell you, the Rector has suspended her monthly grant until she hands in the first half of the thesis and passes to the third year. So she's going to have to survive four months without it . . . I feel ashamed to be part of this university.

James wrote at once to ask if anyone had told Valeria and Federica replied that she didn't know. It was something her supervisors should do. And Preti was the chief supervisor. James forwarded Federica's mails to Antonio and wrote to Preti saying he had heard things had not gone well at the *collegio* and asking whether Dottoressa Lasala had been informed.

'*I did the best I could,*' Preti responded. '*But, a lot of negative things emerged about Lasala's work that I wasn't aware of. If I had been informed earlier, something might have been done. It seems there has been a breakdown in communication. As for telling her, I think this is the duty of those following the thesis closely, yourself or Dottor Furlan.*'

'*Do you want to tell her, or shall I?*' James wrote to Antonio the morning after his father's death, not realising that Antonio already had. The two lovers were sitting by the sea on the Plage de la Voile d'Or, in a daze of sunlight and despair. There was no point in looking for a room in Dakar.

PINOCCHIO

In the ogre's cave, one serves and slaves. The fables don't have much to say about this condition of subjugation; as with other forms of exile, all that matters is how long it lasts. Years usually. Very likely seven. Occasionally, the prisoner, always a young man or woman far from home, will figure out how to escape, tricking the ogre, or even killing him. But this is rare. More often, he or she will be rescued by a sibling or future spouse, who for some reason never succumbs to the same fate, as if immune from danger. Of course the reader knows this is going to happen; but the victim does not. The victim fears a lifetime lost in servitude.

At a conference in Lyons where Antonio has explained his and Valeria's precarious situations to three French colleagues, one asks him is it possible that this man Ottone is such a monster? 'Everyone has some psychological depth,' she protests. 'Isn't that what literature tells us? This woman Modesto as well. The way you tell it, they sound like caricatures.'

Antonio has had a couple of drinks and is on the defensive. 'You mean his cat died in his arms when he was ten, poisoned by an evil stepmother, and as a result I have to lose my job? Does that add complexity?'

His French colleagues laugh. Still, they find it hard to believe someone running a university could be so merely nasty.

Antonio tries to be reasonable. 'Many of the professors love Ottone. He's given them jobs and looks after them. He has a kind of magnetism as well, looking you straight in the eyes, touching your hand or putting an arm round your shoulder. And he's a charismatic speaker. He always presses the right liberal buttons when he has a big audience. But it's also true that these colleagues are ready to obey him in everything. They put their careers entirely in his hands. They switch areas of research at his convenience. They always ask him for permission before publishing. They live in fear.'

The Frenchmen shake their heads. '*Formidable!*'

'No!' Antonio is taken aback. 'No, he's really not! It's just the way we do things in Italy. It's a *role*. There are Ottones all over Italy. If he were in France or Germany or the United States he'd be quite different.'

'But,' the most sceptical member of the group asks, 'if everyone else obeys and admires, why didn't you?'

Antonio sighs. 'I don't know,' he says. 'I really don't know.'

It's true. Neither Antonio nor Valeria can grasp, as the summer approaches, quite how they have wound up like this. They are not rebels by vocation. Antonio is thirty-six now. Having completed three three-year contracts as a researcher, his only way forward in academe is to be invited to take a tenured post as professor (the rule was introduced to prevent universities from keeping researchers on a lifetime of three-year projects). This means that even in the unlikely event that a university were looking for someone from outside, they would probably choose someone younger and cheaper than himself, someone they could offer a three-year contract to. Both Federica and James urge him to toe the line for the coming months and be as helpful as possible toward Modesto, to ask for an interview with Ottone and swear allegiance to him.

'Should I?' he asks Valeria.

She is disturbed by his indecision. What had been wonderful, at the beginning of their relationship, was the feeling, after her two insecure southern boys, that she had found a real man, someone who knew he wanted her, knew his way in life, and knew how to handle, among many other things, her mother. But Antonio seems shaken and uncertain now. In the days after their return from Dakar, he tries to think of ways of pleasing Modesto. He suggests conferences and projects, he offers assistance. But his heart is not in it and Modesto doesn't bite. So he writes to the Rector asking for a meeting to discuss his future. Ottone doesn't reply.

'I don't want to see him anyway,' Antonio decides. 'The hell with him.' He concentrates on an article he is writing about translations of contemporary French poetry. He loves his work and still doesn't quite believe that his university career is over. But when a student asks him to tutor her thesis, he realises that by the time she is ready to graduate he may no longer be at the university. He writes to Modesto for guidance. She replies, after a week, that although nothing has been decided about his future, perhaps it would be wiser not to make commitments that he might not be able to see through.

The lovers have a first falling-out. Even before arriving home from Dakar, on the train from the airport, Valeria had phoned her mother and told her about the disastrous *collegio di dottorato* and the suspension of her grant. There was a long excited conversation between Lombardy and Basilicata, the phone signal coming and going as the train passed in and out of tunnels so that Valeria had to call back twice and explain things all over again. Yes, her grant had been suspended. Cut. Stopped. At least until she handed in the first half of her thesis and it was approved. Yes, that meant writing about a hundred and fifty pages over the summer. No, she hadn't done anything that she could see to deserve this treatment.

Antonio couldn't understand why she was making this call. He hadn't told his own parents about his renewal problem. What was the point of worrying them? 'You have enough money to survive till October, don't you? And you know I can tide you over if you don't.' People who didn't move in the university world couldn't understand these things. 'They'll think you've done something wrong.'

But Valeria couldn't imagine not telling her mother. It was true the older woman had no idea how universities worked; she had wanted to get on a train right away to come and give Ottone a piece of her mind. Valeria smiled. 'Mamma would never doubt I was telling the truth.'

'What's to be gained, though?'

'It's not a question of gaining. It's that I wouldn't feel comfortable talking to her with such an important thing in the background. It's important not to hide, Antò,' Valeria adds. 'We can't pretend it hasn't happened.'

'I'm not hiding.' He spoke sharply, and looked out of the window as the city cemented around them.

Back at the flat in Isola, Paola was more depressed than ever. She listened sympathetically to Valeria's woes, but found it impossible to shift her thoughts away from Paolo. The two had had a *chiarimento*, she said, a showdown. In a pub on the Navigli. He had cried, but still didn't want to come back to her. He felt they had been more brother and sister than lovers. Paola felt insulted.

'Did he say he had someone else?'

'No.' Paola hesitated. She was a handsome girl, but as though quenched or stifled by the turn life had taken. 'He said not to be surprised, though, if he found someone else very soon.'

The summer months were a slog. Valeria had spent three years now studying the journalism and literature of francophone Africa, thinking about the relationships between French and the many indigenous languages, and again between French and English. But she needed experience of the place and the people; she needed to test her ideas and reading against reality. Arriving in Dakar, smelling the smells of Africa, the African air, the traffic, the people, it had seemed to her that everything she had been working towards was about to be realised. Then in a moment she had lost both Africa and her confidence.

For weeks she struggled with anger and resentment. Preti had let her down spectacularly. But Federica and James too, she thought, should have been more careful when they set a collision course with the powers that be. It was all very well their having their jobs for life, but they should have realised that the people helping them would be vulnerable. On the other hand, she should have realised this herself. No, she *had* realised. That was what made the whole thing so strange and even dreamlike. She had watched Cecilia over the last couple of years. She had seen how the Sicilian woman was polite and friendly with Antonio and James, joining in their project and learning all she could from them, but at the same time grovelling to Modesto and grovelling to Ottone. She could easily have followed suit. Why hadn't she? Why had she allowed the story to unfold as if it were inevitable?

Looking at her notes in the library, mapping out the thesis she must now write in haste and without the benefit of fieldwork, this question continued to nag. Sometimes the nagging would morph into a hot heavy lump in her abdomen and she would have to get up from her desk and set off walking in the city's summer heat, under a milky sky, in the pollution haze of Milan's thoroughfares, stopping from time to time to drink at a fountain. Why hadn't she done what was expedient? It was the same question she had asked herself years ago after turning down Don Gabriele's offer of a flat in Milan. I'm not a saint, she thought. I don't have to be better than the others.

One afternoon she stopped in the gardens in Corso Indipendenza and found herself looking at the statue of Pinocchio. On a broad granite base, the puppet sprawls lifeless and prostrate with his long pointed nose, dunce's cap and circus clothes, while atop the polished plinth two metres above stands the handsome, well-groomed fellow he becomes at the end of the tale, a real boy with a book tucked proudly under one arm. '*Com'ero buffo quand'ero un burattino!*' reads the inscription. How funny I was when I was a puppet. Then, '*E tu che mi guardi, sei ben sicuro di aver domato il burattino che vive in te?*' And you who look at me, are you really sure you've tamed the puppet in yourself?

Valeria stared. What was that supposed to mean, *tamed the puppet in yourself*? Her infancy had been quite different from Pinocchio's. She

328

had never skipped her classes or run off to have fun in a world of toys and nonsense. Was that what they meant by the puppet? A rascal, a scamp? Lighting a cigarette, she sat on a bench to contemplate the monument, which had been recently restored, the stone plinth cleaned, the various bronze figures – the puppet, the boy, the cat, the fox – all gleaming and the lettering of the inscription bright with fresh gold leaf. The cat and the fox were lurking behind the plinth, like two assassins responsible for Pinocchio's death. Ottone and Modesto? she thought, and smiled. The Rector the fox, Head of Department the cat? Two frauds pretending to be scholars so they can prey on the young. Pinocchio is accepted into society, she remembered, when he stops listening to foxes and cats, gets serious and picks up a book. Only then does he become real. I was always serious, she thought, always reading, but when I showed more respect for my books than for the fox and the cat, I got shafted.

At some point during these long walks, perhaps after four or five kilometres and as many cigarettes in the oppressive summer air, Valeria would start to write a letter in her mind. It was the letter announcing her withdrawal from the doctoral programme. She imagined interviews with Modesto and Ottone, with Preti and Catrone and Masini, interviews where she told them what she thought of them. *E vaffanculo.*

But the letter was never sent and the conversations were fantasy. She had done two years of her doctorate and she had to finish, if only to have something to show for it all. She must knuckle down, accept the challenge they had thrown her, win them over with her diligence and competence. Mid-July, Valeria wrote to her supervisors, announcing that she had completed her first chapter and asking for help and feedback. Unexpectedly, all replied immediately. All invited her to see them at once. And when she went, all were extravagantly kind.

'I had no idea he might do something so drastic,' Professor Catrone protested, taking Valeria to the university café and offering her freshly squeezed orange juice. 'I don't even think what he did is remotely legal!' Preti began when Valeria appeared at his door. 'Honestly, I do feel a bit of a worm,' Masini confided. 'I'm afraid I'm really not cut out for these bureaucratic meetings, you know.'

'Pathetic,' Antonio commented.

June had been hot and July was hotter. They had no air conditioning. Mosquitoes thrived. With neither time nor money for a holiday, there was every opportunity to grow irritated with each other. There were tiffs, moments of exasperation. But almost at once the couple got on top of it. Paola helped. Their guest finally packed her bags and abandoned her Milanese life to return to her family. 'Fifteen years together and he leaves me with *un pugno di mosche*,' she said. A fistful of flies.

'Thank God we have each other,' Antonio breathed.

Suddenly they were laughing. They were young and healthy, they loved each other's company, adored each other's bodies. What better luck could you ask? All day they worked in air-conditioned libraries and when the evening began to cool they drank a beer down on the canal or at the kiosk in the park near their flat. Years later, Valeria would remember it as a beautiful summer, the summer she and Antonio became inseparable.

VIVE CONDOGLIANZE

Some days after his return from his father's funeral in Bristol, James was called down by the condominium's hall porter for a telegram. He was astonished. He wasn't even aware, in this age of Internet messaging, that telegrams still existed.

'*In the name of all Department members*,' it said, '*I wish to express to you our* sentimento di vicinanza − *feeling of closeness* − *in this sad moment and to communicate our most heartfelt condolences. Prof. Elisabetta Modesto.*'

There was something odd. James reread it. Yes. Modesto had used the formal polite form, *lei*, to address him. *Le esprimo il nostro sentimento …* Yet the two had been on first-name terms and using the informal *tu* for years. Why would Professor Modesto switch to *lei* when sending condolences? Then it dawned on James that the Head of Department must have some pre-prepared script that was sent to all members of staff on these occasions. She hadn't read over what she was sending.

Four days later a courier arrived with a large and colourful plastic package from which James fished out a small white envelope. Inside was a blank postcard with the university logo and three lines of scrawl that he pored over for fifteen minutes but was unable to decipher. He took a photo of the card and emailed it to Federica who solved the mystery in a matter of seconds. '*I have received news of the passing of your father. I am very sorry and want you to know I feel close to you. Con vive condoglianze, Beppe Ottone.*'

Vive – lively – *condoglianze* – condolences! Thinking about these two messages, James realised they were inviting him to remember he had another family, his university. He could decide to fit in and be at home there, if he wanted. In a corridor on the third floor, Modesto buttonholed him with a solemn face. It was exam time and crowds of students were hurrying to their classrooms. 'I was so sorry to hear your news.'

'Thank you,' James said.

'If you need to take some time off.'

James shook his head.

Then, unasked, the Head of Department explained that she really was doing her best to see if there was some way they could keep Doctor Furlan when his contract expired. 'I know you are concerned about this,' she said earnestly.

Tidying the flaps of her jacket pockets, she waited for James to respond.

'I have to get to an exam that kicks off at ten,' he said.

Over the next three hours, watching his forty or so students bent over their work, it occurred to James that he loved his contact with them to the same degree that he hated having to deal with people like Modesto. He loved their naivety and shyness in the first lessons of their first year, when they sat in the front rows and worried whether they would ever catch their teacher's eye, and he loved their brashness and proprietorial airs in the last lessons of their last, when they sat four or five rows further back and barely gave him the time of day, they had so much to talk to each other about. He loved to watch how each year the individual youngsters who had survived the entrance exam gradually formed a group, became friends, or at least acquaintances, offering each other moral support at oral exams and thesis commissions. He loved the inevitable know-all of the class who tried to answer every question he asked, and the smart student who knew the answers but wouldn't speak, and even the lost student who simply had no idea what the questions meant, let alone what the answers might be. They were all endearing, in their ways. Endearing as individuals – Costanza and Roberto and Maddalena – but also as roles, as possibilities. Perhaps someone had to be the know-all and someone had to be lost. The class situation required it. He loved how, over the two years he taught them, four hours a week, month in month out, the group would at first isolate and exclude the know-all, often quite cruelly, then gradually reintegrate the culprit once they had suffered enough and lowered their crest.

Year after year, class after class, these young people changed each other and became a community. And he, James, had been granted the immense pleasure of observing and savouring that process, over and over. So he knew that midway through the first term each class would already have its special feeling, perhaps of obedience, perhaps of rebellion, of intimacy or coolness, harmony or conflict. And he would be waiting for the feeling to emerge, ready to respond and adapt his teaching accordingly. Sometimes he found he had already adapted without realising, discovering the mood of the class through his own changed behaviour. Willy-nilly, one was part of the group oneself.

So each year the students transformed him, in a way. They kept him alive. He loved their flusteredness before exams, the girls chewing their curls, the boys picking at nails, and he loved their shameless opportunism when they came alone to see him in his office, pleading for special treatment perhaps – they needed a higher mark, they needed the deadline for their thesis extended. There was a bright-as-a-button falseness to them at such moments that he always found charming even as he said no to every request. He loved their concentration when a lesson interested them, but also their distraction when they couldn't care less. Every student has a right to be distracted sometimes. He had even learned to love the way they sneaked glances at their phones under the desks, sending messages while he was trying to teach. To mothers and boyfriends, no doubt. And instead of growing tired of hearing the same names time and again, year in year out, the inevitable Chiaras and Carlos, Federicas and Filippos, Claudios and Caterinas, he had come to enjoy this predictability. Likewise the repetition of facial types. After all, these students were all Italian, the DNA was what it was. He enjoyed the way this foxy nose and mouth in 2010 reminded him of another foxy nose and mouth of 1990. Or perhaps 1985. Though she had been a Sara not a Silvia. This earnest, moon-faced Tommaso recalled a moon-faced boy of God knows when who must now be a grown man with a family of his own very likely. James had forgotten his name, forgotten his existence even, until the new arrival brought him back.

He found these feelings of recognition reassuring and sometimes even exciting. There was a special mystery in finding yourself once again in the presence of a face that had been wonderfully unique ten years ago, yet reappeared now in another manifestation. As if at some level they might have been the same person. If he thought seriously about the experience, he realised it ought to be disturbing: class after class, identity and individuality were eroded under a fresh tide of youth, entirely similar to the tides that had come before. It should have been disheartening. Instead he responded with elation to the powerful sense of familiarity, the feeling that in greeting and teaching Ilaria today you were also still in contact with Mariangela of fifteen years before. The similarity kept the past alive. It was a good thing. As when he recognised his grandmother's face in his younger sister's, his father's face in his older brother's. Rather than slipping away, life accumulated. Layer upon sedimentary layer, experience grew richer. And here at the university he was inside this Italian life, he was part of it, gathering it into himself and giving of himself.

The sound of the printer gave him a start. Someone had finished writing and was already printing out her exam. The next ten minutes would be hectic as the weaker students, still writing, tried to use the noise of the printer and the bustle of their companions leaving as cover to ask for answers to the questions they hadn't understood. But he loved this too. He enjoyed its predictability. The scene was always the same. Meantime, Modesto, he realised, was trying to use this sympathy over his father's death to get him to play ball. He was being given a last chance to conform. This was the world all these students were about to join.

ANITA

The exam session ended on 29th June. The last thesis commission wound to a weary close on 22nd July. Then the professors and students were free until September, when there would be exams again before lessons resumed in October. It was a time when the losers in the academic game could lick their wounds. Splashing with children on the beaches of Romagna. Sailing blue seas off the coast of Liguria. Exploring Italy's astonishing cultural heritage in Emilia Romagna and Umbria, Campania and Calabria. Or visiting Sicily perhaps, the hilltop spectacle of Ragusa, the dusty slopes of Etna. In its long summer dazzle, when time seems to slow and work and politics are forgotten, in the rhythmic din of the cicadas and the sultry evening rumble of distant thunder, eating fish at beachside restaurants, drinking chilled Vermentino in the shade of an antique portico, Italy has a thousand destinations where a loser can still feel he, or she, made the right decision coming to live here.

Federica and her husband were exploring the mountains above Turin, the Gran Paradiso Park. Alessio was with wife and family on the north coast of Sardinia. Cecilia had gone home to Palermo, Professor Preti to Lecce. Ottone always spent his summers with his wife in a second or perhaps third house above Bari. Bettina Modesto was with her arthritic father in the spa town of Fiuggi, where various members of a certain Masonic lodge were taking the waters. Only

Valeria and Antonio were sweating it out in purgatorial Milan. And even here all conflict seemed suspended in the still air of the deserted streets, where the occasional empty tram squealed by under the dusty leaves of the city's long-suffering plane trees. They had until October to turn their lives around.

James went to the Adriatic. A new companion had more or less co-opted him. Patrizia was from Chieti in Abruzzo; she taught History at a *liceo scientifico* in Sesto San Giovanni, a northern suburb of Milan, and had a long-term project to write a book on Ana Maria de Jesus Ribeiro da Silva, better known simply as Anita, Giuseppe Garibaldi's Brazilian wife. So what they were going to do, she told James only a day after the dinner party that led to their becoming lovers, was rent a room and a sunshade at Porto Garibaldi, midway between Rimini and Venice, identify the very spot where in 1849 the hero landed his fishing boat fleeing from the Austrian navy with the heavily pregnant Anita, dying from malaria, then visit the places where the two hid and Anita eventually died. One plus, she concluded, was that Porto Garibaldi was hardly a fashionable destination. The pensione would be cheap.

'I thought Garibaldi and his crew were out of fashion,' James observed. 'That it had all been a big mistake uniting Italy.'

Patrizia thought about this, sitting topless in a deck chair on her fourth-floor balcony above the busy Via Padova, examining the varnish on her toenails. 'Garibaldi and Anita were both *fuori dagli schemi*,' she said. 'Completely out of it. They lived as they liked; wore whatever clothes they chose. He went to the first Italian Parliament in Turin in poncho and sombrero. She rode and fought alongside of him like a man. Dressed like a man, cut her hair like a man.'

James smiled. 'You like them because you'd love to be like that yourself.'

'I like them because they're the opposite of all the shits and hangers-on we have in Parliament today.'

James realised at once that this was the kind of woman who would push him around. Like Garibaldi's men, he was being enlisted to serve a cause. All the same her pugnacity was seductive; it was summer time; he had no plans, and after his father's death he needed to feel he was alive.

They spent the mornings on the beach, made love and slept after lunch, and in the late afternoon set off to explore the hinterland where the dying Anita, Garibaldi and a couple of companions had hid in the marshes of the Po delta, crossing the six miles of the Comacchio lagoon in an open boat. The sultry summer air hummed with hornets and mosquitoes. A smell of low tide hung over the dusty roads. Herons flapped over the rice fields. Towards nine they would look for a place to eat.

Every passer-by they met, every waiter who served them, Patrizia engaged in conversation. Nobody was too forbidding, too young or too old, rough or chic. Did they know that this was where Anita passed her last days? Was there anywhere where she could buy rolling tobacco? Was there anything to see in San Romualdo?

Invariably she got answers. Garibaldi and Anita were fools, they should have left Italy as it was. Anita was a saint. Garibaldi was the greatest Italian of all time. But more often than not what people talked about was wine and food. *Anguille marinate e alla brace*, for example. Barbecued eels. 'We say *il capitone*, but actually it's *la capitone* you're eating,' an elderly lady explained. 'The females are bigger and tastier.' 'There you are!' Patrizia cheered, raising her glass of the local Sauvignon. In Comacchio a young man spoke at length about his technique for preparing frog risotto, explaining exactly where to cut the frog at the thigh and warning against too much flour. Creaming with ample butter was a must. 'Roll it round on your tongue before swallowing.'

Patrizia rolled a forkful on her tongue and pulled a face.

'You're a phenomenon,' James laughed.

One day she announced they were going to spend the night sleeping rough in the Bosco Eliceo, the woods between beach and lagoon where Anita and Garibaldi had spent the first night of their flight. 'So I can describe it in my book.'

'Is that an order?'

'You bet,' she said.

They took plenty to eat and two bottles of wine and after a long search for somewhere secluded enough settled down on the sandy soil under a stand of poplars criss-crossed with irrigation canals.

'People are just not courageous enough these days,' she said.

'But they love praising people who are,' he replied.

Wriggling to find a comfortable position amid clumps of coarse grass, he told her how certain colleagues of his – Catrone, Masini, Modesto herself – would encourage their students to write theses about dissenters under Fascism, or poets persecuted in the Third World, yet these very teachers were invariably the same who bowed their heads to the Rector's dictatorship most willingly; they never spoke out when injustice was done under their noses.

It was colder than they expected and they couldn't sleep. The night was full of spooky sounds, trees creaking, animals scuttling through the grass. In the end, they settled for sitting opposite each other, backs resting on tree trunks, while she smoked and he drank. With the whole night before them, he told her then, in detail, what had happened at his university in recent months.

'*Una vergogna*,' she declared.

'What do you think I should do?' he asked.

'Be yourself, say what you think.'

The problem, James observed, was that you never knew who you were until you did whatever it was you were going to do. 'If only we had an Anita in the department,' he sighed.

A marsh bird raised a shrill cry. A breeze began to whisper in the leaves over their heads and the temperature fell further. Towards four, they got to their feet and tramped along a narrow road beside a canal in the direction of the lagoon. Patrizia wouldn't hear of going back to their pensione; at least one night must be spent savouring the discomforts of her heroine. James felt stiff and uncomfortable, but the sky teemed with stars and once you were on the move the breeze was pleasant after the heat of the day. In Comacchio towards six they sat

338

outside a café on the main piazza and waited for the owner to raise his shutters and bring them a cappuccino.

The following afternoon they were dozing under their sunshade on the beach when James received a WhatsApp from Federica to tell him that their friend Domenico Galli had died. Heart attack. The funeral was on Thursday, in two days' time.

'Of course you must go,' Patrizia said.

James was astonished to find himself facing a second funeral in just a couple of months. Domenico was only fifty-six. Not much older than himself.

'He was a rather strange friend, to be honest, always posing as someone who knew more of what was going on than you ever could, always making you feel naive when you tried to do anything about anything. The exact opposite of Garibaldi and Anita.'

'That doesn't mean you don't go to his funeral,' James's new girlfriend said sharply.

LA COPPELLA

There are no funerals in fables. People die by the score, get born and marry by the score. But there are no ceremonies. So James, who loves Basile's fables, sometimes wonders how much these stories can say about Italian life where ceremony is so important, where baptism and first communion, wedding and funeral, impose a conventional narrative that everyone can be comfortable with.

Perhaps what the fable offers, James reflects, is the real story behind the liturgy. An unmasking. Basile's collection is a kind of half *Decameron* with a group of people telling ten stories a day over five days, rather than the *Decameron*'s ten. But unlike Boccaccio, between each of the days, Basile offers his readers an eclogue, which is to say a conversation between two rustics who know how to call a spade a spade. In the first, a certain Iacovuccio shows off his *coppella*, or crucible, to the excited Fabiello. Not just a pot for purifying metals, this particular *coppella* can actually tell you, Iacovuccio claims, what a man is really like beneath the surface. You think that this lord or count or knight is happy because he rides in a carriage and people bow and curtsy to him, and '*even his chamber pot is made of silver*'. In fact, '*put him all in this crucible, and you'll see just how many festering sores lie under the velvet saddle; you'll find how many snakes are hiding in the flowers and grass ... The crows he feeds are all pecking out his eyes; the dogs he keeps all bark at him; he's paying salaries to his enemies, they surround him, swindle him, suck him up alive.*'

Fabiello is delighted as, one by one, Iacovuccio puts different lives into his crucible: the noble soldier (*'his suffering is long and his sweetness short'*), the swashbuckler (*'the thunder of his boasting is the thin shit of fear'*), the courtier (*'labyrinths of fraud and betrayal'*), the good servant (*'he corrupts your maid; he goes through your pockets'*), the flattering friend (*'even if you're an ogre he'll say you're Narcissus'*), the beautiful woman (*'you think she's sparkling wine but really she's infected meat'*), and so on. It seems that without the charm of the fable, to look at reality is to fall into disgust.

Certainly, Domenico Galli, James reflects, loved seeing the conspiracy beneath apparently innocuous behaviour, the shit beneath the silk, though more with pride in the quality of his eyesight than disgust over what he found. He seemed pleased to be able to prove the world so consistently corrupt; perhaps it legitimised some bad behaviour of his own. Or simply no behaviour at all. If the world is irretrievably bad you are exonerated from seeking to do anything about it.

James has been to any number of Italian funerals where the stolid priest puts a positive spin on lives he knows nothing of, painting familiar pictures of traditional virtue and, in general, oiling the gates of paradise. He remembers in particular a very sad funeral of a colleague's son, knocked off his scooter at twenty-two by a driver sending text messages. The priest spoke of a boy dedicated to family and friends, even implying he was a regular churchgoer. In fact Stefano hadn't darkened the proverbial door since infancy, was in conflict with everyone and facing a trial for dealing dope and amphetamines. All of which made his death so much harder for the parents, who had been blaming each other for their son's delinquency. It might have been as well, James had thought, to face that reality and get the pain out in the open. So today he wonders what the priest will find to say about a deeply cynical man like Domenico.

The church was San Cristoforo sul Naviglio. The sun was brutally hot. Seven or eight colleagues had come along and three or four administrative staff. Alessio appeared in a dark suit and black tie. Federica wore a blue dress and sunglasses. Outside the church beside the canal, a small crowd waited for the hearse. Well into her eighties, Domenico's mother was in a wheelchair, a lily in the buttonhole of her black jacket, her face blank. Apparently there was a sister too and even an ex-wife, but James wouldn't have known how to identify them.

The coffin arrived and was slid out of the hearse onto a trolley to be wheeled towards the church, rather as a patient for whom something might still be done is wheeled towards the operating theatre. Only at the steps up to the porch did six black-suited men appear and heave the box onto their shoulders, giving everyone a sense of its unwieldiness and weight. Then it was laid on another, smarter trolley and the priest was walking up the aisle beside it, waving his smoky aspergillum over its polished joinery. He was a big man, breathing heavily under his cassock, but otherwise altogether at ease in the cluttered mysticism of his surroundings, the electric candles beneath fanciful martyrdoms, the general feeling of a tradition that was grateful for its layer of dust.

The ceremony opened with a dull muttering of automatic orisons. The priest announced the versicles, the congregation provided the responses, promptly but without conviction. Then the organ sounded and everyone stood and mouthed the words on their hymn sheets, though no sound came from their lips. It seemed this was always the way, James thought, whether it be the national anthem at the Inauguration of the Academic Year, today's funeral dirge, or a carol at midnight Mass; people felt they should be taking part, they wanted their mouths to be seen to follow the words, but they couldn't quite bring themselves to give voice to those words. Because it would seem ridiculous? Because they didn't believe a word of what they were supposed to be singing? It was a conflictedness that James, who had sung with feeling only a month ago at his father's funeral, could never understand. Why don't Italian congregations sing? And why is no comment ever made about this? The Italian priest never complains, as a more ingenuous English clergyman might, that his congregation isn't singing. Nothing is required of the Italian churchgoer, it seems, beyond his or her presence, or acquiescence perhaps, the way at the university one need not seem enthusiastic about this or that dubious proposal, merely nod, or not object when the Head of Department asked if agreement was unanimous. Everything is done to accommodate a dispirited nominalism, as though to ask for fervour would be to invite revolt.

So James was pleasantly surprised when the priest began his sermon with an engaging smile. This was one of the rare occasions, the man said, when he found himself a mourner as well as the priest. Domenico had been a friend since schooldays. The priest paused and his eye passed over the small congregation. 'Of course you know Domenico, the kind of man he was. He never hesitated to tease me for my vocation, as if only someone naive, or perverse, would want to become a priest. "And since I know you're not perverse, Alberto," he would joke, "I suppose I have to congratulate you on your naivety."

'This was the kind of thing Domenico liked to say,' the priest acknowledged. But of course I had plenty of opportunity to tease my friend too. Domenico always said he was an atheist, it was a boast of his, but, as many of you know, he never failed to bring his mother here to Mass on Sunday mornings. He would wheel in her chair exactly as I began the service – you could set your watch by his arrival – and sit beside her throughout the service, adjusting the blanket on her knees, helping her with her reading glasses and missal. And he gave generously whenever we had cause to make an appeal. After the earthquake in the Marche. Or when we needed to raise funds to restore the organ. So I like to think of Domenico's insistence on his atheism as a caprice, part of his need to seem a little special. But whatever the truth may have been, Sunday after Sunday, my friend's feet brought him to church with his mother. As if his more humble self believed what his pride denied.' The priest paused, heavy jowls lit up with sentiment. 'May that same humility lead him safely now to the gates where his Maker awaits him.'

James was impressed; not just by the eloquence of this little sermon, but by its brevity. When had a funeral oration ever been so brief? 'If

Domenico gets to heaven,' Alessio leaned over to whisper, 'he'll soon figure out the angels are taking bribes and the saints are all Freemasons.'

Six or seven younger people now stepped up to the chancel steps and said an earnest word or two about the man who had been their professor and tutored them through their PhD. A kind man, always attentive to their publications and careers, they said. Two of the women wept. One spoke of Professor Galli as a model of the upright public man in a corrupt world. No one mentioned the rumours that he had a habit of inviting pretty students out for drinks.

Afterwards, leaving the main group of mourners to follow the hearse to the cemetery, the three friends walked back along the Naviglio to their famous bar, ordered Pink Ladies all round and raised their glasses.

'To Domenico.'

'Domenico.'

All, simultaneously, made faces of dismay. Alessio spluttered.

'How bitter would you need to be to drink something as sugary as this.'

'Poor Domenico!'

'To think he always had two.'

Federica asked the waiter for a jug of water.

For a while they sat silently in the sullen air, batting off mosquitoes, watching the flow of tourists along the waterside. Until Alessio lit a cigarette and said:

'Perhaps we'll have to be more cynical ourselves now he isn't here to do it for us.'

'The good thing about Domenico's cynicism,' James said, 'was that it spurred us to prove him wrong.'

'Without much success.'

'But even making an attempt is a kind of success, don't you think?' Federica observed. 'A proof of life.'

'I wouldn't exaggerate.' Alessio blew a smoke ring. 'About life, I mean.'

SCARSA, INCAPACE, PENOSA

With his new girlfriend's hold over his life prematurely interrupted, James was at a loss. Back home, he went through the post that had arrived while he was away; there was a replacement credit card, a reminder that the condominium did not permit people to hang washing on their balconies, a query from the tax office about the health expenses listed in his annual declaration of four years ago.

James pushed the papers to one side. They seemed such trivia beside the fact of being here one minute and gone the next. At his father's funeral, his younger brother had read out John Donne's great sermon – 'Every man is a piece of the continent, a part of the main ... Never send to know for whom the bell tolls ...' His voice had trembled with emotion. 'It tolls for thee.' And throughout the service, beside his mother, James had wondered, did Donne just mean the bell was a warning that you too must die? Indisputable, but banal. Or did he mean, this man was part of your world, *part of you*, and now that part has died? That we make and unmake each other in every moment? The father part of him was gone. His world was less. And now, though it had never amounted to much, the Domenico part was gone too. It had amounted, perhaps, James thought, to an extreme and very Italian take on life: that society is irretrievably conspiratorial, that the only thing to do is to accept this ugliness and burrow down in the dung. But if Domenico had known he was going to go like that, James wondered, like a bulb that pops with no warning, without even collecting his pension, would he have felt the same? Wouldn't he have wanted to do something more, to live more courageously? James thought about it and decided very likely not. Very likely it was fine just getting through and waiting till the axe fell.

Was this, then, the Italian mindset? Am I acclimatised at last? James asked himself.

Certainly he wasn't acclimatised to Milan's summer weather. The city was waiting for one of its summer thunderstorms. Even with all the windows open, the apartment was suffocating. He phoned Patrizia, described the funeral, and told her how down he felt. People should stop going to church altogether, was her brusque response. They only went because they had no imagination, no idea how to do things differently. 'People are hopeless.'

James listened, feeling once again the bulldozer force of her character.

'What are you going to do for the rest of the holiday?' he asked.

'Visit the town archives in Comacchio and Ravenna,' she said. 'And wait for you to get yourself over here for a little action.'

James said he would come soon, but putting down the phone realised he very likely wouldn't. He felt disorientated, as if peremptory voices were calling from different directions.

'Any thoughts of coming back to England?' his brother had asked him. 'I know Mum would be so grateful.'

'You should leave the university, if you're not happy with it,' Patrizia had said.

'*We should launch a petition*,' Antonio proposed in an email, '*to demand the direct election of the Rector and Head of Department. We have to take the battle to them.*'

James turned on the fan to get a little air moving about the room and was just pulling out his tax declaration of four years before when the phone rang. The number was private. Let it go? he wondered. It was after eight o'clock. He still had dinner to cook. Instead he answered, and at first didn't recognise the voice. It was a woman.

'*Buona sera*. Do forgive me if this is not a convenient moment.'

James was astonished.

'Good evening, Bettina.'

'Are you in Milan?'

'I've just been to Professor Galli's funeral.'

'Ah, yes, how sad. I sent a message of condolence on behalf of the department. It was so sudden.'

'Right.'

'Though I believe he had been suffering from heart problems for some time.'

James couldn't think what to reply.

'You'll be wondering why I'm phoning.'

Still James didn't respond.

Modesto cleared her throat. 'As you know there was a meeting of the Senate mid-July and then of the Board of Directors shortly thereafter, meetings at which a number of issues came up. One of them was our application for European Community Certification for our MA in publishing. Since I've now received details of how to make that application, I wanted to ask you if you were willing to take the matter in hand.'

James knew at once that this was not why she had called. Whoever asked anyone to do anything in August?

'I would have mentioned this before, but it had been understood that Professor Galli, as the most senior teacher in the degree, would be doing this.'

'Ah.'

'As soon as they're back, after the break – I think they open on the 26th – the International Relations Office will be sending you an email with the various steps we need to take. It looks rather daunting, I'm afraid. A lot of documentation is required and you'll need to coordinate input from the various professors teaching in the degree. On the bright side it will mean your going to Brussels to represent the university to the various authorising committees.'

347

'Great,' James said.

'Brussels is a wonderful city – you'll be expected to go in October, I think. They have a kind of conference to bring together new applicants. In any event we will all be most grateful if you can get a result there.'

'I'll see what can be done,' James said.

'Frankly' – Modesto lowered her voice – 'this is an excellent opportunity for you to improve your relationship with the Rector. Beppe is extremely sensitive to the international aspect of the university's reputation.'

'Point taken,' James said.

Apparently satisfied that the ground had been prepared, Modesto said, 'The other issue is Doctor Furlan.'

Here we go.

'The Senate had to debate whether there were sufficient motives and financial resources for keeping Furlan, now that we have the arrival of a prestigious associate professor in French Language and Literature, who of course, after a long career, is already at a rather high pay grade, hence expensive. As you can imagine we are all quite excited to have someone of the quality of Professor Contini, whom I recently met at a conference in Livorno. A wonderful person and quite a mind.'

James felt extremely agitated. He got to his feet and started walking about the empty apartment.

'That notwithstanding, I have always been, as you know, very eager to keep Furlan, if possible, given all the years he's worked for us, his excellent student-satisfaction ratings and so on. I know you feel the same. So I insisted with my colleagues, despite their scepticism, that rather than decide right there and then, we should ask the Personnel Office and the Financial Office to assess the pluses and minuses, as it were, above all whether we can afford to have an extra professor in French.'

James found himself in the bathroom, staring at his face in the mirror.

'Well, they sent me their report this afternoon, just before closing for the August break.'

Modesto paused.

'Of course I tried to phone Furlan at once, but his phone must be off. He'll be on holiday, I suppose. I haven't been able to contact him.'

'So you are contacting me.'

There was a silence. Modesto had apparently hoped that the nonsense of the trip to Brussels would have flattered James and reminded him what side his bread was buttered.

'So you are asking me to tell Antonio that you are not renewing his contract.'

Modesto sighed. 'I understand your disappointment, but Antonio has had the advantage of being with us and learning with us for nine years. Now he can move on and find a future elsewhere. He's not from Milan, you know.'

James was at the window in the bedroom, looking out onto a drop of three floors and a spiked railing.

'At the *consiglio*,' he said slowly, his voice trembling with tension, 'where the exchange of professors was first discussed, I explicitly asked you if bringing Professor Contini to the university would damage Furlan's career, and you said that the two issues were quite separate and had to be considered separately.'

'Right. Technically that was correct. We had to consider them separately.'

'But in this way you have destroyed a young man's future. Simply because Professor Busacca wanted to go back to Genoa.'

'Oh, I wouldn't be so dramatic. We are not the only university in Italy.'

'You know that in the position Furlan is in, needing to be taken on as a professor outside his home base, in French, which is attracting fewer and fewer students, no one is going to give him a job at the present time. At the very least you should have warned him months ago that his contract would not be renewed. Now there is no way at all he can find work before the new academic year.'

349

'I cannot understand,' Modesto said sharply, 'why you always suppose that I am not upset by this too. I waited because I hoped to be able to keep him.'

'You are not upset,' James said firmly. Now he was standing by his bookshelf staring at works of Italian literature. *The Tartar Steppe. The Path to the Nest of Spiders. Il Bell'Antonio. The Betrothed. Dear Michele. House of Liars. The Conformist. The Moon and the Bonfires. Fontamara.* All stories of exclusion and betrayal.

'On the contrary, you seized on the opportunity of this exchange as a chance to get rid of someone who wasn't always flattering you and bringing you gifts as others do. Somebody who made the mistake of helping me with our conference.'

Saying this caused a flood of adrenaline to surge through James's body. He was gripping the phone too hard.

'And if you waited all these months before making it official, it was only because you wanted to make sure he would work obediently to the end.'

'I am astonished,' Modesto was protesting. 'If you believe that, you are genuinely sick. What kind of person do you think I am?'

'Exactly the kind that everybody else thinks you are, Bettina. Everybody believes what I believe, and behind your back many of them say it.'

It was as if James had found himself in a gun battle at a street corner, with no time at all to choose a strategy. He was shooting from the hip.

'The department decision to make this exchange was unanimous,' Modesto said icily. 'You voted for it yourself.'

'I did and I'm ashamed. But the votes in department meetings are unanimous for the simple reason that everyone knows that if they vote against you they will be punished for it. They vote for you out of fear.'

'Don't make me laugh,' Modesto said.

'Bettina, let me do you the favour of telling you the truth that your spies will never tell you. Everybody thinks that you are only in your present position at the university thanks to the favouritism of the

Rector. Everybody thinks you are inept and incompetent. *Scarsa, incapace, penosa.* Everybody laughs at you behind your back. And everybody fears you like an ogre in a fable.'

James was in the sitting room again now, looking at a plant, a maidenhair fern that was urgently in need of watering.

'You should think of the consequences, before you start saying things like this,' Modesto said sharply. Her voice was trembling too.

'Is that a threat?' James demanded. He was livid. 'What *are* the consequences for telling the truth, Bettina?'

Modesto was breathing heavily.

'You're dumping a perfectly good teacher because he didn't grovel. And you don't even have the courage to tell him yourself. You are a coward.'

'I can't see any point in our continuing this conversation,' Modesto said. 'You have no idea of the kind of responsibilities I have to shoulder. Perhaps when you have had time to cool down you will see reason.'

'Remember, Bettina' – James hurried to fire his last rounds – 'that people think you are completely and utterly ridiculous. That your publications are pathetic. Your lectures are beyond embarrassing. Don't forget!'

He pressed the red button to close the call. His whole body was shaking and he sank down on the floor and sat for a while with his back against the wall.

After ten minutes or so he picked up the phone again and called Antonio. 'I'm afraid so,' he said. He kept it short, knowing it was a big blow and that the other man would need to take stock. For a while he wondered if he should call Patrizia and tell her about it. Or Federica. He saw the opportunities for boasting about the mad step he had taken, the mad courage of talking to Modesto so openly. But he didn't want to speak to anyone. And he hadn't been courageous. It had just happened.

The relationship with Patrizia would not last, he thought.

AMARCORD

How do Italian stories end? In Leonardo Sciascia's Sicilian crime stories the murderer isn't found, though the reader knows who it is; such is Sicily, he seems to say. In Verga's stories his protagonist victims die acquiescent with the society that has destroyed them. In Brancati's *Il bell'Antonio* only the destruction of his home town allows Antonio to recover his libido and his hope for the future. In Buzzati's *The Tartar Steppe* the hero wastes his whole life serving a meaningless institution. In Svevo's great comedies things eventually work out for the best, but only thanks to some astonishing stroke of good luck. In Natalia Ginzburg's stories the character who tries to forge an independent life outside the family is first destroyed by society, then much missed by those who remained within its safe confines. In Elsa Morante's exuberant cries for help, a young person discovers that what seemed to be a fabulous and wonderful family world is actually a perverse hotbed of thwarted desire and betrayal. In Alberto Moravia's cerebral narratives the hero would like to conform but feels he is a misfit, until, in attempting to be like others, he destroys himself. In Giorgio Bassani's stories anyone opposing the collective vocation for denial will sooner or later disappear: drowned, deported, or simply untraceable.

Let us take leave of our Gang of Four, in Italy today.

Federica Motta, professor of German, wins recognition as *abilitata* – qualified – to become a professor *ordinario*. But she knows the authorities at her university will never confer that honour on her, or its corresponding salary. She is asked to teach courses that have little to do with her studies. She is increasingly sidelined and ignored. Colleagues acknowledge her presence, but will not open up to her. Any small administrative roles she had are taken away from her. The upside is that this gives her more time to focus on her own interests. She begins to translate eighteenth-century German literature for a small publishing house based in Trento. Rather remarkably one book becomes a minor bestseller and she receives invitations to travel around Italy presenting it and talking about Mitteleuropa past and present. Consequently, she is asked to produce a small weekly radio programme on German culture. She begins to write occasional articles for the newspaper *La Repubblica* and to do some freelance editing; so after three or four years, and with only a small loss of income, she is able to leave the university. All things considered, Federica is happy with this outcome, though she does miss the teaching and the research. She had felt she had something to offer students, a particular take on Germany and German literature. It wasn't to be.

Having heard that he had lost his job from James, Antonio Furlan received no official communication from the university. The logic of this, he realised, was that being on a fixed-term contract, it was self-evident that his employment would cease when the contract expired. Indeed on that very day, his university email address was disabled, leaving a number of students and colleagues who were still in contact with him over this or that project unable to get in touch. So, after nine years, he removed his books and papers from his office, returned to his apartment in Isola and wondered how the rent was going to be paid. 'Take them to court,' friends said. Antonio's father agreed. Having read the small print of his contract, a lawyer assured him he had a strong case. But after much agonised reflection, Antonio decided against. A year for the first decision, he told Valeria, another year for the appeal, another year for the *cassazione*, all to work with people he loathed. He wasn't going to do it.

Doctor Furlan applied for jobs all over Italy and found only poorly paid contract teaching. He applied for jobs in France, in Belgium, in Senegal. He fell into depression. He struggled with poor self-esteem. From time to time he drank more than he should. He borrowed from his parents. Valeria worried for him, and encouraged him to keep studying and publishing. The rent was nine hundred euros a month, plus expenses. They contemplated moving to a cheaper place further out of town, until the good news came that Valeria's grant had been restored. The first half of her thesis had been approved with excellent reports from all her tutors. She also received all the money for the months when it had been suspended, and a year later completed her PhD with flying colours. The thesis was to be published with a small academic publisher. But no offer of collaboration of any kind was forthcoming from the university. For a year she worked as a supply teacher in a *scuola professionale*, which is to say a high school for adolescents who were not on track for the university.

The school was on the southern outskirts of Milan. On two occasions police entered her classroom with dogs to search for drugs. Students arrived with knife wounds. Parents threatened her if she gave low grades. In one class a third of the students were certified dyslexics. Many others were seeking such certification; with it came lower expectations and easier exams. Often it was the best students, Valeria noticed, who were certified dyslexics. She realised at once that she was not cut out for this. She didn't have the authority, the physical presence, the sheer balls, the voice, the age, to control twenty and more adolescents who weren't remotely interested in learning French.

The two had health problems. Antonio smoked too much. His sinuses troubled him. Valeria always seemed to have a stomach ache, particularly when she boarded the crowded tram of a morning, or just before going into the classroom. Yet they were happy together. They would not retreat to their respective homes in Padova, in Basilicata. They spent Christmas together, in Milan, to the dismay of their respective families. Then at last, some three years after his firing,

Antonio received an invitation to teach on a yearly contract in Dakar, the very university where Valeria was supposed to have done her fieldwork. And they left the country. They went with mixed feelings, joining the 285,000 Italians, mostly young, more than a third graduates, who left Italy that year. So Valeria finally met the professor she was to have met three years before, and was given a little teaching. It was a beginning. It was exciting to be in Dakar. It was good to feel there was everything to play for. A year later a child arrived, in Africa.

James saw them again two years later in Milan when they stopped over in August on the way to their wedding, in Basilicata. Federica was there too. And Alessio. They met in the usual bar, on the Naviglio. James was late and Antonio asked Alessio how he was, and how things were going at the university. 'Well, Ottone has awarded himself a new Mercedes as official car,' he smiled, 'with a driver from Palermo. That's the big news.'

'From strength to strength,' Antonio said.

'But we want to know about you,' Valeria protested.

'Oh, we soldier on,' Alessio said, with his wry smile.

Did James have a girlfriend? Valeria asked.

'No doubt he whores around,' Alessio thought. 'Or maybe not. I don't know. But then I never knew what you two were up to either.'

Valeria blushed. Antonio stretched his arm around her.

'I've never understood why he didn't go home,' Federica observed.

'Because he's hooked. Poor fool's convinced if he just hangs on a little longer, one day he'll understand.'

'What?' Antonio asked.

'Italy! He told me he'd applied for citizenship.'

The four shook their heads and chuckled, clinking their drinks, at which the baby began to cry and had to be lifted from his carriage. Then they were all making such a fuss of the pretty child that none of them noticed James had arrived and was standing there beside them with a book in his hand.

'*Carissimi!*'

He moved round the table embracing and kissing them all, congratulating the youngsters on their child.

'Someone has translated Giambattista Basile!' He slapped the big book on the table. 'Can you believe it? A crazy American woman. Listen to this!' He turned to the young couple, opened the book and read.

'*When I had journeyed half of my life's way, a new spirit inflamed in me the desire for higher study, and although I knew I was a swamp bird, I strived to equal the most noble swans. But when I thought most surely that my fatherland was going to confirm me in winning laurels, I then saw that those who should have loved me most ignored me . . . And so I arranged to flee the ungrateful shores and search for my fortune elsewhere.*'

There was a brief silence. Absurdly a gondolier was paddling up the canal, as if Milan were Venice.

'*Amarcord*,' Valeria said, and then she said, 'Please do come to our wedding, everyone. We really want to have you with us.'